COLLIN

TOP
WILDLIFE SPOTS

THE BEST 200 PLACES TO SEE WILDLIFE IN THE UK

HarperCollins*Publishers*

The Wildlife Trusts' Nature Reserves Guide

HarperCollins*Publishers*
77–85 Fulham Palace Road
Hammersmith
London W6 8JB

The HarperCollins website address is:
www.**fire**and**water**.com

Collins is a registered trademark of HarperCollins*Publishers* Ltd.

2 4 6 8 10 9 7 5 3 1

00 02 04 03 01 99

ISBN 0 00 220178 X

Edited by Geoffrey Young
Designed by Julien & Bernadette Lightfoot, Media 4 Graphix
Additional line illustrations by Julien Lightfoot

All photographs © RSNC The Wildlife Trusts Partnership apart from the
following: p.32 Adonis Blue © Chris Newton, FLPA; p.92 English Oak leaf and
fruit © Silvestris, FLPA; p.123 Common Bittern © David Hosking, FLPA

Printed and bound in Great Britain by The Bath Press

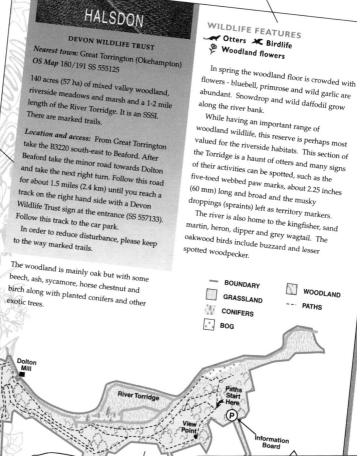

HALSDON

DEVON WILDLIFE TRUST

Nearest town: Great Torrington (Okehampton)
OS Map 180/191 SS 555125

140 acres (57 ha) of mixed valley woodland, riverside meadows and marsh and a 1-2 mile length of the River Torridge. It is an SSSI. There are marked trails.

Location and access: From Great Torrington take the B3220 south-east to Beaford. After Beaford take the minor road towards Dolton and take the next right turn. Follow this road for about 1.5 miles (2.4 km) until you reach a track on the right hand side with a Devon Wildlife Trust sign at the entrance (SS 557133). Follow this track to the car park.

In order to reduce disturbance, please keep to the way marked trails.

The woodland is mainly oak but with some beech, ash, sycamore, horse chestnut and birch along with planted conifers and other exotic trees.

WILDLIFE FEATURES
Otters   Birdlife
Woodland flowers

In spring the woodland floor is crowded with flowers - bluebell, primrose and wild garlic are abundant. Snowdrop and wild daffodil grow along the river bank.

While having an important range of woodland wildlife, this reserve is perhaps most valued for the riverside habitats. This section of the Torridge is a haunt of otters and many signs of their activities can be spotted, such as the five-toed webbed paw marks, about 2.25 inches (60 mm) long and broad and the musky droppings (sprints) left as territory markers.

The river is also home to the kingfisher, sand martin, heron, dipper and grey wagtail. The oakwood birds include buzzard and lesser spotted woodpecker.

--- BOUNDARY   WOODLAND

GRASSLAND   --- PATHS

CONIFERS

BOG

Dolton Mill

River Torridge

Paths Start Here

View Point

P   Information Board

P   Information Board

300 yards

To Dolton

40

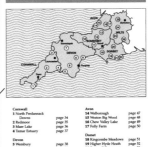

SOUTH-WEST ENGLAND

33

9

Information and guidance for visitors

HRH Prince Charles, patron of The Wildlife Trusts, visiting Wiltshire Wildlife Trust.

Introduction

The Wildlife Trusts welcome visitors on all our nature reserves. However, the prime purpose of our reserves is the conservation of wildlife and habitats, and their interests must come first. The following information is intended to make sure that you and your family have an enjoyable and safe day out when visiting a Wildlife Trust reserve.

Opening hours

The opening times are given for each reserve. However, it is advisable to check with the relevant Wildlife Trust before you set off, as these may change, particularly on a seasonal basis. Opening times for reserve visitor centres, toilets and other facilities may not be the same as opening hours for the reserve.

Visitor costs

Most reserves have free access for visitors. However, there may be a small charge at some, to help with the upkeep of the reserve, or at a visitor centre providing several facilities.

Where you can go

At most reserves we ask visitors to keep to marked paths and trails. This is to ensure that wildlife is not disturbed too much, and that plants or fragile habitats do not suffer heavy trampling. This is also often for the visitors' own safety as many reserves are on steep hillsides or alongside tidal estuaries or cliff tops, so wandering from the paths is not advisable. On Skomer Island, for example, the ground is pockmarked with puffin burrows and anyone straying from the path is likely to tread on a nesting puffin.

The Wildlife Trusts are continually working to improve facilities for visitors, building new bird hides and improving trails. Where the terrain is suitable, some reserves have paths suitable for wheelchairs or pushchairs. However, some reserves are too hilly or the construction of paths is not appropriate for the sensitive habitat of the reserve.

Many reserves have trail leaflets available for visitors, and interpretation boards to help people's understanding and enjoyment of the site.

Families and schoolchildren

Families and children are welcome at all nature reserves. Throughout the year, local Wildlife Trusts arrange a wide range of events at their reserves, including dawn chorus walks, tree planting, wild flower walks, hay making, and fungal forays. Every year in June, The Wildlife Trusts hold Wildlife Week, including hundreds of family events around the UK.

Among these are guided walks, rockpool rambles, face painting, plant fairs and many other activities.

Some reserves have special facilities and programmes of events for schoolchildren. Please check the information on individual reserves or phone the relevant local Wildlife Trust to find out what it can offer (see pages 15-17).

Refreshments

Some reserves have visitor centres with shops or cafés, or there may be a kiosk selling snacks, or a café nearby. Otherwise, visitors are welcome to bring picnics, and some reserves provide picnic areas. We ask that people do not light barbecues, as they could be a hazard to wildlife and habitats of the reserve.

Where possible toilets are provided, including toilets with wheelchair access. This is stated in the information on individual reserves.

Visitors and special needs

As already stated, many reserves have trails and hides suitable for wheelchair access. Some, such as Rutland Water, lend out electric buggies for people with restricted mobility. The Anglian Water Birdwatching Centre at Rutland Water has a sound system that people with hearing aids can tune into, enabling them to enjoy bird sounds being broadcast from around the reserve.

Some reserves have sensory gardens, rich in sounds, scents and textures, especially delightful for visually impaired visitors. Brandon Marsh in Warwickshire has a sensory garden with a babbling stream, raised flower beds, and a tactile geological map of the county.

Dogs

Visitors may bring their dogs to some reserves, but are asked to keep them on leads. At some reserves, visitors are requested not to bring dogs at all, even on leads, as they disturb ground nesting birds. Some reserves are grazed by sheep and it is important that they are not worried by visitors' dogs, particularly at lambing time. It is also worth bearing in mind that some reserves have cattle grazing on them, and while cattle will probably leave human visitors alone, they are quite likely to chase canine visitors, purely out of curiosity.

Very few reserves provide dog waste-bins so visitors are asked to take any waste away with them, and dispose of it responsibly. Dog fouling could seriously spoil a family's day out at a reserve.

We would ask visitors not to leave their dogs in cars unattended, as on a warm day they can suffer heatstroke and possibly die, even if they are left with open windows and water.

Rare Konik ponies grazing Redgrave and Lopham Fen, Suffolk.

Rare breeds

As well as spectacular wildlife, visitors can enjoy the unusual sight of rare farm animal breeds grazing on many reserves. Where conventional breeds find the grazing too poor, many rare breeds are perfectly adapted to graze the rough terrain or unimproved grassland of many Wildlife Trust reserves. The Lancashire Wildlife Trust grazes Hebridean sheep on heathland at Mere Sands Wood, as the sheep nibble on scrub such as young birch, and leave the heather. On Cranham Common, Gloucestershire, Welsh Black cattle have replaced sheep to control scrub invasion and to help improve the chalk grassland habitat for the Duke of Burgundy fritillary butterfly. Several reserves use native ponies such as the Exmoor, while Redgrave and Lopham Fen in Suffolk uses the Konik pony from Poland - descended from the now extinct wild Tarpan pony - which is suited to the wet, boggy conditions of the fen.

The Wildlife Trusts' widespread use of rare breeds in reserve management is helping to keep many of these endangered breeds alive.

What to wear

Please be prepared for changeable weather, even in summer, especially on upland or island reserves. Waterproofs and warm clothes are advisable. Sensible footwear such as walking boots or wellies are usually recommended, as paths can be bumpy or boggy and some have streams crossing them.

Working as a volunteer

If you're interested in helping on a Wildlife Trust reserve, or generally getting involved with Trust activities, there are lots of opportunities. Please see page 21 for more details.

The Wildlife Trusts' address list

Avon Wildlife Trust
The Wildlife Centre, 32 Jacob's Wells Road,
Bristol, BS8 1DR
Tel: (0117) 9 268018 Fax: (0117) 9 297273
Email: avonwt@cix.co.uk

**The Wildlife Trust for Bedfordshire,
Cambridgeshire, Northamptonshire &
Peterborough**
3B Langford Arch, London Road, Sawston
Cambridge, CB2 4EE
Tel: (01223) 712400 Fax: (01223) 712412
Email: cambswt@cix.co.uk

**The Berkshire, Buckinghamshire &
Oxfordshire Wildlife Trust**
The Lodge, 1 Armstrong Road, Littlemore,
Oxford, OX4 4XT
Tel: (01865) 775476 Fax: (01865) 711301
Email: bbontwt@cix.co.uk

**The Wildlife Trust for Birmingham & The
Black Country**
Unit 310, Jubilee Trade Centre, 130 Pershore St,
Birmingham, B5 6ND
Tel: 0121 666 7474 Fax: (0121) 622 4443
Email: urbanwt@cix.co.uk

Brecknock Wildlife Trust
Lion House, Bethel Square, Brecon, Powys,
LD3 7AY
Tel/Fax: (01874) 625708
Email: brecknockwt@cix.co.uk

Cheshire Wildlife Trust
Grebe House, Reaseheath, Nantwich,
Cheshire, CW5 6DG
Tel: (01270) 610180 Fax: (01270) 610430
Email: cheshirewt@cix.co.uk

Cornwall Wildlife Trust
Five Acres, Allet, Truro, Cornwall, TR4 9DJ
Tel: (01872) 273939 Fax: (01872) 225476
Email: cornwt@cix.co.uk

Cumbria Wildlife Trust
Brockhole, Windermere, Cumbria, LA23 1LJ
Tel: (015394) 48280 Fax: (015394) 48281
Email: cumbriawt@cix.co.uk

Derbyshire Wildlife Trust
Elvaston Castle, Derby, DE72 3EP
Tel: (01332) 756610 Fax: (01332) 758872
Email: derbywt@cix.co.uk

Devon Wildlife Trust
Shirehampton House, 35-37
St David's Hill Exeter, Devon, EX4 4DA
Tel: (01392) 279244 Fax: (01392) 433221
Email: devonwt@cix.co.uk

Dorset Wildlife Trust
Brooklands Farm, Forston, Dorchester, DT2 7AA
Tel: (01305) 264620 Fax: (01305) 251120
Email: dorsetwt@cix.co.uk

Durham Wildlife Trust
Rainton Meadows, Chilton Moor,
Houghton-le-Spring, Tyne & Wear, DH4 6PU
Tel: (0191) 584 3112 Fax: (0191) 584 3934
Email: durhamwt@cix.co.uk

Essex Wildlife Trust
Fingringhoe Wick Nature Reserve, Fingringhoe,
Colchester, Essex, CO5 7DN
Tel: (01206) 729678 Fax: (01206) 729298
Email: admin@essexwt.org.uk

Glamorgan Wildlife Trust
Nature Centre, Fountain Road, Tondu,
Mid Glamorgan, CF32 0EH
Tel: (01656) 724100
Fax: (01656) 729880
Email: glamorganwt@cix.co.uk

Gloucestershire Wildlife Trust
Dulverton Building, Robinswood Hill Country
Park, Reservoir Road, Gloucester, GL4 6SX
Tel: (01452) 383333 Fax: (01452) 383334
Email: gmcg@cix.co.uk

The Wildlife Trusts' address list

Gwent Wildlife Trust
16 White Swan Court, Church Street,
Monmouth,
Gwent, NP5 3BR
Tel: (01600) 715501 Fax: (01600) 715832
Email: gwentwildlife@cix.co.uk

Hampshire & Isle of Wight Wildlife Trust
8 Romsey Road, Eastleigh,
Hampshire, SO50 9AL
Tel: (01703) 613636/613737 Fax: (01703) 612233
Email: hampswt@cix.co.uk

Herefordshire Nature Trust
Lower House Farm, Ledbury Road, Tupsley,
Hereford, HR1 1UT
Tel: (01432) 356872 Fax: (01432) 275489
Email: herefordwt@cix.co.uk

Hertfordshire & Middlesex Wildlife Trust
Grebe House, St Michael's Street, St Albans,
Herts, AL3 4SN
Tel: (01727) 858901 Fax: (01727) 854542
Email: hertswt@cix.co.uk

Kent Wildlife Trust
Tyland Barn, Sandling, Maidstone,
Kent, ME14 3BD
Tel: (01622) 662012 Fax: (01622) 671390
Email: kentwildlife@cix.co.uk

Lancashire Wildlife Trust
Cuerden Park Wildlife Centre, Shady Lane,
Bamber Bridge, Preston, Lancs, PR5 6AU
Tel: (01772) 324129 Fax: (01772) 628849
Email: lancswt@cix.co.uk

Leicestershire & Rutland Wildlife Trust
1 West Street, Leicester, LE1 6UU
Tel: (01162) 553904 Fax: (01162) 541254
Email: leicswt@cix.co.uk

The Lincolnshire Trust for Nature Conservation
Banovallum House, Manor House Street,
Horncastle, Lincolnshire, LN9 5HF
Tel: (01507) 526667 Fax: (01507) 525732
Email: lincstrust@cix.co.uk

London Wildlife Trust
Harling House, 47-51 Great Suffolk Street,
London, SE1 0BS
Tel: 0171 261 0447 Fax: 0171 261 0538
Email: londonwt@cix.co.uk

Manx Wildlife Trust
Conservation Centre, The Courtyard,
Tynwald Mills,
St Johns, Isle of Man
Tel: (01624) 801985 Fax: (01624) 801022
Email: manxwt@cix.co.uk

Montgomeryshire Wildlife Trust
Collott House, 20 Severn Street, Welshpool,
Powys, SY21 7AD
Tel: (01938) 555654 Fax: (01938) 556161
Email: montwt@cix.co.uk

Norfolk Wildlife Trust
72 Cathedral Close, Norwich, Norfolk, NR1 4DF
Tel: (01603) 625540 Fax: (01603) 630593
Email: nwt@cix.co.uk

Northumberland Wildlife Trust
The Garden House, St Nicholas Park, Jubilee
Road, Newcastle upon Tyne, NE3 3XT
Tel: (0191) 284 6884 Fax: (0191) 284 6794
Email: northwildlife@cix.co.uk

North Wales Wildlife Trust
376 High Street, Bangor, Gwynedd, LL57 1YE
Tel: (01248) 351541 Fax: (01248) 353192
Email: nwwt@cix.co.uk

Nottinghamshire Wildlife Trust
The Old Ragged School, Brook Street,
Nottingham, NG1 1EA
Tel: (0115) 958 8242 Fax: (0115) 924 3175
Email: nottswt@cix.co.uk

Radnorshire Wildlife Trust
Warwick House, High Street, Llandrindod
Wells, Powys, LD1 6AG
Tel: (01597) 823298 Fax: (01597) 823274
Email: radnorshirewt@cix.co.uk

The Wildlife Trusts' address list

Scottish Wildlife Trust
Cramond House, Kirk Cramond, Cramond
Glebe Rd, Edinburgh, EH4 6NS
Tel: (0131) 312 7765 Fax: (0131) 312 8705
Email: scottishwt@cix.co.uk

Sheffield Wildlife Trust
Wood Lane House, 52 Wood Lane,
Sheffield, S6 5HE
Tel: (0114) 231 0120 Fax: 0114 231 0120
Email: sheffieldwt@cix.co.uk

Shropshire Wildlife Trust
167 Frankwell, Shrewsbury, Shropshire,
SY3 8LG
Tel: (01743) 241691 Fax: (01743) 366671
Email: shropshirewt@cix.co.uk

Somerset Wildlife Trust
Fyne Court, Broomfield, Bridgwater,
Somerset, TA5 2EQ
Tel: (01823) 451587   Fax: (01823) 451671
Email: somwt@cix.co.uk

Staffordshire Wildlife Trust
Coutts House, Sandon, Staffordshire, ST18 ODN
Tel: (01889) 508534 Fax: (01889) 508422
Email: staffswt@cix.co.uk

Suffolk Wildlife Trust
Brooke House, The Green, Ashbocking, Nr
Ipswich, Suffolk, IP6 9JY
Tel: (01473) 890089 Fax: (01473) 890165
Email: suffolkwt@cix.co.uk

Surrey Wildlife Trust
School Lane, Pirbright, Woking, Surrey,
GU24 0JN
Tel: (01483) 488055 Fax: (01483) 486505
Email: surreywt@cix.co.uk

Sussex Wildlife Trust
Woods Mill, Shoreham Road, Henfield,
West Sussex, BN5 9SD
Tel: (01273) 492630 Fax: (01273) 494500
Email: sussexwt@cix.co.uk

Tees Valley Wildlife Trust
Bellamy Pavilion, Kirkleatham Old Hall,
Kirkleatham, Redcar, Cleveland, TS10 5NW
Tel: (01642) 759900 Fax: (01642) 480401
Email: clevelandwt@cix.co.uk

Ulster Wildlife Trust
3 New Line, Crossgar, Co. Down, BT30 9EP
Tel: (01396) 830282 Fax: (01396) 830888
Email: ulsterwt@cix.co.uk

Warwickshire Wildlife Trust
Brandon Marsh Nature Centre, Brandon Lane,
Coventry, CV3 3GW
Tel: (01203) 302912 Fax: (01203) 639556
Email: warkswt@cix.co.uk

The Wildlife Trust: West Wales
7 Market Street, Haverfordwest, Dyfed,
SA61 1NF
Tel: (01437) 765462 Fax: (01437) 767163
Email: wildlife@wildlife-wales.org.uk

Wiltshire Wildlife Trust
19 High Street, Devizes, Wiltshire, SN10 1AT
Tel: (01380) 725670 Fax: (01380) 729017
Email: wiltswt@cix.co.uk

Worcestershire Wildlife Trust
Lower Smite Farm, Smite Hill, Hindlip,
Worcester, WR3 8SZ
Tel: (01905) 754919 Fax: (01905) 755868
Email: worcswt@cix.co.uk

Yorkshire Wildlife Trust
10 Toft Green, York, YO1 6JT
Tel: (01904) 659570 Fax: (01904) 613467
Email: yorkshirewt@cix.co.uk

The more you send, the more you save.

How your donation could help protect Wildlife for the future.

In your lifetime, hundreds of species of British wildlife have come under threat, and thousands more acres of our ancient woodland and flower meadows have been lost. At this rate, your children might never see an enchanting bluebell wood or hear the beautiful song of a skylark.

The Wildlife Trusts fight to protect all of the UK's wildlife. We spend our money where it matters - in the field. (Last year our volunteers spent a million hours there).

We have, for example, helped raise otter numbers fourfold, increase the barn owl population and re-establish rare species of butterfly. We have many similar success stories but more and more new challenges to fund.

Please send whatever you can afford. And start saving now.

Name: MR/MRS/MISS/MS ....

Address: ....

....

....

County: .... Postcode: ....

I enclose a donation of £ 100 ❑ , £ 50 ❑ , £ 25 ❑ , £ 10 ❑ , £ 5 ❑

Please make cheques payable to The Wildlife Trusts', or complete the credit card details below, and send with this form to:

The Wildlife Trusts, Dept. MSFR, FREEPOST MID20441, Newark NG24 4BR.

Access ❑   Visa ❑   Mastercard ❑   CAF Charity Card ❑   *(Please delete as applicable).*

Expiry Date .... / ....   Signature ....

Card No.

Registered Charity 207238.   Code : RG/DON

The Wildlife Trusts need your support

Since 1912, The Wildlife Trusts have been speaking out for nature in the U.K. Our organisation is unique with a strong national voice and practical action taking place at a very local level in every county in the country. We have more than a third of a million members and many more supporters, all of whom are committed to helping The Wildlife Trusts in their mission to secure a future for wildlife. Using the specialist skills of our staff and volunteers, we manage more than 2,300 nature reserves, each one a very special place for wildlife.

As a charity, we can only be truly effective with the support of people who care about their environment. Please join us in our fight for the UK's wildlife by becoming a member of your local Wildlife Trust, or if you prefer, by making a donation (see previous page).

I would like to join as:

☐ Individual member   £18 per year
☐ Joint member   £22 per year
☐ Family member*   £30 per year
(*Includes up to four members of the Children's Club, Wildlife Watch)

Name: MR/MRS/MISS/MS ....

Address: ....

....

....

County: .... Postcode: ....

I enclose a cheque/postal order or Visa/Access order payable to: The Wildlife Trusts.

Expiry Date: ..../........... Signature ....

Date ....

Card No: | | | | | | | | | | | | | | | | | |

Send this form to: **The Wildlife Trusts, Dept. MSFR, Freepost MID 20441, Newark NG24 4BR**

Registered Charity No 207238   Code: RG/MEM

Photocopy page or cut along dotted line ✂

A UK richer in wildlife is a legacy worth leaving

The Wildlife Trusts are working to safeguard the future of wildlife in the UK. Even with the help of many thousands of volunteers, this costs money. Legacies are a very important source of our income. Would you remember us in your will? Ask your solicitor or financial advisor for help. Or request a free copy of our useful booklet How to make or change your will. You'll be helping to make wildlife in the UK much better off.

Please send me: ☐ Details on making a bequest   ☐ A copy of your booklet

To : **The Wildlife Trusts, Dept. MSFR, Freepost MID20441, Newark NG24 4BR.**

Name: MR/MRS/MISS/MS ....

Address: ....

....

....

County: .... Postcode: ....

I am a member of the following Wildlife Trust:

....

Working as a volunteer

The Wildlife Trusts offer lots of opportunities for people to get involved with their vital work Anyone with some spare time is welcome, and each Trust tries to match people's skills with what they would like to do. You might like to help out on a reserve, meeting visitors, taking guided walks, or helping with practical conservation work. If you have an in-depth knowledge of plants or animals you could become a recorder and let the Trust know what you've seen, either on a reserve or where you live.

Or you could help in a Trust office, shop or visitor centre. If you are a photographer or illustrator, the Trust would welcome your help with the production of leaflets, displays or publications. Accountants, public relations people, writers, editors - the list of skills needed by The Wildlife Trusts is endless. Administrative experience is always in demand, you might like to offer your telephone skills, organise a fund-raising event, or help with mailings. Whatever you feel you can offer, The Wildlife Trusts will make you feel welcome. Hopefully you will meet new friends, as well as making a vital contribution to wildlife conservation in the UK.

Visitor centres and shops

From restored barns and water mills, to the latest eco-friendly buildings, Wildlife Trust visitor centres offer a whole range of experiences and facilities. They often have fascinating displays and exhibitions explaining the wildlife and habitats of our fabulous reserves. Some have cafes and shops, and most have toilets, some with wheelchair access.

Dorset Wildlife Trust's Purbeck Marine Wildlife Centre has an underwater video link to take you beneath the waves at Kimmeridge Bay without getting wet. You'll see spectacular marine life, including many crabs and several species of brightly coloured wrasse. Cameras also come in handy at the Anglian Water Birdwatching Centre at Rutland Water, Leicestershire. Viewers can zoom in on some of the best bird life in Europe, using remote control cameras placed around the reserve. Microphones also pick up bird sounds which are played in the visitor centre, a special sound system is adapted so that people with hearing aids can listen in. A shop sells birdwatching equipment, which can also be hired.

Warwickshire Wildlife Trust's new Brandon Marsh Nature Centre has an Ecozone with interactive displays, and is powered by a wind pump on the roof.

Several visitor centres are purpose built for viewing life on the reserve. The Montrose Basin Wildlife Centre in Scotland has unbeatable views of life on the South Esk estuary, including the internationally important population of pink footed geese that overwinters there, plus it has a display extolling the glories of mud and its importance for wildlife. And Essex Wildlife Trust's Fingringhoe Wick Conservation Centre has an observation tower with first-rate views around the estuary reserve. At the award-winning Welsh Wildlife Centre, near Cardigan, you can eat in the Nuthatch Restaurant while enjoying panoramic views of the surrounding reserve.

For details of all Wildlife Trust shops and visitor centres, please contact the local Wildlife Trust.

What are nature reserves?

Apart from certain coastal areas, little of our countryside is natural - it has been influenced by man for many thousands of years. And, in fact, this management is often the reason behind the great variety of wildlife (the word includes plants as well as animals) that we see today.

Nature reserves are places where wildlife is protected for its own sake, and this often means continuing or restoring the old-time practices which made them rich in the first place.

One example is the coppicing of woodland. When the last ice age eased, a tangled wildwood spread across much of the lowlands. This was cleared for farming, and by medieval times the remaining woodland was patchy. Much of it was worked as "coppice"; every seven to 15 years trees and shrubs were cut to stumps which threw up a new head of straightish branches or "small wood" for many uses. Set through this coppice were tall timber trees.

Strengthened by the open light after the cut, woodland flowers flourished and many woodland reserves are now coppiced to keep the bluebells strong. Butterflies too; previously they were restricted to the few natural glades of the wildwood. And birds; the nightingale for example likes the dense low growth of new coppice, but deserts it after seven years when it becomes more mature.

Another example of an old habitat is chalk downland; regular grazing by sheep keeps the ranker grasses at bay and allows wild flowers to flourish.

Most nature reserves have had that kind of history and they have somehow escaped the farming revolution of the last 60 or so years. The green of the countryside disguises the damage it has suffered this century. Many woodlands have been felled and replanted with conifers. Grassland is sprayed to weed out the wild flowers, but it is just as damaging to feed it with fertilisers or slurry, for then the aggressive fodder grasses smother the flowers. But, anyway, most grassland is now ploughed and resown every five or so years and few flowers or butterflies survive. The old hay meadows are no longer cut for hay, giving the flowers time to seed; instead, green silage is closely cropped earlier in the year.

By and large, nature reserves are places where this has not happened.

In addition, there are places such as quarries, railway cuttings and canals, which although originally "industrial" have become populated by a variety of plant and animal life. Some of these are now nature reserves, or part of one.

And there are reserves of a third kind - planned and planted like a garden, but with wildlife and ecological principles in mind, a kind of showcase. Some Wildlife Trusts have one alongside their HQ. There are a couple of examples in this Nature Reserves Guide.

Conservation in action
WOODLAND

● Fallen boughs are left
lying to rot.
In nature, decomposition
creates new nutrients, and is a
vital part of a balanced system. Specialist
decomposers, beetles and fungi among them,
attack dead timber.

● The wood is being cleared of sycamore and
rhododendron (planted as pheasant cover).
These trees are non-natives and of little value
to native wildlife. Oak, for example, hosts 284
insect species, sycamore only 15.

● Clearings and open rides are being created.
This benefits butterflies. Many birds nest in the
bushes which thicken around a glade (which is
why many adopt gardens!).

● Volunteer work parties are coppicing parts of the
woodland.
This strengthens the "field" layer of the
wood, encouraging the wild flowers. It
also creates sunny glades, encouraging
butterflies.

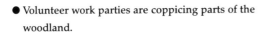

● Oak and other native trees are
being planted.

● Where relevant nest and bat boxes are being placed.

Conservation in action
GRASSLAND

Old grassland is usually easy enough to spot. It is a tawny colour, the result of a marvellous diversity of wild plants and grasses, maybe as many as 30 different species in a square yard.

● Sheep are grazing.
On chalk downland, and with the right stocking rate, sheep produce a fine sward, ideal for the shorter wild flowers and hence many of the downland butterflies. (Cattle, being heavy animals, are unsuitable; they "poach" wet ground and their cow-pats develop rank thistles!)
Sometimes, on nature reserves, you may see unexpected sheep, speckle-faced Welsh beulahs for example, which can deal with invasive scrub. Some Wildlife Trusts organise "sheep sponsoring" to raise funds for this, and more than one rely on Monday shepherdesses - volunteers to help manage the flocks.

● Encroaching scrub is being cleared by hand.
Along with sheep grazing, many Wildlife Trusts organise volunteer work parties.

● Rare plants are being guarded.
To safeguard the flowers, some Wildlife Trusts have orchid wardens who sleep on site while the plants are in bloom and seeding.

● Hay is mown.
Hay meadows, often found alongside a stream or river, are now a rare treasure in the countryside and the variety of flowers and butterflies can match the old downland pastures. After the traditional hay cut in June or July, animals graze the "aftermath".

WETLANDS

MIRES

Many rivers have separate "ages", from the "young" rushing beck in the hills full of trout and minnows to the "old" winding giant on its last miles to the sea, inhabited by coarse fish. A different type is the chalk river, fed by springs and with low banks - but unlike clay rivers, it rarely floods.

- **River banks are left wild in nature reserves.**
  In the countryside as a whole, river management causes controversy. Farmers and others desire swift flow to avoid flooding. Rivers and streams are canalised, which is bad news for wildlife.

- **The open water is being dredged.**
  Ponds and lakes tend to infill from the edge, eventually drying out. Dredging is often necessary to keep smaller ponds open.

- **Small ponds are being dug.**
  Small ponds are often created to add to the habitat variety of a reserve. In medieval and Tudor days, many woods contained fish ponds.

Wherever water is held up on its journey to the sea, wetlands or "mires" of different types form. On the large scale, fens can be created. Most lowland mires are fens. Here reeds colonise the open water, dying down to create peat which eventually fills the basin, topped with a multitude of growing plants. Left to itself, a carr woodland of willows and alders takes root on what is becoming dry land.

- **Reeds are being cut.**
  This is a regular winter task on many wetland reserves. The reedbeds often need harsh cutting to prevent them invading open water. The cut reeds are sold for thatching, bringing in funds for the reserve.

- **Hay is being mown.**
  In many fen areas, a hay crop was cut from the fen which was then grazed. It was rich grazing, and as a result many fenlands, such as the Somerset Levels, were ditched and drained for permanent pasture which has since been ploughed.

Bogs are another kind of mire, often a feature of moors and heaths (see opposite).

Conservation in action
HEATHS AND MOORS

These have developed where forest clearance on poor and acid soils has been followed by centuries of grazing, perhaps with frequent fires destroying any invading trees. The sight of a solitary relic tree, perhaps growing from rocks out of reach of the sheep, is a clue that the natural cover would be woodland (and many areas are now planted with conifers).

There is no clear distinction, but heaths are typically found in the lowlands or moors in the uplands. Both have heather accompanied by bilberry and other shrubs. Heaths often carry some gorse.

- Heathland is being cleared by hand.
  Weekend volunteers are often at work on this task. Heathland quickly becomes self-sown with gorse, birch and also pine if there is a conifer plantation nearby.

- Bare-soil areas are created.
  These are important for heathland insects, and basking places for snakes and lizards.

BOGS

Bogs are mires which develop on both moors and heaths. In sodden acid conditions in upland areas, sphagnum mosses thrive and create bogs. The mosses can tolerate poor surroundings, relying on slight traces of nutrients brought down by the rain, which they soak up like a sponge. The living moss surface of the bog may hide a considerable depth of peat below. The bog may be a mosaic of mossy pools and drier hummocks on which heathers grow.

Bogs may also form on heathlands on sandy acid soils in the lowlands.

- Paths are made.
  Bogs are neither muddy nor smelly, but a very fragile habitat, and paths are often created on reserves to steer visitors from sensitive areas.

THE COAST

Many different habitats are found where the land meets the sea: cliffs, rocky shores, shingle banks, sand dunes, estuary mudflats, saltmarsh. It is a restless interface and many habitats are in the process of change. Loose sand dunes, for example, become fixed by marram grass and then other plants, scrub and eventually trees take root.

The tides have a major influence. Where the shore (perhaps in an estuary) is covered for only a few days a month, saltmarsh is likely to develop, colourful with wild flowers. Fed by a whole river system, the base mud is rich, and saltmarshes have often been banked and drained to create rich grazing marsh.

This rich mud holds vast numbers of small worms and shellfish which attract large flocks of waders, some resident, others passing on migration, others arriving to spend the winter here. Duck and other waterfowl are also attracted - many feed on the green eel grass growing on the mud below low-water mark.

● The Wildlife Trusts do not own any marine nature reserves but work in protecting the marine environment in partnership with others.

● Boardwalks are being created across dunes. Sand dunes are fragile areas.

● Loose sand dunes are being planted with marram grass to bind them.

● There are no-go areas.
These protect nesting terns and other birds.

● Birdwatching hides are installed.

● There is strict control of shooting.

A Conservation Glossary

Some words used in this book

Bog - a fragile wetland area of waterlogged acid peat blanketed by bog moss.

Community - an interlinked assembly of plants (and animals) relatively independent of others; one community may be part of another. The aim of conservation is often to protect and maintain the character of a community.

Conservation - maintenance of (often ancient) communities of plants and animals and/or management to protect certain species.

Coppice - woodland cropped for poles; this benefits many butterflies and wild flowers.

English Nature - the official adviser to the Government on nature conservation in England. It is paralleled by the Countryside Council for Wales, Environment and Heritage Service (Northern Ireland) and Scottish Natural Heritage.

Forest - in medieval times an area of land set aside for hunting, with trees on all or part. Generally, a large area of woodland.

Grassland - except for some mountain slopes, grassland would revert to woodland if not grazed or cropped. Traditionally, grassland was long term pasture (grazed) or meadow (cut for hay, but also grazed afterwards). However, much of today's grassland is "ley", regularly ploughed and resown and cut for silage. The nature of the soil (acidic, neutral etc) is reflected by the species of grass and other plants found growing.

Habitat - the "address" of an animal or plant, its living place; the complex of soil, climate etc to which it adapted. Like a human address, the word can be large scale (woodland, moor = town) or small scale (clearing, bog = street or house number).

Heath - a (usually lowland) British habitat with heather prominent.

Herb - unlike its kitchen meaning, in this book a herb is a green, non-woody plant that dies down to a rootstock or low rosette, or survives the winter as seed.

Introduction - non-native species now established in the wild. Many are a nuisance in conservation, swamping or competing with native species (eg rhododendron, mink).

Lammas - the 2nd August, when traditional hay meadows were opened up to grazing animals.

Ley - grassland ploughed and sown as a crop.

Local Nature Reserve (LNR) - local council land, managed along conservation lines.

Management - use and care of a site for farming or conservation.

Meadow - unploughed grassland cut for hay.

Moor - (usually) upland open ground kept open by grazing; heather is usually a feature.

National Nature Reserve (NNR) - site of national importance, sometimes managed jointly with the local Wildlife Trust.

Pasture - grazing grassland.

Peat - "soil" of part-decayed plant matter.

Plantation - planted timber woodland, and largely uninviting to native wildlife.

Pollard - a tree cropped of its branches; of little timber value and frequently ancient.

Pollution - disturbance or damage to a habitat, usually by contamination as a result of people's domestic or industrial activities.

Primary - woodland that has never been anything but woodland (although usually managed) since the last Ice Age. Secondary woodland occupies once-open ground, but may by now have been established for centuries.

Ramsar site - a site of international importance to birdlife (named after the venue of a key International Convention).

Semi-natural - a habitat which although modified by people has a rather natural character. Ancient chalk turf is one example, although it rapidly changes if grazing finishes.

Shrub - a woody plant branching near ground.

Silage - grass cut young and green and stored as cattle fodder.

SSSI - a Site of Special Scientific Interest, of outstanding value for its plant and animal life, or geology, with some legal protection.

Understorey - shrubs, young trees in a wood.

Wildlife - wild animals, but usually meant to include plant life too.

Wildwood - the ancestral woodland which naturally colonised most of Britain at the end of the last Ice Age.

Regional breakdown of reserves

SCOTLAND

ULSTER

ISLE OF
MAN

NORTH

NORTH
MIDLANDS

EAST

WALES

SOUTH
MIDLANDS

SOUTH-EAST

SOUTH-WEST

South-west England

From the exposed plateau of the Lizard in Cornwall, to the gentle chalk downland of Wiltshire, this section covers a huge variety of habitats. The Lizard supports unique plantlife including Cornish heath, while the River Tamar, which almost cuts off Cornwall from the rest of England, has a tidal estuary rich in birdlife. Across the border in Devon, rivers like the Teign and the Dart, rush off Dartmoor through steep sided valleys, offering the chance to spot otters as well as birds such as the dipper and grey wagtail. The Somerset Levels were once under the sea, now they are pastures, some rich in plants, while thousands of wildfowl gather there in winter. Parts of Dorset have remained unchanged for centuries and you can still find traditional meadow farmland with ancient hedges and copses. Brownsea Island in Poole Harbour is a haven for a red squirrel population as well as nesting nightjar, little grebe and little egret. Much of the chalk downland once typical of Dorset and Wiltshire has been lost, but the unimproved grassland that remains can contain up to 40 species of plant, including a dozen orchid species; several species of blue butterfly can also be seen, including the chalkhill blue and Adonis blue.

SOUTH-WEST ENGLAND

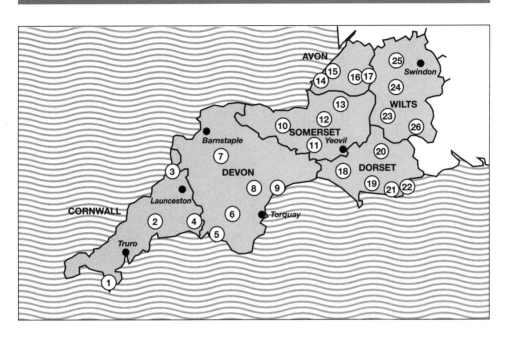

NORTH PREDANNACK DOWNS

CORNWALL WILDLIFE TRUST

Nearest town: Helston

OS Map 203 SW 695165 (start of bridleway with limited parking)

99 acres (40 ha) of prime Lizard heathland with some wet willow woodland and pools, lying within an SSSI. There is an interpretation board.

Location and access; The reserve is 2 miles south-east of Mullion, to the west of the A3083 which runs south from Helston to Lizard village. Travelling south on the A3083, turn right 1 mile south of the B3296 junction to Mullion. Take the bridlepath on the right just before the airfield gates.

The Lizard peninsula is mainly composed of serpentinite rock which provides conditions for the development of several plant communities, notably two types of Lizard heathland: short heath and tall heath. These occur in a mosaic across the reserve, with pools and some woodland or scrub around its boundaries.

The short heath develops on serpentinite which is overlain by sand and silt. The soils here are fairly well drained and acidic and the heath has a low, stunted form where heather (ling), bell heather and cross-leaved heath all grow.

WILDLIFE FEATURES
- Lizard heathland
- Emperor moth and other insects

The tall heath develops on the often wet and peaty soils which are formed directly from the serpentinite. An important plant is the beautiful Cornish heath. It is native only to the Lizard - its long flower spikes add a distinctive splash of pale pink and lilac in late summer. Here too, greyish tussocks of bog-rush stand out above the other plants.

In both types of heath you find low hummocks of very prickly western gorse.

There are often dragonflies by the pools, and this is a good place to see the spectacular emperor moth flying fast on sunny days in April and May. Its large eye spots make it unmistakable.

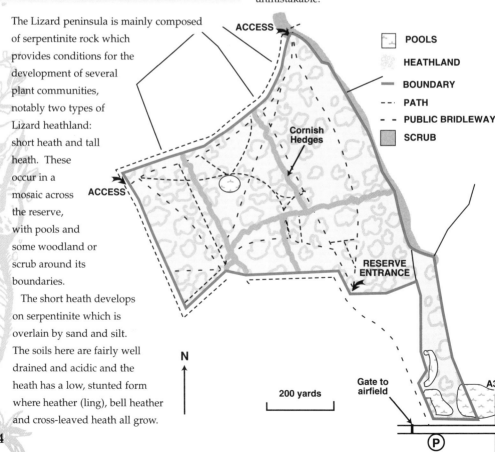

ACCESS

ACCESS

Cornish Hedges

POOLS
HEATHLAND
BOUNDARY
PATH
PUBLIC BRIDLEWAY
SCRUB

RESERVE ENTRANCE

N

200 yards

Gate to airfield

A3

P

REDMOOR

CORNWALL WILDLIFE TRUST

Nearest town: Bodmin/Lostwithiel
OS Map 200 SX 076623

A complex reserve of 235 acres (95 ha) with dry heath, bog and open water together with some mixed woodland and scrub. It is an SSSI. There are four interpretation boards.

Location and access: the reserve is about 2.5 miles (4 km) south of Bodmin and 2 miles to the north-west of Lostwithiel. There is limited car parking at the north-eastern end, but more at Helman Tor car park (SX 063614) to the west of the reserve.

Redmoor reserve is in a valley on the north-eastern edge of the St Austell granite. Its gravels were worked for alluvial tin until the end of the 19th century.

It supports a wide variety of habitats. The northern area is mainly dry, cut by open water while the low lying south is mainly marshy grassland and wet heath merging into peaty bog. There are also areas of mixed woodland and willow carr.

There are a number of interesting flowers.

WILDLIFE FEATURES
🌾 **Heathland**
🌸 **Royal fern and other wetland plants**

Bog asphodel, for example, its bright yellow flowers being followed by orange seed pods (and in fact the rest of the plant also becomes orange). There is cotton grass of course, and another flower to look for is marsh cinquefoil, with striking red-purplish flowers.

Royal fern grows extensively, in places forming an understorey in the willow carr. This is a distinctive and stately fern, growing up to chest height in a dense bushy clump, with the brownish fertile fronds sticking up above the rest.

There are a good number of dragonflies and damselflies, including the scarce blue-tailed damselfly. The nightjar nests here, together with tree pipit, willow tit, sparrowhawk and other birds.

The heath is managed by grazing with rare breeds of ponies and sheep.

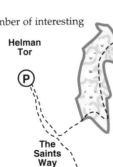

Helman Tor

The Saints Way

Redmoor

— **BOUNDARY**

WET WILLOW WOODLAND SCRUB

MOSAIC OF HEATHLAND AND BOG

PONDS

- - - **PATH**

SCRUB

200 yards

35

MAER LAKE

CORNWALL WILDLIFE TRUST

Nearest town: the reserve is in Bude
OS Map 190 SS 206076

24 acres (9.8 ha) of seasonally flooded grazing meadow. There is an interpretation board.

Location and access: Maer Lake is in Bude. Take Crooklets Road out of Bude (alongside the golf course), and veer left to the car park at Crooklets. Do not park on the road running to the west of the reserve. The reserve itself is not accessible, but the whole site and its bird life can be viewed easily from this road along the western edge; the interpretation board is on the boundary of the reserve.

The reserve is a wet grazing meadow. It is particularly important as a feeding and roosting refuge for large numbers of passage and wintering duck and waders and sea birds, and a marvellous bird-watching site. Among the birds to be seen are lapwing, herring gull, common gull, snipe, curlew, wigeon and teal. Visitors include Bewick swan, white-fronted goose and golden plover.

WILDLIFE FEATURES

- Wintering duck and waders
- Stands of yellow flag

The distinctive plant of the wetter parts, the seasonally flooded area, is the yellow flag (iris). It occurs with bogbean, common reed, marsh horsetail and starwort.

Management involves the maintenance of open water areas by clearing vegetation and sluice operation. Horses are grazed to maintain the grassland.

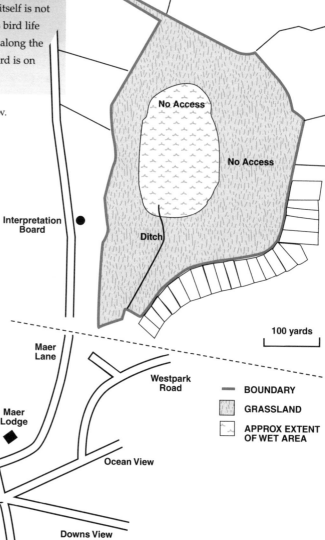

100 yards

BOUNDARY

GRASSLAND

APPROX EXTENT OF WET AREA

TAMAR ESTUARY

CORNWALL WILDLIFE TRUST

Nearest town: Saltash (Plymouth)
OS Map 201 SX 434631 (northern boundary)
421604 (southern boundary)

Nearly 1,000 acres (404 ha) of wetland, and intertidal zone SSSI. There are information boards at Cargreen and Landulph.

Location and access: The map shows the reserve's shape and location, on the west shore of the Tamar north of Saltash (and reached by side roads from the A388). There is some (very limited) parking at Landulph, near the church, and some parking in Cargreen village, north east of Landulph.

There is no access along the sea wall at Landulph. From the information board follow the public footpath along the edge of the marsh.

This reserve is of national and international ornithological importance.

There is some saltmarsh, but the site in the main is tidal mudflat which is rich in shellfish and in worms

WILDLIFE FEATURES
🦅 Winter wildfowl and waders

(the mud is fed by a whole river system) and hence attracts waders and other birds.

It is a very good birdwatching reserve. There is a wintering population of the uncommon avocet - a striking black and white wader with a noticeable upturned bill - they sift the mud with this, sweeping it from side to side.

Other passage and wintering waders for which the estuary is nationally important include snipe, black-tailed godwit, redshank, dunlin, curlew and whimbrel. Other birds to be seen include greenshank, spotted redshank, green sandpiper and golden plover. The kingfisher also.

And the otter may also be seen!

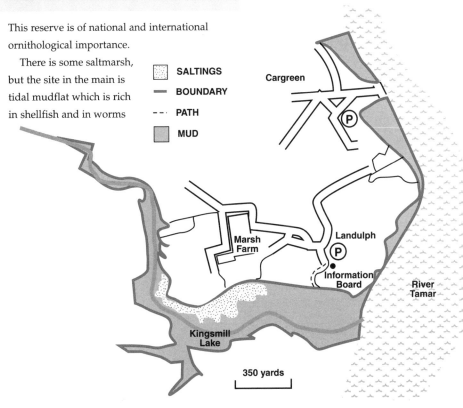

Legend:
- SALTINGS
- ▬ BOUNDARY
- - - - PATH
- MUD

Cargreen

Marsh Farm

Landulph

Information Board

River Tamar

Kingsmill Lake

350 yards

WEMBURY

DEVON WILDLIFE TRUST & PARTNERS

Nearest town: Plymstock (Plymouth)

OS Map 201/202 SX 520485

4 miles (6.4 km) of seashore and the adjacent coastal waters with a variety of wildlife habitats, protected as a result of voluntary agreements between all users to ensure sympathetic use of the area. There is a visitor centre and a warden in summer, who provides day to day management of the area.

Location and access: The visitor centre is at the western edge of the coastal village of Wembury, reached by leaving the A379 at Elburton on the east side of Plymstock and following signs for Wembury and Wembury beach. Park in the National Trust car park

The Wembury Voluntary Marine Conservation Area (VMCA) was set up in 1981.

WILDLIFE FEATURES
🐦 Varied shore life

The four miles of shore from Fort Bovisand to Gara Point embrace sandy beaches and rocky reefs, as well as numerous underwater gullies and crevices. All in all, the diversity of plant and animal species can be found in few other parts of the country. Further out to sea, for example, there are coral gardens as beautiful as any tropical reef.

Out in the bay, the Mewstone provides a safe nesting place for hundreds of cormorant, shag and greater black-backed gull, feeding on the plentiful fish in the surrounding waters.

Wembury Point is also an important landmark for waders and migratory birds.

The area is popular for scuba diving, sailing and surfing and the challenge of the VMCA initiative has been to reconcile this with the conservation of the wildlife.

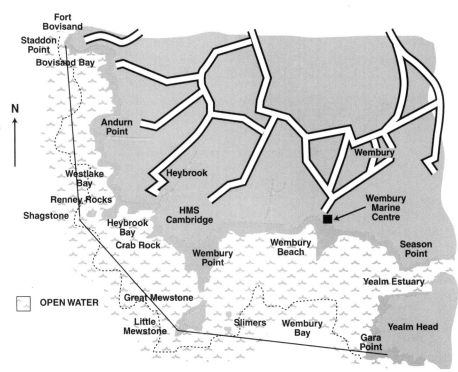

DART VALLEY

DEVON WILDLIFE TRUST

Nearest town: Ashburton
OS Map 191 SX 680727

717 acres (290 ha) of upland moor and unspoilt valley oakwood, together with the River Dart, pools and some bog. It is an SSSI.

Location and access: There are two main access points, via the New Bridge and Dartmeet car parks.

For New Bridge and the southern end of the reserve take the Dart Valley Country Park exit off the A38. Follow the signs to the country park and then continue past the park and onwards to New Bridge. Follow the road over the bridge and park in the car park on the left. A track leads north from here into the reserve.

The entrance to the northern end of the reserve is at Dartmeet, which can be reached from the south by taking the first road left just after the New Bridge car park and following it past Poundsgate. It can also be reached from the north by taking the B3357 from Two Bridges. Once at Dartmeet, park in the large car park by the sign to the 'Badgers Holt' pub, cross the road and follow the track which will take you into the reserve.

This enormous reserve occupies one side of the spectacular Dart gorge. Large areas of oakwood fill the valley bottom. Above the woodland,

WILDLIFE FEATURES
- Unspoilt moorland and
- riverside oakwoods

bracken-covered slopes give way to open moorland.

The woodland is old neglected oak coppice with birch, rowan and holly growing among the scattered moss-covered rocks.

The reserve is rich in mosses and lichens as well as ferns (two species of which are very rare) - which give the place a prehistoric feel. Bilberry and hard fern are plentiful, typical of acid soil, and grazing by sheep has encouraged large patches of Yorkshire fog grass. It's an attractive grass, with a soft feel, the heads often flushed pink. The boggier areas are home to the attractive ivy-leaved bellflower, with sky blue flowers.

The Dart Valley also supports a wealth of birds, mammals and insects. The pied flycatcher nests in the woodland, while the river is home to the nesting dipper and is also used by otters. Rarities such as the high brown fritillary butterfly and the blue ground beetle rub feelers with commoner beasts such as the ferocious green tiger beetle, while the buzzard soars overhead.

P Dartmeet

P

N

River Dart

P Poundsgate

— BOUNDARY
WOODLAND
MOORLAND

P New Bridge

750 yards

HALSDON

DEVON WILDLIFE TRUST

Nearest town: Great Torrington (Okehampton)
OS Map 180/191 SS 555125

140 acres (57 ha) of mixed valley woodland, riverside meadows and marsh and a 1-2 mile length of the River Torridge. It is an SSSI. There are marked trails.

Location and access: From Great Torrington take the B3220 south-east to Beaford. After Beaford take the minor road towards Dolton and take the next right turn. Follow this road for about 1.5 miles (2.4 km) until you reach a track on the right hand side with a Devon Wildlife Trust sign at the entrance (SS 557133). Follow this track to the car park.

In order to reduce disturbance, please keep to the way marked trails.

The woodland is mainly oak but with some beech, ash, sycamore, horse chestnut and birch along with planted conifers and other exotic trees.

WILDLIFE FEATURES
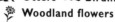
Otters ✖ Birdlife
Woodland flowers

In spring the woodland floor is crowded with flowers - bluebell, primrose and wild garlic are abundant. Snowdrop and wild daffodil grow along the river bank.

While having an important range of woodland wildlife, this reserve is perhaps most valued for the riverside habitats. This section of the Torridge is a haunt of otters and many signs of their activities can be spotted, such as the five-toed webbed paw marks, about 2.25 inches (60 mm) long and broad and the musky droppings (spraints) left as territory markers.

The river is also home to the kingfisher, sand martin, heron, dipper and grey wagtail. The oakwood birds include buzzard and lesser spotted woodpecker.

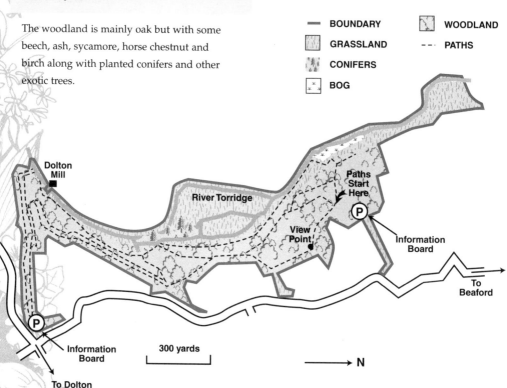

— BOUNDARY			WOODLAND
GRASSLAND		- - -	PATHS
CONIFERS			
BOG			

DUNSFORD

DEVON WILDLIFE TRUST

Nearest town: Exeter
OS Map 191 SX 798875

140 acres (56 ha) of river valley woodland, flood plain grassland and scrub and heathy rocky slopes, part of a larger SSSI.

Location and access: There are two entrances, one at Steps Bridge, the other not far from Clifford Bridge. The former lies on the Dunsford to Moretonhampstead road about 3 miles (5 km) from Moretonhampstead. Park in the Dartmoor National Park car park next to the Steps Bridge tea rooms. The reserve entrance is just past Steps Bridge itself, on the Exeter side of the bridge. For the opposite end of the reserve take the road from Dunsford towards Clifford Bridge and Clifford Cross. The reserve entrance is on the southern side of the road, half a mile from Boyland Farm.

A path runs along the valley floor between the two entrances.

WILDLIFE FEATURES
 Wild daffodil
 **Woodland butterflies**

This riverside woodland is lichen-encrusted sessile oak with stands of ash and birch - ash predominates on the extensive flood plain and the lower, wetter slopes and there are thickets of blackthorn and hawthorn with some spindle and the occasional crab apple.

The reserve is famous for its superb spring show of wild daffodil in the clearings on the valley floor. But there are many wild flowers apart from the daffodil, such as wood anemone, wood sorrel, bluebell, ramsons (wild garlic) and pignut.

There are no less than six species of fritillary butterflies to be seen here, and dragonflies are common. Dunsford is also home to the wood cricket, rarely found outside the New Forest.

As for birds, pied flycatcher, green and great spotted woodpecker, dipper and buzzard all nest on the site while dormouse and otter are also resident.

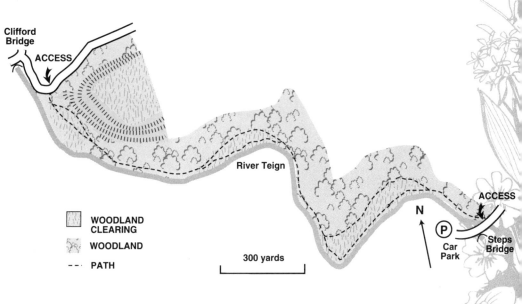

WOODLAND CLEARING
WOODLAND
PATH

Clifford Bridge
ACCESS
River Teign
300 yards
N
P Car Park
Steps Bridge
ACCESS

OTTER ESTUARY

DEVON WILDLIFE TRUST

Nearest town: Budleigh Salterton
OS Map 192 SY 076822

An estuary reserve of 57 acres (23 ha) with tidal mudflats and saltmarsh. It is an SSSI. There is a bird hide.

Location and access: Take the B3178/B3179 from Exeter to Budleigh Salterton and follow the road along the sea front. At the far (eastern) end bear off right to the public car park.

There is no access to the estuary itself but footpaths lead along either side with two viewing platforms on the western side and a hide on the east. The estuary can be crossed at its northern end at White Bridge.

Although fairly small, the estuary of the River Otter has the largest area of saltmarsh remaining in Devon. There are many typical plants - sea aster is among the flowers making a show on the middle marsh. In the upper marsh where the influence of fresh river water pre-dominates over the salt, there are areas of reeds and other wetland plants - the very poisonous hemlock water dropwort, of the cow parsley clan, is one of them.

The rich pickings of shellfish and worms to be had in the estuary mud support a good wintering population of wildfowl and waders including redshank, greenshank, dunlin, common sandpiper, ringed plover, grey plover, curlew, snipe, water rail, wigeon, teal, shelduck, brent goose, red-breasted merganser and little grebe. Reed warbler, reed bunting and sedge warbler nest on the reserve and it is a regular stop-off place for migrant birds.

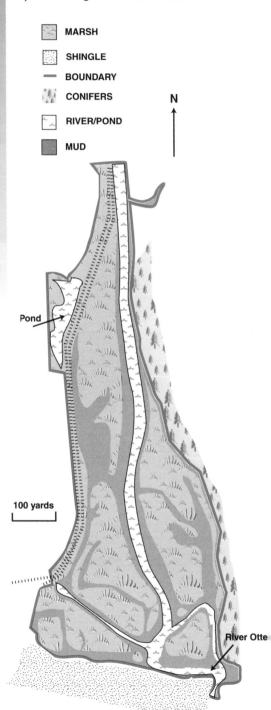

WILDLIFE FEATURES
Wintering wildfowl and waders

MARSH
SHINGLE
BOUNDARY
CONIFERS
RIVER/POND
MUD

N

Pond

100 yards

River Otter

HURSCOMBE

SOMERSET WILDLIFE TRUST

Nearest town: Minehead
OS Map 181 SS 974320

46 acres (19 ha) of scrub, marsh, rough grass and old and new woodland and water. There is a waymarked trail and nature trail leaflets are available on site.

Location and access: The reserve, which is within the Exmoor National Park, is at Wimbleball Lake, a reservoir in the Brendon Hills 1.5 miles east of Brompton Regis on a minor road from that village to the B3190. The entrance is at SS 969 317 on the west side of Bessom Bridge - the large bridge across Wimbleball Lake - and the reserve occupies the northern end of the lake, above the bridge. The map shows the location of the car park and picnic site.

This is an oasis of a site, set as it is in intensively farmed land. French Combe is a sheltered meadow and East Hurscombe a secluded marshy area where the Bessom and another small stream enter the reservoir.

There is some interesting botany, including wild cherry and wild service trees (these have been planted although they are native) and wild raspberry which does grow wild on the Brendon Hills. For wild flowers (more than 100 species have been logged here) the marsh and the rabbit-grazed sward are the richest sites: look for abundant meadow-sweet, kingcup, ragged robin, lousewort (wort means plant) and bird's- foot-trefoil among them.

WILDLIFE FEATURES

🦋 Birdlife   🦋 Butterflies/moths
🌼 Flowers

Thirty species of butterflies have been seen here - pearl-bordered, silver washed and marsh fritillaries occasionally with small and large skippers and common and holly blue among those seen frequently.

Nesting birds include kestrel, buzzard, raven, tawny owl, whinchat, redstart, pied flycatcher, all three woodpeckers, willow warbler and blackcap. Great crested grebe, wigeon, teal, pochard and tufted duck are seen on the lake - they winter here.

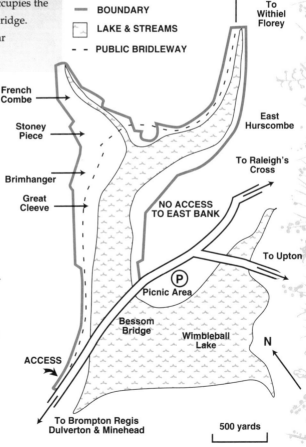

─── BOUNDARY
▨ LAKE & STREAMS
- - PUBLIC BRIDLEWAY

To Withiel Florey

French Combe

Stoney Piece

Brimhanger

Great Cleeve

East Hurscombe

To Raleigh's Cross

NO ACCESS TO EAST BANK

To Upton

(P) Picnic Area

Bessom Bridge

Wimbleball Lake

N

ACCESS

To Brompton Regis Dulverton & Minehead

500 yards

43

FYNE COURT

Nearest towns: Bridgwater and Taunton
OS Map 182 ST 223321

Basically an old estate (the bulk of the house burnt down in the 1890s) with an arboretum, woodland, lake, ponds and an old quarry. It is the Trust's HQ and visitor centre.

Location and access: Fyne Court is in Broomfield, about half way between Bridgwater and Taunton, reached (from Bridgwater) via side roads past Enmore. The route is well signposted.

The estate is notable for the variety of habitats, all easily accessible. The arboretum (planted in the 1780s) has had 50 new tree species added a couple of decades ago. The slopes here have been planted with daffodils, and there is snowdrop in the valley.

There are about 22 acres of woodland, much of which has been replanted with oak and ash, more typical of the Quantock Hills than the original sycamore and laurel - both of these are invasive foreigners and work is ongoing to reduce their spread.

There are various paths, picnic sites and trails with accompanying leaflets for the visitor.

Among the nesting birds are long-tailed tit, marsh tit,

WILDLIFE FEATURES
🖢 **A good variety of plant and animal life**

treecreeper, nuthatch, chiffchaff and blackcap, while a pair of great spotted woodpecker regularly nests each year in the vicinity of the old quarry.

The woodlands support a great variety of fungi and deadwood invertebrates.

- **━━** BOUNDARY
- **▢** OPEN WATER
- **▧** WOODLAND
- **⁂** CONIFERS
- **- - -** PATH

Quarryland

Quarryland

Boat House

Walled Garden

N

P

Arboretum

Warden's Cottage

Arboretum

Fyne Court Farm

The Old Post Office

100 yards

44

CATCOTT HEATH & LOWS

SOMERSET WILDLIFE TRUST

Nearest town: Bridgwater
OS Map 182 ST 399 414

A fragment of overgrown rich fen and arable land which has been restored to seasonally wet grassland. There are bird hides and information boards.

Location and access: About half way between Bridgwater and Glastonbury, on the A39, take the signposted turning north for Catcott. Go north through the village past the war memorial and down onto the moors. After a sharp left and right turn, go straight ahead to the car park or park at the drove end as the road next goes sharp left. Catcott Lows has no access but can be viewed from two hides. For Catcott Heath walk eastwards down Leather Drove for three quarters of a mile; the entrance is on your right.

WILDLIFE FEATURES

❀ **Wetland wild flowers**
✿ **Dragonflies** 🦅 **Wintering wildfowl and waders**

Catcott Lows, restored to wet grassland since 1991, has winter flooding and provides sightings of wildfowl and waders in thousands, especially lapwing, mallard, teal, wigeon, pintail and shoveler. Lapwing and redshank breed here and whimbrel is one of the passage waders seen. Garganey and marsh harrier are often present.

Catcott Heath has areas of carr woodland, bog myrtle scrub and tall fen (milk parsley is one plant to look for here) and purple moor grass. There are some interesting management experiments taking place; and these are explained on site. For example sundew and marsh pea are being encouraged in nursery beds, and cut areas sport devil's-bit scabious, southern marsh orchid and meadowsweet. The raft spider and great crested newt haunt the pools, which are patrolled by dragonflies.

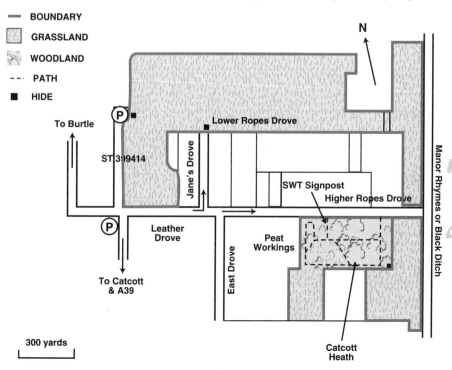

- — **BOUNDARY**
- **GRASSLAND**
- **WOODLAND**
- --- **PATH**
- ■ **HIDE**

To Burtle

ST 399414

Lower Ropes Drove

Jane's Drove

SWT Signpost

Higher Ropes Drove

Leather Drove

Peat Workings

East Drove

To Catcott & A39

Manor Rhymes or Black Ditch

N

Catcott Heath

300 yards

45

BLACK ROCK

SOMERSET WILDLIFE TRUST

Nearest town: Wells

OS Map 182 ST 482545

181 acres (73 ha) of limestone grassland, scree and scrub with some woodland and plantation, part of the Cheddar Gorge SSSI. There is a waymarked trail, owned by the National Trust.

Location and access: The reserve is at the head of the Cheddar Gorge about 1.5 miles (2.5 km) from Cheddar on the B3135 from Cheddar towards Priddy and Bath. There is parking at the Black Rock gate, where trail leaflets are available. Visitors are asked to keep to the paths and to control their dogs.

The main botanical interest in this reserve lies with the grassland with a myriad of flowers, such as lesser meadow rue, rock stonecrop, spring cinquefoil, thyme, rockrose, violet, small scabious and salad burnet. The old drystone walls (and scree) of limestone are an interesting feature - there is one wall immediately from the car park for example which is probably 200 years old. The exposed stone carries many lichens and ferns including the uncommon limestone fern (or limestone polypody) and brittle bladder fern.

There are many butterflies to find - maybe the dark green fritillary in the sheltered glades on a sunny summer day and Black Rock Drove, the northern section, is good for small and common blues together with their close relation the brown argus; the last has no blue colour in either sex

WILDLIFE FEATURES
❀ **Limestone flowers**
🦋 **Butterflies and moths**

(many female blue butterflies are brownish in colour).

Much of the grassland has been invaded by scrub since the rabbits were decimated by disease in the 1950s and sheep grazing eased. However in recent years, scrub clearance, fencing and sheep grazing have been introduced with the bonus of offering nest sites for birds.

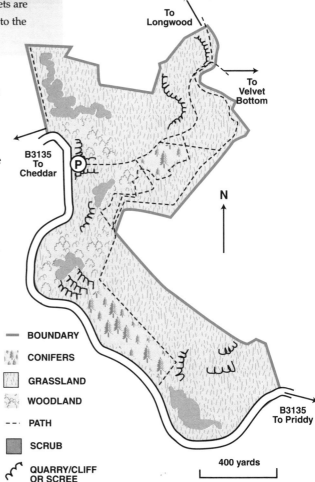

BOUNDARY
CONIFERS
GRASSLAND
WOODLAND
PATH
SCRUB
QUARRY/CLIFF OR SCREE

400 yards

AVON WILDLIFE TRUST

Nearest town: Weston super Mare
OS Map 182 ST 315580

52 acres (21 ha) of mudflats and saltmarsh, backed by wet grassland, a strip of woodland and limestone grassland.

Location and access: The reserve is at Uphill on the southern edge of Weston super Mare, at the mouth of the River Axe. The map explains its position. There is parking at the lay-by (see map).

WILDLIFE FEATURES
🐦 **Wildfowl and waders** 🌼 **Wild flowers**

as the fragile pinkish-flowered green-winged orchid which joins the pyramidal and common-spotted orchids here.

These flowers encourage butterflies - 23 species breed here, not only on the limestone grassland but also benefiting from the mosaic of scrub and nearby woodland. The chalkhill blue is one of the grassland butterflies (its host plant is horseshoe vetch) - this is one of its only sites in Avon.

This is a prime reserve, with an amazing diversity of landscape, habitats and species. Mudflats and saltmarsh border the River Axe. The rich estuary mud, teeming with worms and shellfish, provides ideal feeding and roosting for wildfowl and wading birds from August to April. Shelduck are perhaps the most obvious, but there are also dunlin, redshank and curlew. The saltmarsh itself can also be alight with sea aster, sea lavender and other flowers. Skylark and finches feed on the seed heads here, sometimes to be scattered by a swooping peregrine or the occasional merlin.

Further inland wet grassland shelters wintering snipe and sometimes lapwing; this zone is backed by a strip of scrub beyond which rises Walborough Hill, with wonderful views but also a good display of wild flowers in the limestone turf. Kidney vetch, rockrose, wild thyme, and small scabious are common, but there are also several rarities growing, such

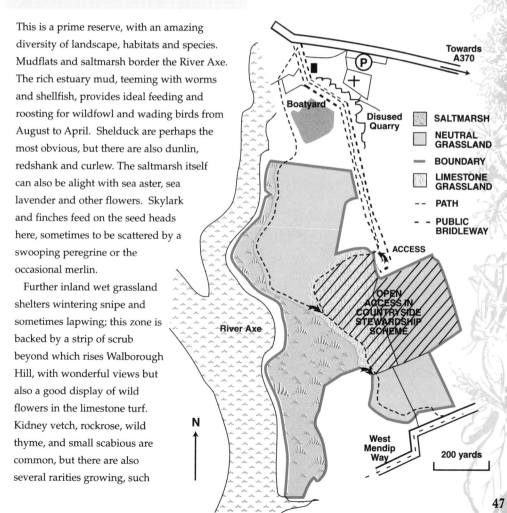

Towards A370

Boatyard

Disused Quarry

	SALTMARSH
	NEUTRAL GRASSLAND
—	BOUNDARY
	LIMESTONE GRASSLAND
--	PATH
- -	PUBLIC BRIDLEWAY

ACCESS

OPEN ACCESS IN COUNTRYSIDE STEWARDSHIP SCHEME

River Axe

N

West Mendip Way

200 yards

WESTON BIG WOOD

AVON WILDLIFE TRUST

Nearest town: Clevedon
OS Map 172 ST 456750

94 acres (38 ha) of ancient woodland; it is an SSSI.

Location and access: From the B3124 Clevedon to Portishead road, turn into Valley Road. Park in the lay-by approximately 300 yards along on the right and walk up the hill. Steps lead into the wood from the road. A circular path links with the ride, but paths can be slippery and steep sided; keep away from the quarry sides.

This is one of Avon's largest ancient woodlands, having never been anything but woodland since the end of the last Ice Age. It has been worked - and the stones, ditches and banks are probably medieval woodland compartment boundaries.

The slopes of this limestone ridge bear the uncommon small-leaved lime, while oak and hazel are more abundant at the top of the hill. Rare whitebeam species and wild service trees

WILDLIFE FEATURES
🌼 **Whitebeam and other limestone species**
🦅 **Woodland birds**

are also dotted throughout the woodland.

In spring the ground is speckled with wood anemone and violet, and with blankets of bluebell. The presence of herb Paris and yellow archangel, together with the rare purple gromwell, underline the fact that this is an ancient woodland. (The small-leaved lime is also an indicator of ancient woodland.)

The ride is excellent for butterflies such as orange tip, speckled wood and silver-washed fritillary.

The wood is also very good for birds, including woodpeckers, nuthatch and tawny owl. Bats also find roost sites in the trees. The many setts indicate a large badger population.

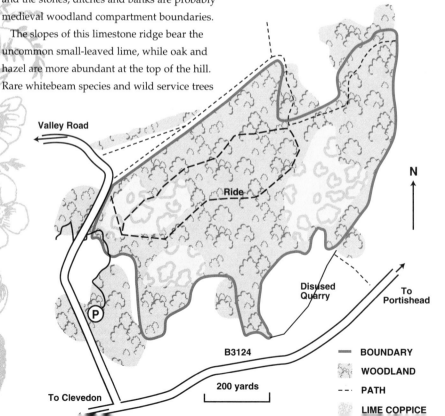

Valley Road

N

Ride

Disused Quarry

To Portishead

P

B3124

To Clevedon

200 yards

— **BOUNDARY**

🌲 **WOODLAND**

-- - **PATH**

🌿 **LIME COPPICE**

48

CHEW VALLEY LAKE

AVON WILDLIFE TRUST

Nearest town: Bristol
OS Map 172 ST 570582

207 acres (83.5 ha) of the southern end of the large Chew Valley Reservoir are managed by the Wildlife Trust. There are bird hides and a visitor centre.

Location and access: Chew Valley Lake lies about 8 miles (13 km) due south of central Bristol. Take the B3114 south from Chew Stoke, bear left for West Harptree and head north-east on the A368. There are good views of the reserve from the causeway at Herriott's Bridge where there is car parking.

There is a visitor centre run by Bristol Water at the picnic site near the dam.

Should you wish to use the bird hides, you need a daily or annual permit from Woodford Lodge (Bristol Water). The Lodge is reached via the metalled track which heads towards the lake about half a mile south of Chew Stoke on the B3114.

WILDLIFE FEATURES
➤ **Wildfowl and waders**
✿ **Lime-rich grassland**

Chew Valley Lake, the largest artificial fresh-water lake in the south-west, is edged by extensive reed beds. It is extremely important for migrating birds including warblers and swallows and martins, and for wintering wildfowl and waders. Large numbers of reed warbler nest in the reedbeds, which are also a vital autumn feeding station for both it and the sedge warbler.

Wintering and passage wildfowl include important numbers of shoveler, gadwall, teal and tufted duck. Numbers of fish-eating birds such as goosander, great crested grebe and cormorant are also high (the autumn grebe numbers can be amongst the highest in Britain). The winter gull roost is also a spectacular sight with up to 50,000 or more birds at a time.

Breeding birds include great crested and little grebe, gadwall, tufted duck, shoveler and pochard. The hobby often feeds over the area in late summer and large numbers of dragonflies hunt over the water. When the water level falls, the mud can attract waders such as dunlin, ringed plover and green sandpiper.

Chew often attracts rare birds, including osprey!

Chew Valley Lake

To West Harptree

Herriott's Bridge

A368

N

REEDBEDS
BOUNDARY
WOODLAND
LAKE

300 yards

49

FOLLY FARM

AVON WILDLIFE TRUST

Nearest town: Bristol
OS Map 172 ST 610603

A peaceful and unspoilt 17th century farm of 250 acres (101 ha), with flowery meadows and woodlands offering splendid views. The meadows and Dowlings Wood are SSSI.

Location and access: The farm is about 8 miles (13 km) due south of the centre of Bristol, to the east of Chew Valley Lake. Locate the village of Bishop Sutton, on the A368 running east of the lake. About half a mile (1 km) north-east of Bishop Sutton take the track to the right and follow the signs. Park in the car park.

There is open access to all parts of the farm, but please remember to close the gates. Dogs are not allowed.

There is disabled parking next to the farmhouse, and there is a walk suitable for wheelchair users.

WILDLIFE FEATURES
❀ **Traditional meadow flowers**
✘ **Woodland birds**

The pasture is of a kind now rare in the area. It is unspoilt by pesticides and fertilisers (the latter encourage the rank grasses at the expense of the slighter plants) and in summer is brimming with flowers such as betony, oxeye daisy and heath spotted orchid. In late summer it is covered with drifts of black knapweed and devil's-bit scabious.

Many butterflies can be seen throughout the summer, including ringlet, gatekeeper and marbled white. The rare marsh fritillary butterfly has also been seen here, flying in early summer.

Of the two woodlands, Dowlings Wood is largely an ancient hazel coppice. Its floor is rich in springtime with primrose, bluebell and early purple orchid.

Among the many birds to be seen are marsh tit, buzzard and great spotted woodpecker. The tawny owl also nests on the reserve.

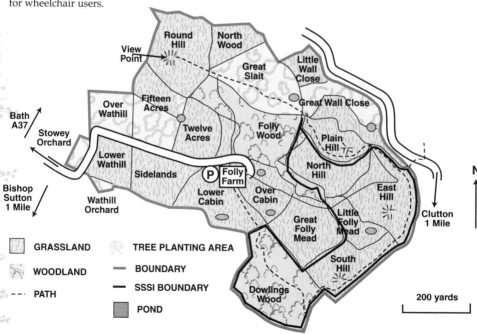

KINGCOMBE MEADOWS

DORSET WILDLIFE TRUST

Nearest town: Dorchester
OS Map 194 SY 554990

371 acres (150 ha) of traditional meadow farmland with ancient hedges and copses, three quarters of which is SSSI status. There is an information centre and a warden to hand.

Location and access: From Dorchester, take the A356 north-west towards Crewkerne. 1 mile past Maiden Newton (which is about 7 miles, (11 km) from Dorchester) take the side road to the left for Toller Porcorum. Turn right at the Old Swan pub, and as you enter the hamlet of Lower Kingcombe, Pound Cottage Information Centre is the first building on the right, up a short, steep drive. There is a small car park here (please do not park in the hamlet).

All dogs must be kept under close control. You can often walk where you will, but bulls are run with the cattle, and notices are posted on gates when this is happening. Keep to the paths in the hay fields.

This is a reserve of national importance but also a working farm, a lovely example of England as it was before the intensive farming of this century. With its patchwork of small named fields, ancient hedges, old tracks and corners of boggy land, it is quite unlike the surrounding modern countryside. The Wildlife Trust maintains it as a grazing-hay complex (with cattle and sheep).

It is bursting with wildlife.

WILDLIFE FEATURES
 **Butterflies** **Wild flowers**

Some of the meadows have 150 plant species growing - lady's mantle and devil's-bit scabious among them, with the marshy areas alight with yellow flag iris, ragged robin and water forget-me-not. The flowers are matched by the butterflies: of 56 native species, 36 have been seen here at various times, including the scarce wood white and marsh fritillary. The birdlife, of course - which includes buzzard, dipper and nuthatch - is superb.

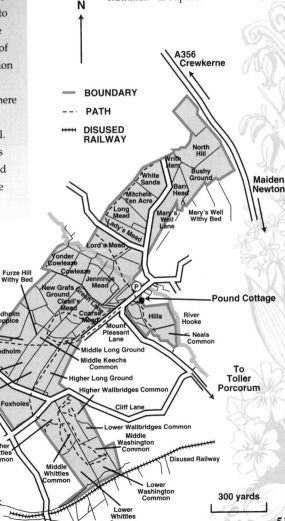

51

HIGHER HYDE HEATH

DORSET WILDLIFE TRUST

Nearest town: Wareham
OS Map 194 SY 853902

100 acres (40 ha) of Dorset lowland heath, part
of which was dug for sand and gravel.
It is an SSSI.

Location and access: Leave Wareham to the
west on the A352 for Dorchester, and after about
2 miles (3 km) take the unclassified road to
Puddletown on the left. The reserve is about
3 miles along this road, on the right.

There was sand and gravel digging here (and
the neighbourhood is still extensively
quarried); a series of mounds and water-filled
hollows mark the older workings in the western
corner - an interesting example of how past
industrial workings can revert to nature.

WILDLIFE FEATURES
- Snakes and lizards
- Birdlife including Dartford warbler

The reserve sits on infertile sands and gravels
with lenses of clay. With the original forest
cover cleared (possibly from the Bronze Age
onwards) heathland developed, its exact make-
up of plants influenced by the ground water.
Here at Higher Hyde we have areas of dry
heath dominated by heather (ling) and bell
heather and wet heath dominated by cross-
leaved heath and purple moor grass. In the wet
heath there may be noticeable carpets of bog
mosses. Here the nutrient level is really low
and sundews and pale butterwort both add to
their intake by trapping and digesting
small insects.

Paradoxically, however, it is in the wet that
you look for the handsome flowers - the
yellow bog asphodel (seed cases and stems
turn vivid orange in autumn) and the
pink spikes of early marsh orchid. The
purple moor grass may form large
tussocks.

There is abundant insect life -
dragonflies and damselflies, bog
bush cricket and emperor moth
are to be seen. Of the
butterflies, there is a good
population of the rare
silver-studded blue.

As well as snakes
and common lizard,
the rare smooth snake
and sand lizard are
here, although
reclusive. Birds
include the nightjar,
in pine areas and
Dartford warbler
(nesting in the gorse).

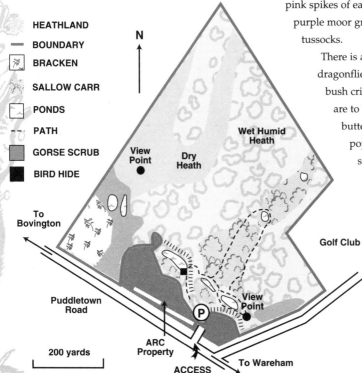

KEY
- HEATHLAND
- BOUNDARY
- BRACKEN
- SALLOW CARR
- PONDS
- PATH
- GORSE SCRUB
- BIRD HIDE

N

View Point

Dry Heath

Wet Humid Heath

To Bovington

Golf Club

Puddletown Road

View Point

P

ARC Property

200 yards

ACCESS

To Wareham

FONTMELL DOWN

DORSET WILDLIFE TRUST

Nearest town: Shaftesbury
OS Map 183 ST 884176

145 acres (58 ha) of chalk downland, scattered scrub and woodland. It is an SSSI.

Location and access: The reserve is adjacent to the upper Shaftesbury to Blandford road, the unclassified road running about 2 miles (3 km) to the east of the A350. It can be reached by leaving the A350 at Fontmell Magna. Parking is as shown on the map.

The reserve is one of the best remaining stretches of chalk downland, a steep sided valley which drains into the Blackmoor Vale. The turf is alight with flowers - in spring and early summer you will find lady's bedstraw, common bird's-foot-trefoil, wild thyme and salad burnet together with less common species such as early gentian and clustered bellflower. With careful searching you may also find early purple and bee orchids and the less obvious frog orchid. Later in the year restharrow, small scabious, pyramidal orchid and the delicate harebell come into their own. The prickly, straw-coloured 'everlasting' carline thistle is another flower to look for. A speciality of the down is the spiral-flowered coconut-scented autumn lady's tresses.

The reserve is also good for butterflies - the marbled white, common and Adonis blue, brown argus, large skipper and often painted lady (a butterfly which is probably largely migrant).

Jerry's Hole is an additional small

WILDLIFE FEATURES
❀ **Wild flowers** ☙ **Downland butterflies**

reserve to the south of Fontmell Down, worth visiting (the map shows its location). It is a partly scrubbed-up meadow, managed for its population of knapweed broomrape. The broomrapes are strange, parasitic plants, the knapweed broomrape having a rather yellowish spike of flowers.

There is quite a good bird population in this area, 35 species nesting, largely in the thickets and woods. They include nightingale and yellowhammer.

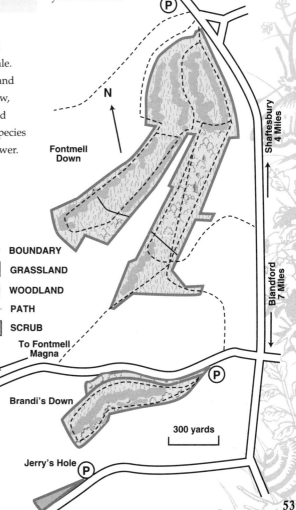

- — **BOUNDARY**
- **GRASSLAND**
- **WOODLAND**
- - - - **PATH**
- **SCRUB**

53

PURBECK MARINE WILDLIFE RESERVE

DORSET WILDLIFE TRUST

Nearest town: Wareham
OS Map 195 SY 905790

An unofficial reserve, about 5 miles (8 km) of coast protected by voluntary agreement between the owners and regular users and the Wildlife Trust. There is an information centre and aquarium and a warden.

Location and access: Leave Wareham southwards in the direction of Swanage and at Stoborough Green take the turning right for East Creech and Kimmeridge (the turning is about 1 mile from the centre of Wareham). Go through Kimmeridge and the information centre and car parking are reached, via a toll road.

The reserve is backed by army firing ranges and warning notices should be respected: do not pass the warning notice on the beach when a red flag is flying on the cliff top.

To any geology student worth their hammer, Kimmeridge is a textbook illustration of revealed strata - one of the rocks being a greasy shale that was once mined for its oil.

But geology apart, another bonus is an

WILDLIFE FEATURES
🐚 Marine life

extraordinary range of seashore life. The rocky layers shelve gently out to sea in ledges like rotten piano keys and on these at low tide you can study the succession of more than a hundred seaweeds growing in the often crystal clear water. The unusual tidal cycle makes it an ideal place to explore - at times of spring tide the low water lasts for most of the afternoon.

The shallow waters of Kimmeridge Bay are virtually clear of kelp so that the marine life is visibly abundant, not only crabs galore, but several species of brightly coloured wrasse which wouldn't look out of place on a coral reef. Visitors can observe them using the live remote subsea TV system.

The 'reserve' includes not only the famous rocks and ledges but also the deeper water beyond the low tide mark where the rocks are smothered with a bewildering variety of marine life. Here there is an underwater nature trail for divers!

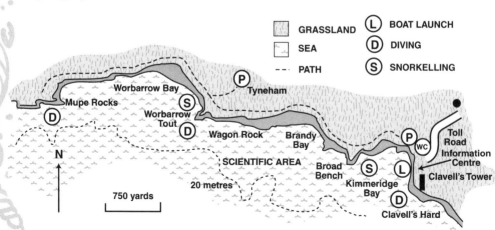

BROWNSEA ISLAND

DORSET WILDLIFE TRUST

Nearest town: Poole
OS Map 195 SZ 028878

The Wildlife Trust reserve consists of 250 acres (100 ha) of this island, with Scots and maritime pine woodlands, two lakes with some reedbeds and some wetland carr with sallow and alder; and a brackish lagoon. It is SSSI status. There are guided and self-guided tours and bird watching hides.

Location and access: The island is in Poole Harbour; it is open from 1st April until the first week of October (the end-of-season details may vary).

Access is by boat from Sandbanks or Poole quay - run by an independent operator. In addition to the ferry charges there is a National Trust landing fee payable.

The first boats run from 1000 am; the island closes at 1700 pm, or 1800 during the high season.

Access to the reserve is restricted; in July and August there is a guided tour every day; in April, May, June and September there is a daily self-guided trail. There is an additional charge for guided tours and self-guided trails in the reserve area.

WILDLIFE FEATURES

🐿 Red squirrel   🐦 Wildfowl and waders

Brownsea Island is the largest of the islands in Poole Harbour, occupying about 550 acres in all, the Trust reserve occupying the northern half.

Renowned for its red squirrel population, the reserve also boasts many other important wildlife features - a flourishing colony of common and sandwich terns and important flocks of over-wintering ducks and waders including shelduck, avocet and black-tailed godwit. There is a large heronry with 70-100 nesting pairs.

In addition the island has nesting nightjar, little grebe, reed warbler and little egret.

Twenty three species of dragonfly have been recorded, notably downy emerald, ruddy darter and small red damselfly.

▬	BOUNDARY
▨	WETLAND
▨	BRACKISH LAGOON
▨	CONIFERS
▨	LAKE & OPEN WATER
- - -	PATH
■	HIDE

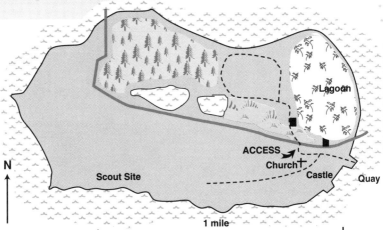

SMALLBROOK MEADOWS

WILTSHIRE WILDLIFE TRUST

Nearest town: Warminster
OS Map 183 ST 878443

The reserve is made up of wet meadow and linked wet habitats, including an area of willow woodland.

Location and access: The reserve lies in a valley just south of Warminster town centre, adjacent to the Lake Pleasure Grounds. It can be reached by walking through the park from Weymouth Street or from the car park on Smallbrook Road. There is access for wheelchairs into one of the meadows from here.

Smallbrook Meadows were water meadows, created two or three centuries ago in the chalk-stream regions of Wiltshire and Hampshire. The meadows lay alongside streams or rivers and with a system of sluices and dug channels, they were flushed with warm, silty water to promote an early growth of spring grass for sheep grazing. The ridges and furrows of the channels can still be seen here in winter but get hidden by plant growth in the summer.

The reserve has plants that are now generally rare because of the widespread draining and ploughing in the wider countryside, plants such as water avens and

WILDLIFE FEATURES
❀ Marsh marigold and other wetland flowers

ragged robin. The handsome bright yellow marsh marigold flowers where the ground is wet and the lovely flowers of yellow flag are followed by the pink and cream of great willow herb. By the end of July, the meadowsweet forms a shoulder-high mass of cream coloured and sweet scented flowerheads.

There are many dragonflies and damselflies, and small copper, small tortoiseshell and meadow brown butterflies are abundant in some years. The tall vegetation provides cover for snipe in winter and nesting sedge warbler in summer.

The woodland, mainly of white willow, is of interest. The trunks and branches of the trees are covered with mosses, lichens and ivy. Some have polypody ferns growing on them. Conditions here are just right for the woodpeckers, nuthatch and tree creeper.

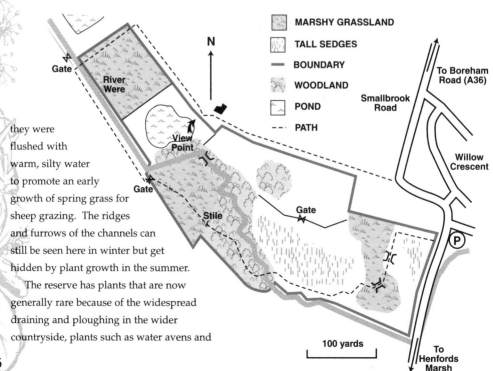

MORGAN'S HILL

WILTSHIRE WILDLIFE TRUST

Nearest town: Calne
OS Map 173 SU 019671

A good example of chalk downland, with several uncommon species of plants and animals to be found. There is a picnic area.

Location and access: This reserve lies between Calne and Devizes, next to the North Wiltshire Golf Course. Park in the Smallgrain Plantation picnic site car park and walk down the steps at the far end of the picnic area. The main part of the reserve is about a quarter of a mile along the track.

An extensive network of paths links the Roman road with Cherhill Down and Avebury. The Wansdyke can be followed across the top of the Pewsey Downs to Savernake Forest.

Please keep dogs on a lead at all times.

This reserve is on a north-facing slope of the Marlborough Downs with commanding views over the countryside of north Wiltshire. Much of Britain's chalk grassland has been lost to improved farming, but Wiltshire has some of the best remaining sites, including this reserve. Much of it has escaped the plough (the old anthills are the clue).

WILDLIFE FEATURES
✿ Downland flowers

There is some scrub including guelder rose and wayfaring tree, both typical of chalk. Of great interest are the juniper bushes on the bank just inside the gate; they are now quite rare in Britain. Deeper into the reserve is a shoulder of woodland of ash and birch, colonising an area which saw little grazing in the past.

The wild flowers provide an ever-changing display of colour, from the first cowslip and violets of spring to the summer abundance of orchids, wild thyme and bird's-foot-trefoil. The purple heads of devil's-bit scabious and small scabious persist well into autumn. One rarity is the lesser butterfly orchid with creamy white flowers.

Small tortoiseshell, common blue and marbled white are just three of the butterflies to be seen here.

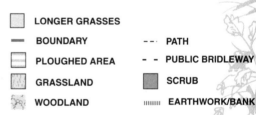

	LONGER GRASSES		
—	BOUNDARY	- - -	PATH
	PLOUGHED AREA	- -	PUBLIC BRIDLEWAY
	GRASSLAND		SCRUB
	WOODLAND	ⅢⅢ	EARTHWORK/BANK

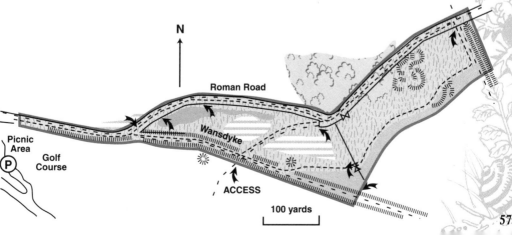

N

Roman Road

Wansdyke

Picnic Area

Golf Course

(P)

ACCESS

100 yards

RAVENSROOST WOOD

WILTSHIRE WILDLIFE TRUST

Nearest town: Malmesbury
OS Map 173 SU 024877

A mainly oak woodland, wet in places and with a wide variety of wildlife.

Location and access: The reserve is to the west of Swindon, approximately 1.5 miles (2.5 km) south of the village of Minety and 2.5 miles north of Brinkworth. At the crossroads on the B4040 to Malmesbury, turn south and in a short while take the right hand road for Brinkworth.

The car park is at the southern end of the wood: continue south along the Brinkworth road and turn right for the car park which is tucked away behind a steep bank. Access is by way of a kissing gate in the car park.

This is a very varied wood; some traces of ridge and furrow shows that it was once farmland in part, but the plants elsewhere point to ancient woodland. The land slopes gently down from the western boundary and being poorly drained, the lower-lying heavy clay has a distinctive community with oaks planted about 100 years ago being the main tree. Because of the waterlogging they have grown slowly with spreading crowns (the bushes have been coppiced). The conifers were also planted but the ash is probably self-seeded. However there are small-leaved lime and wild

WILDLIFE FEATURES
✿ Woodland flowers

service trees in the older parts; they are indicators of ancient woodland. Midland hawthorn is another.

In spring the wild flowers can be spectacular, with bright yellow lesser celandine, bluebell and pignut. The edges of the main ride have primrose, sanicle, wood sorrel and goldilocks buttercup.

There are many butterflies (white admiral and silver-washed fritillary among them), songbirds too. The ponds, dug as clay pits, mean plenty of dragonflies are to be seen, often hunting along the rides.

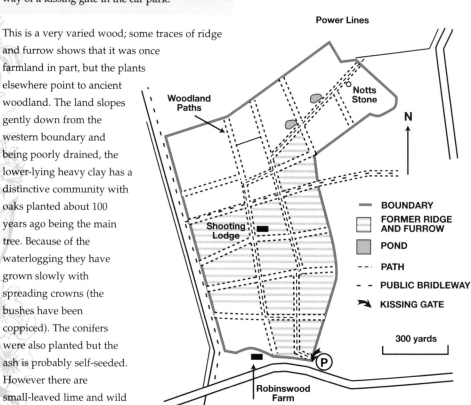

COOMBE BISSETT DOWN

WILTSHIRE WILDLIFE TRUST

Nearest town: Salisbury
OS Map 184 SU 111256

A chalk grassland reserve of nearly 90 acres (35 ha).

Location and access: This reserve is very straightforward to find. From Salisbury head south-west on the A354 Blandford Forum road as far as Coombe Bissett. In the village turn left (east) immediately after you cross the river. After a short distance turn right up Pennings Drove. The gate into the reserve is a short distance up the hill on the right.

This is well worth a visit, tucked away in a quiet secluded valley on the downs south of Salisbury. There is something to be seen at all times of year.

It is basically a chalk downland reserve with species-rich chalk banks and lynchets; lynchets are the broad flat wedges cut into the slopes in Wiltshire, Dorset and other chalk counties by ploughing in the past. Maybe in the very distant past, for while some authorities count them as medieval, others think they are prehistoric. Some of the area has been ploughed recently but is now being restored to flower-rich grassland, a process which will take many years to complete. There are also small areas of scrub and a beech woodland.

Coombe Bissett is one of the top sites in the county for the rare burnt orchid; and there are also other scarce plants such as the dwarf sedge.

The Adonis blue, brown argus, small blue and chalkhill blue butterflies are all seen here. The Adonis blue is much rarer than the chalkhill blue, which puzzled the experts because they both have horseshoe vetch as host plant on which the

WILDLIFE FEATURES
❀ **Chalk grassland flowers**

eggs are laid. But research showed that the Adonis blue chose only short plants in real sunspots - nooky hollows on south facing slopes. So far so good, but that was only part of the reason. These sheltered patches were found to be those chosen by an ant species, which 'adopts' the caterpillar - in exchange for sugary 'nectar' exuded by the caterpillar they protect it from parasitic wasps and other threats.

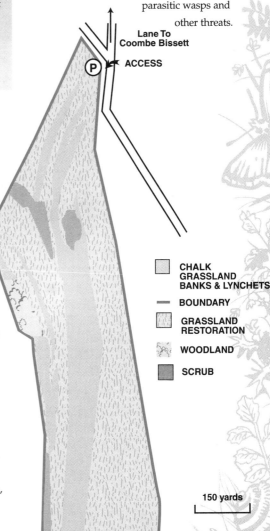

Lane To
Coombe Bissett

Ⓟ ◄ ACCESS

☐ CHALK GRASSLAND BANKS & LYNCHETS

— BOUNDARY

▨ GRASSLAND RESTORATION

WOODLAND

■ SCRUB

150 yards

South-east England

There are many surprisingly wild and unspoilt areas in this heavily populated part of the UK. Hampshire's coast has internationally important places for birds, such as Farlington Marshes, part of Langstone harbour where thousands of Brent geese overwinter each year. The Weald clay country of Sussex has hundreds of hectares of mature oak forest including the Mens and Ebernoe Common. Huge beech trees are also found there, as well as spectacular wild flowers and rare woodland butterflies. To the west of London, Surrey heathlands are probably the county's most important habitat, created by forest clearance thousands of years ago, while Sandwich on the east coast of Kent, is the first port of call for thousands of birds

arriving from continental Europe including shelduck, oystercatcher, dunlin and sanderling. Even in London you can get away from it all. Sydenham Hill Wood was once part of a much larger wood that stretched from Deptford to Selhurst and is rich in birdlife including three species of woodpecker, goldcrest, chiffchaff and treecreeper as well as wild flowers such as bluebell, wild garlic and wood anemone. Former industrial sites have also been reclaimed by nature - for example, Camley Street Natural Park to the rear of King's Cross Station was once a coal depot - now it has wildlife habitats including a meadow, pond and wetland area.

SOUTH-EAST ENGLAND

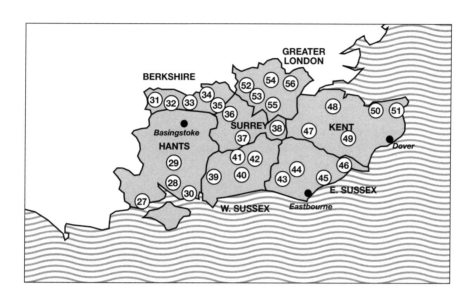

LYMINGTON REEDBEDS

HAMPSHIRE & ISLE OF WIGHT WILDLIFE TRUST

Nearest town: Lymington
OS Map 196 SZ 308917

80 acres (32 ha) of wetland with one of the largest reedbeds in southern England, bordered by wet 'carr' woodland of alder and willow with some oak on drier ground. It is an SSSI.

Location and access: The reserve is a short distance from the centre of Lymington, on the east bank of the river, stretching up from the A3054 road to Beaulieu. Parking places are shown on the map.

WILDLIFE FEATURES
↝ **Otter** *✹* **Birdlife**

Until Victorian times, this area formed part of the Lymington estuary. Then a causeway was built to exclude seawater from the river, and grazing meadows began to form upstream where rich deposits of silt built up. During this century, grazing has declined and reeds soon took over the meadows. The reeds are still cut for thatching, and also cut to prevent the wetland habitat drying out.

Reedbeds are an important habitat for a number of birds, including sedge and reed warblers and the bearded tit (not of the tit family, despite its name). While closely related, sedge and reed warblers have distinct patterns of nesting and feeding. The former builds its nest in the reeds close to firmer ground while the reed warbler slings its mug-shaped nest around the stems of reeds growing in water. The rare Cetti's warbler regularly nests here, while in winter snipe, duck, cormorant and heron are frequently seen.

Although close to a town, otters regularly use the river. The dense cover of the reeds provides ideal sites for lying up and breeding.

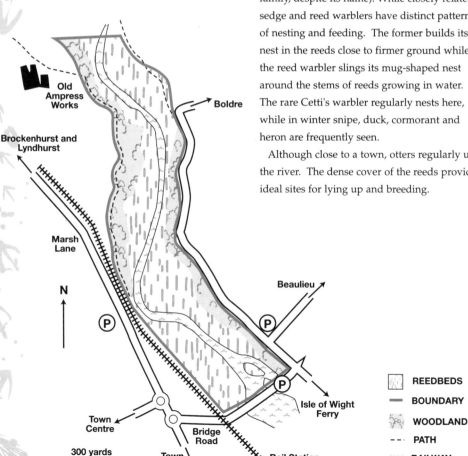

Old Ampress Works

Boldre

Brockenhurst and Lyndhurst

Marsh Lane

N

Beaulieu

Town Centre

Bridge Road

Town Centre

300 yards

Isle of Wight Ferry

Rail Station

▨	REEDBEDS
—	BOUNDARY
▨	WOODLAND
- - -	PATH
┼┼┼	RAILWAY

SWANWICK

HAMPSHIRE & ISLE OF WIGHT WILDLIFE TRUST

Nearest town: Southampton
OS Map 196 SU 507097

70 acres (28 ha) of former clay diggings, from which a varied patchwork of woodland, scrub, grassland and open water has been created which now teems with wildlife. There is a study centre and a full time warden.

Location and access: The reserve is on the north-east edge of Southampton, signposted off Swanwick Lane as the map shows. There is a car park by the study centre. Please keep dogs under control at all times.

Swanwick provides a marvellous example of nature fighting back. Dramatic changes in land use over the last hundred years have created today's varied landscape. Until 1974, clay was dug here for nearby brickworks, which resulted in steep-sided quarries, now partly filled with water. As digging moved on, so oak and birch woodland began to take over.

Formerly a deep flooded pit, Centre Lake was partly filled in 1991-2 to vary its depth and within a year dragonflies, toads and newts had

colonised it. Nearby is New Hill, created in 1991 and sown with meadow grasses and wild flowers which attract butterflies in summer and flocks of finches in winter.

East Valley had, in fact, once been a soft fruit farm and its strawberry ridges still line the woodland floor. Four deep lakes, fished by a local angling club, are a feature of North Meadow; this area is being managed to maintain a balance of open grass and scrub.

Sensitive management has been rewarded with the reappearance of orchids, the return of the nightingale each year, and more than a dozen different dragonflies.

WILDLIFE FEATURES
- **Waterlife**
- **Dragonflies**

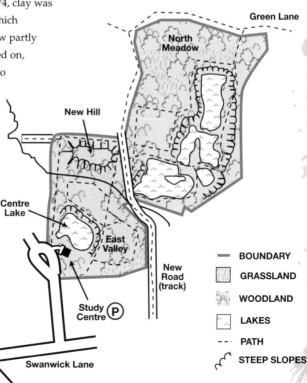

—	BOUNDARY
	GRASSLAND
	WOODLAND
	LAKES
- - -	PATH
	STEEP SLOPES

63

ST CATHERINE'S HILL

HAMPSHIRE & ISLE OF WIGHT WILDLIFE TRUST

Nearest town: Winchester
OS Map 185 SU 485275

116 acres (47 ha) of old chalk downland with various archaeological features including a hill fort, an old 'Troytown' maze, burial mounds and ancient trackways. New areas of chalk grassland are being created, particularly along the route of the old Winchester by-pass which has been infilled and sown with seed collected from local wild plants. The reserve is an SSSI.

Location and access: This steep knoll stands about 1.25 miles (2 km) south of the centre of Winchester. The main access is from the car park on Garnier Road; from here a path climbs up to the original entrance to the hill fort with steps and handrails on the steepest sections. Please keep to the path to prevent erosion.

Old chalk turf is one of the prize habitats of Britain. To keep downland such as this in prime condition requires grazing animals. They ensure that the ground is kept open and doesn't disappear under layers of scrub. Since the 1950s when myxomatosis drastically reduced rabbit numbers, scrub has invaded, and today cattle and sheep are vital to the management of this reserve.

WILDLIFE FEATURES
❀ Chalk flowers   ▶ Butterflies

Grazing enables the more delicate plants to survive by suppressing more rampant species. The top of the hill and areas facing north support taller plants while the dry, south-facing slopes are packed with herbs. Here the thin dry soil is ideal for yellow rockrose, yellow horseshoe vetch and fine grasses which attract chalkhill blue, brown argus and marbled white butterflies.

The long established plant community, which has developed over hundreds of years, also includes clustered bellflower, frog orchid and the rare musk orchid.

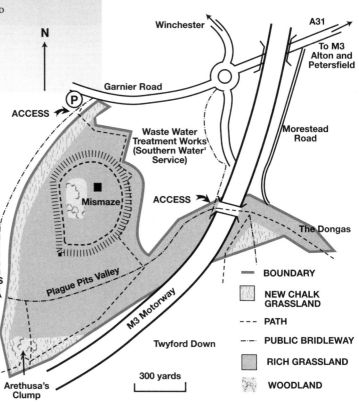

N

Winchester   A31

To M3 Alton and Petersfield

Garnier Road

ACCESS ⓟ

Waste Water Treatment Works (Southern Water Service)

Morestead Road

Mismaze

ACCESS

The Dongas

ACCESS

Plague Pits Valley

M3 Motorway

Twyford Down

Arethusa's Clump

300 yards

— BOUNDARY

NEW CHALK GRASSLAND

--- PATH

—·—· PUBLIC BRIDLEWAY

RICH GRASSLAND

WOODLAND

FARLINGTON MARSHES

**HAMPSHIRE & ISLE OF WIGHT
WILDLIFE TRUST**

Nearest town: Havant
OS Map 196 SU 685045

A 300 acre (120 ha) promontory of coastal
grazing marsh with lake and ponds; an SSSI
and Ramsar site.

Location and access: Lying to the east of
Portsmouth, the marshes form part of
Langstone Harbour. The best access is from
Broadmarsh car park which is reached by
taking the Waterlooville turning (from west) on
the A27 and following the signs for Broadmarsh
Coastal Park.

The map shows open access areas, the rest is
managed as a wildlife sanctuary. There is a
good circular walk around the perimeter, with
excellent views from the sea wall. The section
which lies north of the A27, reached by an
underpass, has facilities for educational groups.

WILDLIFE FEATURES
➤ Migrating waders and wildfowl

The site is reclaimed land; in 1773 a sea wall
was built across the creeks here and saltmarsh
and mudflats (as can still be seen out in the
harbour) were converted to pasture.

It has always been grazed, never ploughed
(the ant hills are a clue to this) and as a result it
has a good list of plants, many rare and only to
be found on coastal marshes. They can erupt
into colour: the yellow rattle in the hayfield in
early summer and the crimson grass vetchling
through the summer months, while the lake
shore and river edges turn deep red as the
swollen succulent fronds of glasswort take on
their autumn hue. Butterflies are sometimes
plentiful, including migrant red admiral and
clouded yellow stopping to refuel on thistles
after their Channel crossing.

But it's for the birds
that this reserve and
the open flats of
Langstone Harbour are
renowned. It is of
international
importance, attracting
thousands of migrant
waders and wildfowl
every year. Through the
winter, thousands of Brent
geese, for example, feed on
the large beds of eel-grass in
the harbour. There are flocks
of dunlin, curlew and
lapwing, the most numerous
of the 27 species of waders
seen here in the course of a
year. Regular wintering
duck include pintail,
goldeneye, shelduck and
wigeon.

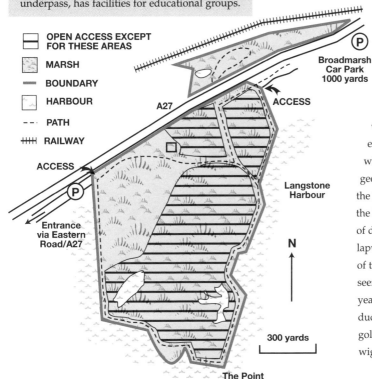

**OPEN ACCESS EXCEPT
FOR THESE AREAS**

MARSH

BOUNDARY

HARBOUR

PATH

RAILWAY

ACCESS

Entrance
via Eastern
Road/A27

A27

ACCESS

Broadmarsh
Car Park
1000 yards

Langstone
Harbour

N

300 yards

The Point

INKPEN COMMON

THE BERKSHIRE, BUCKINGHAMSHIRE AND OXFORDSHIRE WILDLIFE TRUST

Nearest town: Hungerford
OS Map 174 SU 382643

26 acres (10.4 ha) of heathland with bog and areas of woodland. It is an SSSI.

Location and access: About 3.5 miles (5.5 km) east of Hungerford, leave the A4 on the road leading south to Kintbury. Take the second turning to the left in Kintbury village, following the road to East and West Woodhay for about 1.25 miles, and bear right at Rooksnest Farm, signposted Inkpen Common. The main part of the reserve is on the left, opposite a row of houses. Cars may be parked on the verge as shown on the map.

The reserve is a remnant of the former Inkpen Great Common. In the past it was kept more or less open and clear of trees because local people with 'commons' rights could graze livestock, collect firewood, heather and bracken (for bedding) and gorse (for firing bread ovens). When this ceased, birch and oak and other trees seeded themselves in.

The acid soil encourages heathland plants and in the larger eastern part an area of damp heathland survives. It is a 'wilderness' of

WILDLIFE FEATURES
❧ Wild flowers & heathland

heather and gorse of a kind now rare in Berkshire. Look for dwarf gorse, flowering July to September (the taller bushy common gorse is in flower in every month. "When gorse is out of bloom, kissing is out of fashion" ran the old saying).

Apart from the heathers, lousewort flowers abundantly in places and the uncommon pale dog-violet can be seen at midsummer.

The reserve contains a small area of bog fed by water seepage. The most dramatic flower here is bog asphodel with a flag of bright yellow flowers in August - later both seed pods and leaves become a striking orange. It's an unusual plant treasure for Berkshire.

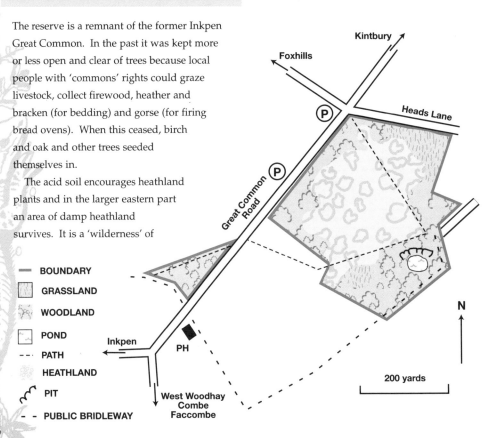

BOUNDARY
GRASSLAND
WOODLAND
POND
PATH
HEATHLAND
PIT
PUBLIC BRIDLEWAY

BAYNES RESERVE & BOWDOWN WOODS

THE BERKSHIRE, BUCKINGHAMSHIRE AND OXFORDSHIRE WILDLIFE TRUST

Nearest town: Newbury

OS Map 174 SU 511651/501655

Two close reserves totalling 94 acres (38 ha), the first ancient woodland, the second more varied and with some heathland. Both are SSSI.

Location and access: These reserves are about 2 miles (7 km) east of Newbury, south of the canal and river. The least complicated directions start from Thatcham, taking the road past Thatcham station over the river and taking the narrow right fork after about 0.75 mile. Baynes Reserve is reached down the gravel track to the right, Bowdown Woods after passing Bowdown House.

WILDLIFE FEATURES

✕ Woodland birds 🦋 Woodland butterflies
🪰 Dragonflies

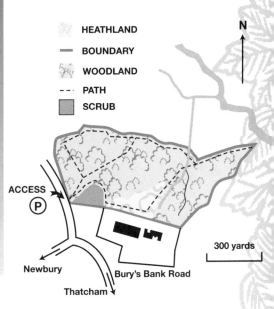

HEATHLAND
BOUNDARY
WOODLAND
PATH
SCRUB

ACCESS
(P)

Newbury
Bury's Bank Road
Thatcham

300 yards

Baynes Reserve is ancient woodland - it has probably not been anything but woodland since the end of the last Ice Age, although it has been worked for coppice (which opens up a wood and encourages the flowers). It is a rather diverse wood - two stream valleys converge to the north-east and, cutting down through layers of gravel and clays, provide several distinct habitats. The higher well-drained slopes for

example have birch and rowan with patches of oak and hazel. Further down, wetter soils are marked by alder and hazel. Look here for the unusual five-ways facing flowers of moschatel (town hall clock). Where springs emerge, the wet flushes are marked by splashes of golden saxifrage.

Bowdown Woods stretch along a slope between a gravelly plateau and the river, and streams have cut sharp valleys along it. There is some dry heathland on the gravel plateau.

Both these reserves are alive with birdsong - the nightingale is heard from low cover in May and June. White admiral, fritillaries and purple emperor are among the butterflies to be seen at times in the summer and 15 species of dragonfly have been recorded, flying in from local ponds!

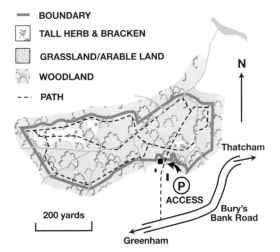

BOUNDARY
TALL HERB & BRACKEN
GRASSLAND/ARABLE LAND
WOODLAND
PATH

N

Thatcham

(P)
ACCESS
Bury's Bank Road

200 yards

Greenham

67

MOOR COPSE

THE BERKSHIRE, BUCKINGHAMSHIRE AND OXFORDSHIRE WILDLIFE TRUST

Nearest town: Reading

OS Map 175 SU 633738

67 acres (27 ha) of varied woodland with a length of the River Pang. It is an SSSI.

Location access: The reserve is about 2 miles (3 km) due south of Pangbourne, on the A340 just before it crosses the motorway. Parking is in the lay-by.

WILDLIFE FEATURES

✿ Woodland flowers ✕ Woodland birds

This magnificent reserve presents you with several different areas of woodland. The first to greet you is Hogmoor Copse, a wet wood on peat and gravel with willows and a few oak and ash trees. There are some drainage ditches, but it is not clear why they were dug. The southern two thirds of this area was thinned or coppiced in 1990, the rest left alone.

Cross the river (a habitat in its own right of course) to reach Park Wood. This gives you a type of landscape very familiar to our ancestors, though not at all like film versions of the greenwood. This ancient wood has areas of coppiced alder and hazel, overshadowed by giant single-trunked 'standard' oak trees. By regularly opening up the woodland floor, coppicing here encourages a breathtaking display of primrose and bluebell.

A five acre hayfield comes next, before you reach Moor Copse itself, an old coppiced ash wood with widely spaced oak and ash tree standards. Look for early purple orchid in late spring.

For other life, look out for the white admiral butterfly; it lays its eggs on the abundant honeysuckle. Fallen and cut wood is left to rot, to encourage beetles and other invertebrates. Grass snakes are often seen, basking in the sunshine of the newly cut coppice. There is usually plenty of birdsong in spring; you might also get a glimpse of a sparrowhawk.

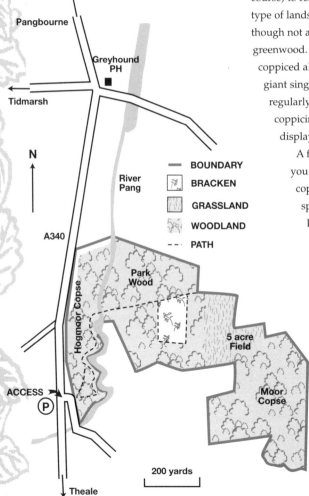

Pangbourne

Greyhound
PH

Tidmarsh

N

River
Pang

A340

Hogmoor Copse

Park
Wood

5 acre
Field

Moor
Copse

ACCESS
P

200 yards

Theale

— BOUNDARY
▨ BRACKEN
▧ GRASSLAND
▩ WOODLAND
--- PATH

LODDON RESERVE

THE BERKSHIRE, BUCKINGHAMSHIRE AND OXFORDSHIRE WILDLIFE TRUST

Nearest town: Twyford
OS Map 175 SU 785758

One of the largest of a group of flooded gravel pits, about 34 acres (14 ha) in extent.

Location and access: The reserve is just south of the Old Bath Road, on the edge of Twyford. Park in the public car park in Polehampton Close and walk west along the main road, past the railway. Just before the factory (old mill site) is the access path, as shown on the map. To avoid disturbing the birds, please do not go too close to the lake edge, and keep dogs away from it.

WILDLIFE FEATURES
🐦 Wildfowl   🦅 Songbirds

The River Loddon frets its way in numerous channels around Twyford. This braiding is the normal behaviour of a river, but river engineering in recent centuries has largely destroyed these meanders and resulted in the loss of a vast amount of water and waterside-habitat.

This reserve, however, is one example of how some of that loss can be made good: gravel diggings have been allowed to flood and revert to nature. The contours of the shallow diggings have created a lake with an attractively scalloped edge, several islands and a bordering strip now covered with scrub. These islands are a bonus for waterfowl, giving some protection against foxes and rats. As a result, terns and lapwing have nested safely. Heron, coot and great crested grebe are regulars - these last are particularly interesting in spring with their remarkable 'present giving' courtship displays. The scrub margin attracts blackcap, whitethroat and other birds. Winter is also a busy time with a greater variety of waterfowl, including tufted duck, pochard, smew andgadwall - and sometimes cormorant! In all, 70 species have been seen here.

The reserve is also valued for its dragonflies and damselflies, and 16 species of butterfly have been recorded.

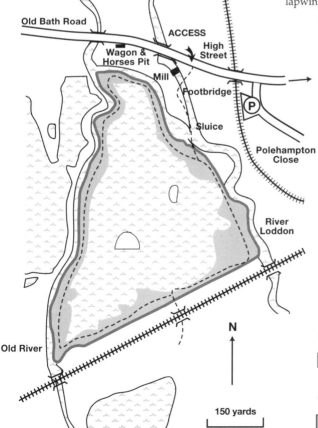

Old Bath Road
ACCESS
High Street
Wagon & Horses Pit
Mill
Footbridge
P
Sluice
Polehampton Close
River Loddon
Old River
N
150 yards

— BOUNDARY

RIVERS & LAKES

--- PATH

++++ RAILWAY

SCRUB

69

WILDMOOR HEATH

THE BERKSHIRE, BUCKINGHAMSHIRE AND OXFORDSHIRE WILDLIFE TRUST

Nearest towns: Camberley and Bracknell
OS Map 175 SU 838629

210 acres (85 ha) of heathland, bog and woodland, part of the Sandhurst to Owlsmoor SSSI.

Location and access: The reserve lies south of Bracknell, between Crowthorne and Sandhurst. The car park is situated off Crowthorne Road, about half a mile (1 km) south of Crowthorne village.

BBONT owns the northerly third of this SSSI (Owlsmoor Bog) and recently purchased the southerly Wildmoor Bottom.

The intention is that, in partnership with Bracknell Forest Borough Council, who own the middle piece, BBONT will manage the whole SSSI, named Wildmoor Heath.

This reserve is mainly on infertile acid soil and in the low-lying areas a thin layer of peat has formed, allowing a

WILDLIFE FEATURES
✿ Bog plants 🦋 Emperor moth

bog to develop. The key plant here is bog moss (Sphagnum species) which can more or less survive on nutrients carried down by the rain. Their floppy stems create a living sponge which traps not only rain but organic matter, which allows other plants to grow. One bog plant to look for here is the round-leaved sundew, which feeds on small insects trapped by the sticky hairs on the leaves.

Look also for the three different species of heather (heather or ling, bell heather and cross-leaved heath, this last being found on wetter ground). The emperor moth, a handsome relative of the silk moth can be seen quickly skimming over the heather tussocks in the May sunshine. Lizards, slow-worm and adder are most likely to be seen sunning themselves in nooky spots after emerging from hibernation in spring (adders are shy rather than dangerous).

Birds liking the open heath with scattered cover and known to nest here include the tree pipit, stonechat - and also woodlark, Dartford warbler and the nightjar. Many others nest in the woodland.

As with all heaths, invasive scrub must be kept at bay. Light grazing by cattle helps control this.

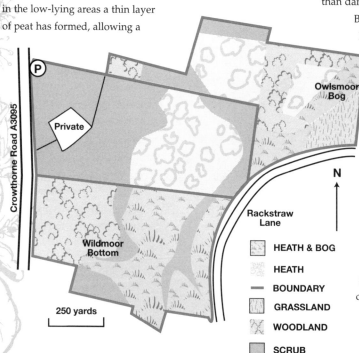

Crowthorne Road A3095

P

Private

Owlsmoor Bog

Wildmoor Bottom

N

Rackstraw Lane

250 yards

HEATH & BOG
HEATH
BOUNDARY
GRASSLAND
WOODLAND
SCRUB

BRENTMOOR HEATH

SURREY WILDLIFE TRUST

Nearest town: Camberley
OS Map 186 SU 936612

A 148.7 acre (60.3 ha) reserve of heathland, woodland, grassland and ponds.

Location and access: This reserve runs alongside the A322 Guildford to Bagshot road, at its intersection with the A319/B311 between Chobham and Camberley. The best access is by Brentmoor Road which runs westwards from West End past Donkey Town.

The reserve occupies the north-east corner of an extensive block of lowland heathland that includes extensive Ministry of Defence lands.

There's a subtle difference in the heathers here. In the dry heath areas, heather (ling) is dominant: its small leaves overlap, close pressed in four rows up the stem, whereas in

WILDLIFE FEATURES
- ❀ Heath habitats
- ✕ Birdlife including nightjars

the wet heath you find cross-leaved heath, its leaves make a cross where they spring off the downy stem in whorls of four. Also, there are scatters of gorse in the dry heath while in areas of open ground in the wet heath you see the white tufts of cotton grass and tussocks of purple moor grass. Here too you may be able to find the insect-eating sundew.

Stands of mature Scots pine and an area of young oak and birch add to the diversity of habitats here, but management is needed to prevent trees predominating in the areas of open heath and shading out the heathland plants. Small clumps of trees and scrub or wooded fringes are valuable, however, and encourage the nightjar, which is fairly common in the area. This bird spends the day motionless on the ground, to fly at dusk, catching moths. It has a strange, rather mechanical churring call, changing pitch when it moves its head.

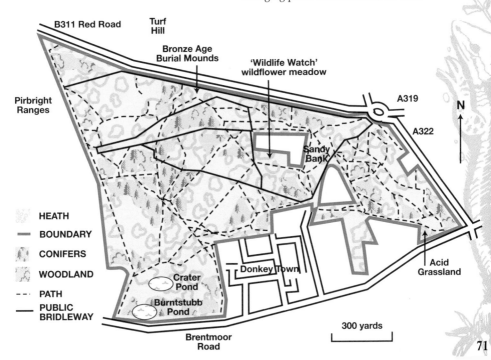

HEATH
BOUNDARY
CONIFERS
WOODLAND
PATH
PUBLIC BRIDLEWAY

B311 Red Road
Turf Hill
Bronze Age Burial Mounds
'Wildlife Watch' wildflower meadow
Pirbright Ranges
A319
N
A322
Sandy Bank
Acid Grassland
Donkey Town
Crater Pond
Burntstubb Pond
Brentmoor Road
300 yards

WALLIS WOOD

SURREY WILDLIFE TRUST

Nearest town: Horsham
OS Map 187 TQ 121388

33 acres (13 ha) of oak woodland.

Location and access: Wallis Wood Village is (as the crow flies) about 5 miles (8 km) north-west of Horsham. The reserve is about 0.5 mile north of the village, on the east side of Walliswood Green Road running up to Forest Green.

The core of this reserve is a superb example of the oak-hazel coppice woodland which once clothed the Weald of Surrey and Sussex. Other features are the stream and small pond and the surrounding pasture.

WILDLIFE FEATURES
✿ Spring flowers 🦋 Butterflies
✕ Woodland birds

The coppice compartments are of different ages, cut in rotation, and the light flooding the ground when they are newly cut encourages the wild flowers. (Together with this the tall 'standards' are spaced out to about 12 trees to an acre.) So here you can see sheets of bluebell, the robust broad-leaved and violet helleborine orchids (both can be tall, the latter having a cluster of stems), primrose and wood anemone. There are also wild daffodil to be seen.

You can find both the native oaks (common oak with lobes where the leaf joins the short stalk, the sessile joining the long stalk smoothly - but they do hybridise) and wild apple and cherry, the Midland hawthorn (with blunter leaves than its hedgerow cousin) and the wild service tree.

With the ancient wood come butterflies - purple emperor, and purple hairstreak, usually in the crowns of the trees, the former often flying around a master tree (so take binoculars) and silver-washed fritillary and speckled wood in the glades. Birds too, though they are attracted more by the wood's structure than its plant list - many of the migrant birds like the thick cover a few years after the cutting of the coppice.

Walliswood Green Road

Coppice
Coppice
Hazels
P
Bryony Copse
Barns
Studio
Shed
Coppice
Coppice
Dam
Chapel Lane

— BOUNDARY
FIELD
WOODLAND
--- PATH
STREAM
— FIELD BOUNDARY

100 yards

72

BAY POND

SURREY WILDLIFE TRUST

Nearest town: Caterham
OS Map 187 TQ 353516

A 17 acre (6.8 ha) reserve of hay meadow with a 6 acre lake. A smaller field study pond has also been dug out. There is a field studies shed and an observation platform (the local angling club has fishing rights on the lake).

Location and access: This reserve is at the edge of the village of Godstone, just south of the M25, about 2 miles (3.5 km) south of the centre of Caterham. You can park opposite the White Hart hotel; a footpath runs east from the hotel past the village hall which gives a good view of the reserve across the lake. Access is by the lane known as "Path to Little Place" at the side of Godstone Place off the A22.

The lake may date back to the early 17th century, as one of a chain feeding a mill downstream. Over the years a mature alder swamp has developed on the eastern side, with what can be a splendid luxuriance of emergent and marginal growth. In what can seem a

WILDLIFE FEATURES
🐦 **Wildfowl**   🦟 **Dragonflies**

tangle, the plants quite carefully position themselves - the bur marigolds are found where water stands in winter but not summer, for example, while the reedmace stands in still water. The latter with its sausage head is often called bulrush - the result of a mistake made by the Victorian artist Alma Tadema, who used it for his famous painting of "Moses amongst the bulrushes". It can crowd out other plants and has to be thinned from time to time; the common reed has been planted as an alternative. The brilliant yellow kingcup flowers here in spring, the native yellow water lily later.

There is a good bird life, with great crested grebe, mute swan and coot and moorhen nesting, while visitors include goldeneye, pochard and tufted duck. The heron is often seen fishing the water. There can also be a fair variety of dragonflies and their daintier cousins the damselflies.

	MARSH		WOODLAND
—	BOUNDARY	⌂	POND
	GRASSLAND	---	PATH

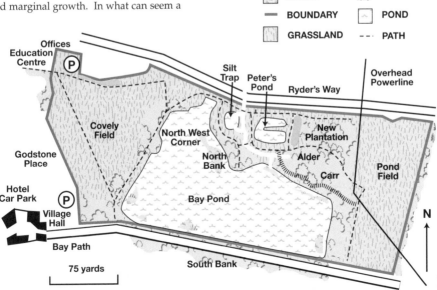

STEDHAM COMMON

SUSSEX WILDLIFE TRUST

Nearest town: Midhurst
OS Map 197 SU 856218

An 87 acre (35 ha) reserve of sandy heathland with pine, birch and bracken. It is an SSSI and a Local Nature Reserve.

Location and access: The reserve is 1.5 miles (2.4 km) west of Midhurst on the A272 Petersfield road. Access is by the footpath opposite the Iping Common car park, on the Elsted road as the map shows.

This area of light sandy soils was being cleared of woodland as early as Mesolithic times, around 5000 BC, allowing heather to spread. Commons grazing kept the area open in medieval times but when it stopped in the 1940s, birch and pine began to seed themselves in. The Wildlife Trust has cleared a good deal of

WILDLIFE FEATURES
- Heathland reptiles
- Birdlife including hobby & nightjar

this, restoring the open heath, and bracken is also being controlled.

There is a subtle mosaic of different areas. Wetter ground, for example, is signposted by tussocks of purple moor grass and colonised by the paler purple of cross-leaved heath rather than heather. But in general heathlands have low plant cover, nooky sheltered corners created by the heather and a light sandy soil which heats up rapidly. These make heathlands ideal for reptiles such as the adder and common lizard and for mining bees and other insects and a great number of spiders.

Nesting birds expected include meadow pipit and stonechat, with the excitement of the nightjar in summer with its churring call.

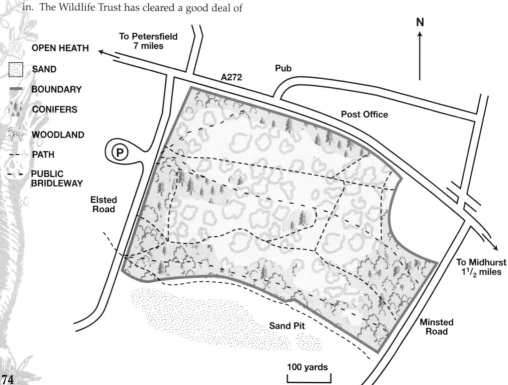

74

BURTON POND WOODLANDS

SUSSEX WILDLIFE TRUST

Nearest town: Petworth
OS Map 197 SU 978181/982173

A 67 acre (27 ha) reserve of woodlands enclosing areas of bog and heath, and surrounding a large millpond. It is an SSSI and LNR.

Location and access; The reserve is 2.25 miles (3.5 km) due south of Petworth, reached via the A285 Chichester road. There is a small car park just below the old mill, from which both sides of the reserve are within easy reach.

This is a marvellously varied place - as the map shows it consists of four blocks of woodland with a large millpond between them.

Though much altered in the past, the four woods all derive from oak and birch woodlands typical of the sandstone parts of the Weald. Where the trees were cleared, the acidic nature of the soil has created heathy areas. There are also some boggy areas, including The Black Hole, now partly overgrown by alder and willow. Here among the carpet of bog moss, you might see the white fringed flowers of bogbean, perhaps our most handsome native flower (it has oval grey-green leaves) and our native cranberry which grows prostrate with threadlike stems.

Management includes keeping this bog open by removing the alder and willow. A boardwalk crosses the bog.

In the drier woodlands, felling of oak and lime and other established trees in recent centuries has left the

WILDLIFE FEATURES
❀ **Bog flowers**   ⬀ **Wildfowl**

ground open to pioneering birch, now the most common tree. It is often first on the scene in newly created glades but soon shaded out when the oaks and others grow over it.

Reedbeds lap the margins of the pond which is often bright with yellow water lilies. It is fished, but birds seen here include great crested and little grebe, water rail and reed and sedge warblers - they all nest here. Many pochard are often present in winter.

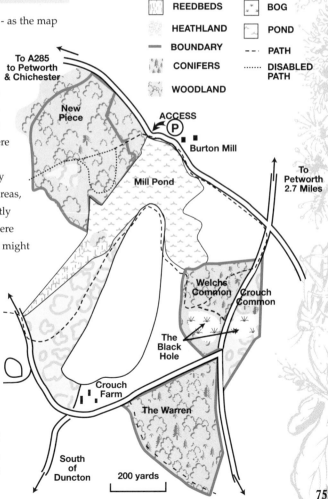

	REEDBEDS		BOG
	HEATHLAND		POND
—	BOUNDARY	- - -	PATH
	CONIFERS	....	DISABLED PATH
	WOODLAND		

To A285 to Petworth & Chichester

New Piece

ACCESS Ⓟ

Burton Mill

Mill Pond

To Petworth 2.7 Miles

Welchs Common Crouch Common

The Black Hole

Crouch Farm

The Warren

South of Duncton

200 yards

75

EBERNOE COMMON

SUSSEX WILDLIFE TRUST

Nearest town: Petworth
OS Map 197 SU 976278

187 acres (75.9 ha) of ancient woodland with glades, ponds and archaeological interest. It is an SSSI. The meadow at the north edge is also managed by the Trust on behalf of Plantlife.

Location and access: The reserve is about 4 miles (6.5 km) due north of Petworth, reached via the A283 taking the first right for Gunters Bridge and Balls Cross, or by taking the second right for Balls Cross. This is the top road on the map. There is a car park near the church, as the map shows.

The indications are that this reserve has been woodland since the last Ice Age. For centuries it

WILDLIFE FEATURES
❀ Unimproved neutral grassland
🦋 Butterflies

has been a "common", wood pasture with livestock grazed under huge oak and beech trees. When this grazing ended earlier this century there was an explosion of holly scrub under the trees. There is a furnace pond used in the 16th century Wealden iron industry and a brick kiln which used local clay and firewood for 200 years until the 1930s.

As for the woodland itself, it is remarkably varied. You could say that every part is different, with wild service tree (usually only found in old woodland) in one place and wild daffodil in another, scatters of bluebell in another (there are over 300 species of plants). The nightingale nests in the thickets and the elusive woodcock hides by day in the dense woodland. There are frogs and toads in the ponds. Woodland butterflies are fairly frequently seen - purple emperor, white admiral and silver-washed fritillary for example. The holly is a problem because it shades out the profuse lichens on the tree trunks (and hinders visitors). The Trust plans to reintroduce grazing on parts of the reserve, but the woodland areas are deliberately left to their natural cycle of growth and decay. The flower-rich meadow to the north is grazed.

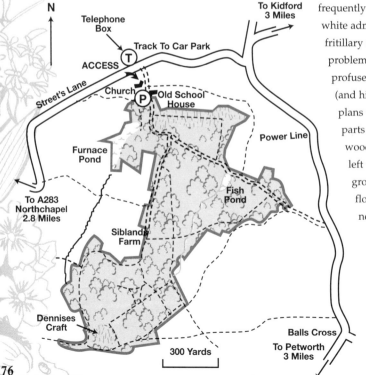

BOUNDARY

MEADOW

WOODLAND

POND

PATH

THE MENS

SUSSEX WILDLIFE TRUST

Nearest town: Petworth
OS Map 197 TQ 023237

297 acres (160 ha) of ancient woodland together with an area of meadow. An SSSI, much of it is a registered common.

Location and access: The reserve is about 3.25 miles (5 km) east-northeast of Petworth, on the A272 road to Billinghurst. Access is easiest from the car park on the minor road to Hawkhurst Court from the A272.

This is an old common and its varied structure echoes that ancient history, with old wood banks and assarts (land cleared in medieval times) which are still open today. In fact the reserve is made up of different pockets of woodland.

On the Bedham ridge to the south, where the soil is lighter, the canopy is of beech with some holly below. Elsewhere there is more oak, with wild service tree and Midland hawthorn - both the latter are linked to ancient woodland. There are areas where the trees are tall and narrow crowned, indicating dense forest conditions for a long time, while elsewhere there are wide-spreading giants which must have grown in more open conditions. The massive Idehurst Hurst Oak is one example.

There has been little management since the 19th century - so it resembles a 'wildwood' with trees in all stages

WILDLIFE FEATURES
🍄 Fungi 🌸 Meadow flowers

from seedlings to tall forest trees.

There are comparatively few open areas, so that glade species of plants and butterflies and others are outweighed by an immense variety of fungi and insects reliant on rotting timber. And there are true woodland birds, such as the three species of woodpeckers. However, the Badlands Meadow offers a stunning list of grassland flowers.

Management is restricted to maintaining the paths and edges (there is a problem with horse riders straying onto the footpaths from the bridleways). Badlands Meadow is grazed, however.

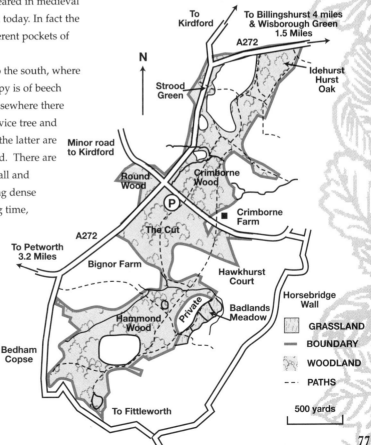

77

MALLING DOWN

SUSSEX WILDLIFE TRUST

Nearest town: Lewes
OS Map 198 TQ 423107

94 acres (38 ha) of chalk grassland. It is an SSSI.

Location and access: The reserve is virtually on the eastern edge of Lewes with access as shown on the map. The principal access points are from the top of Mill Lane and the Ringmer Lane lay-by. For the former, park at the top by the ESCC chalkpit, follow the track and turn almost immediately right over a stile. For the latter, follow the main track through two gates.

The reserve consists of a steep north-facing slope pitted with old chalk pits together with a dramatic west-facing coombe (a dry valley) running down to the outskirts of Lewes at Malling Street.

Until about 40 years ago the whole area was

WILDLIFE FEATURES
🌸 **Chalk flowers**   🦋 **Downland butterflies**

closely grazed by sheep and cattle and the grass was among the richest in downland flowers, orchids and butterflies to be found in Sussex. Since then scrub has spread over much of the site, thickly in some areas.

However, much rich grassland remains, notable for its wild orchids and such chalk specialities as wild thyme, basil, round-headed rampion ('The Pride of Sussex' with an Oxford blue flower head), dropwort, and autumn gentian (with purplish flowers).

The yellow horseshoe vetch (so called from the shape of its seed pods) is the crucial food plant for chalkhill blue butterfly and the rare Adonis blue. This last has a stronghold here on Malling Down. The marbled white also flies here.

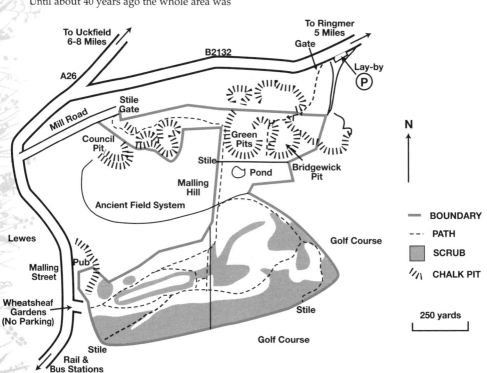

OLD LODGE

SUSSEX WILDLIFE TRUST

Nearest town: Maresfield
OS Map 198 TQ 460302

239 acres (96.8 ha) of heathland with birch and pine woodland. It is an SSSI and LNR.

Location and access: The reserve is 4 miles (6.5 km) north of Maresfield on the B2026 to Hartfield, about 500 yards north of the junction with the B2188. There is a small parking area. No dogs are allowed on the reserve.

Prehistoric clearance of oak woodland on the sandy soils of Ashdown Forest followed by long centuries of grazing and burning created this heathland. Left to itself it would scrub up - birch and pine trees would be early colonists, and eventually oak and other "forest" trees would seed themselves in. The never-ending task on a heathland reserve, therefore, is to keep it open, controlling bracken and birch and usually reintroducing grazing which encourages young heather growth.

WILDLIFE FEATURES
✿ **Heathland** 🦎 **Lizards**
🦅 **Birdlife**

The north half of this reserve is grazed by sheep and cattle in spring and summer.

In addition, the October 1987 hurricane devastated plantations on the western side; the debris has been cleared and it is being left so that Scots pine will regenerate naturally.

In close up, the heath here is a mosaic of slightly different plant communities - the drier areas marked by ling and bell heather, the wetter by cross-leaved heath and tussocks of purple moor grass. Stonechat, tree pipit and hobby are attracted to heathland such as this, while the sparrowhawk has been seen coursing the woodland.

The boggy pools are a good breeding ground for dragonflies and hawkers may be seen in late summer cruising well away from them, searching the pines for prey.

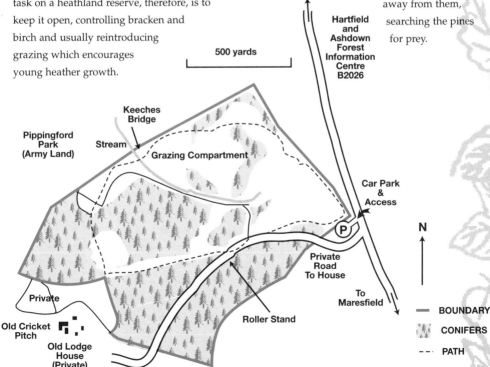

500 yards

Hartfield and Ashdown Forest Information Centre B2026

Keeches Bridge

Pippingford Park (Army Land)

Stream

Grazing Compartment

Car Park & Access

Private Road To House

To Maresfield

Private

Old Cricket Pitch

Old Lodge House (Private)

Roller Stand

N

— **BOUNDARY**
🌲 **CONIFERS**
--- **PATH**

MARLINE & PARK WOODS

SUSSEX WILDLIFE TRUST

Nearest town: Hastings
OS Map 199 TQ 783123

99 acres (40 ha) of coppice and ghyll woodland with meadows. It is an SSSI and LNR owned by Hastings Borough Council.

Location and access: The reserve is just west of Hastings, and the map explains its position in relation to nearby roads. Cars should be parked where shown in Napier Road.

WILDLIFE FEATURES

🦇 **Woodland birds**   🌿 **Mosses and ferns**
❀ **Meadow flowers**

The woodlands extend across the steep sided sandstone ghyll which holds the stream. It's a picturesque place with its rock outcrops, wild-looking too, as storm damage has left trees uprooted and strewn to rot along the valley floor. But the real interest is that the shelter and humidity create conditions more to be expected in an oakwood in the milder west of Britain than here in Sussex, with plenty of mosses and ferns rooted in the damp crevices. Some of these are relics from the Atlantic climate period of about 7000 years ago.

On the gentler slopes above, large oak trees stand over a coppice which has been worked for centuries. The coppice is largely of hornbeam (it has beech-like leaves): hornbeam is usually only found as coppice in the south-east of Britain. Mixed with it are ash, sweet chestnut and hazel - the more usual coppice species. Coppice cutting continues as part of the Trust's management here.

Between these woods and the road are ancient hay meadows and pastures, never ploughed or fertilised (this last would encourage the rank grasses and they would smother out the wild flowers). Apart from the marvellous flowers, these fields are notable for butterflies of various species. Ideally these fields should be grazed in the traditional way, but this is no longer practical, so they are mown for hay annually, which prevents scrubbing up.

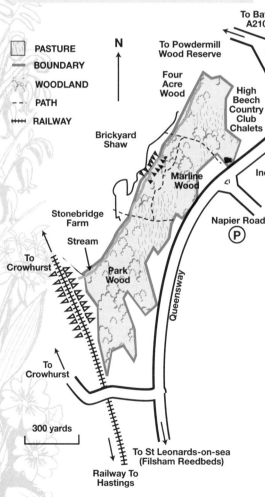

PASTURE
BOUNDARY
WOODLAND
PATH
RAILWAY

N

To Battle
A2100

To Powdermill
Wood Reserve

The Ridge   To Hastings
A2093

Four
Acre
Wood

High
Beech
Country
Club
Chalets

Approx. 0.8 Miles
to reserve from
this junction

Brickyard
Shaw

A2100

Marline
Wood

Industrial
Site

Battle Road

Stonebridge
Farm

Napier Road
Ⓟ

To
St Leonards

Stream

To
Crowhurst

Park
Wood

Queensway

To
Crowhurst

300 yards

To St Leonards-on-sea
(Filsham Reedbeds)

Railway To
Hastings

CASTLE WATER, RYE HARBOUR

SUSSEX WILDLIFE TRUST

Nearest town: Rye
OS Map 189 TQ 925185

216 acres (88 ha) of shingle ridges, grassland and flooded gravel and shingle diggings. It is an SSSI and part of the Rye Harbour Local Nature Reserve. There is an information centre nearby. Screens and hides are planned.

Location and access: This reserve forms part of the Rye Harbour complex, about 2.5 miles (4 km) south-east of Rye. There is parking at the LNR information centre. Access to most parts of the LNR is restricted to certain paths - there are details of this at the information centre.

Rye Harbour, which includes Castle Water, is one of the most important conservation sites on

WILDLIFE FEATURES
✕ **Birdlife**   ✶ **Rare insects**

the south coast. It contains a natural shingle system and tidal mudflats, saltmarsh and grazing marsh and all phases of plant succession can be seen. In addition gravel diggings have flooded to provide areas of open water, with reedbed and willow scrub around the water margins.

The specialised plant life of Rye Harbour as a whole is fascinating, but more for the specialist maybe - examples are five species of glasswort and the rare sea mouse-ear on the Castle Water grassland. However, there are flowers for everyone – sea aster for example and yellow horned-poppy on the shingle. The birdlife is superb: on the reserve nest reed and sedge warblers and redshank and lapwing. Lengths of ditch have been fenced off to encourage reeds to spread. There are also plans to develop an island as a nesting site for the common tern. The shallow open water often attracts heron when they nest in a nearby wood. The general area of Rye Harbour is noted for its winter wildfowl and birds on migration - from dunlin and curlew to pochard, shoveler and other duck. As well as these, yellow wagtail, oystercatcher, and common, little and Sandwich terns among others have been known to nest in the harbour complex.

To Rye
Harbour Road
River Rother
Public Telephone
Castle Farm
Castle Water
Rye Harbour
Castle
Camber Sands
River Brede
Castle Farm
Harbour Farm
River Mouth
Ternery Pool
Shoreline
N

■ HIDE
— LNR BOUNDARY
SHINGLE
OPEN WATER
- - - PATH
ARABLE

1000 yards

BOUGH BEECH

KENT WILDLIFE TRUST

Nearest town: Tonbridge
OS Map 188 TQ 496489

80 acres (32 ha) of the northern end of Bough Beech Reservoir, including a separate small lake, fields and woods. There is a visitor centre open 1100—1630 Wed, Sat, Sun April-October inclusive.

Location and access: About 6 miles (9 km) due west of Tonbridge, north of the B2027. The whole of the reserve may be viewed from the road just south of Winkhurst Green (496494). Park on the roadside.

WILDLIFE FEATURES
🦅 Waders and wildfowl

Following the construction of a dam with a sluice gate across transfer pipes to the main reservoir, it has become possible to control the level of North Lake after it has fallen in the reservoir. Beyond the boundary of the reserve, the reservoir is busy with dinghies and is stocked for fishing, but the reserve offers a retreat to many birds. Sixty-five species of birds have been recorded as breeding in the area. Fluctuating water level (which also affects the sedges and reeds around the margin) affects bird life: great crested grebe for example cannot cope with the fall in the water level in summer, but lapwing and little ringed plover which nest on the bank have an advantage. It's interesting that the grey wagtail is now being attracted to the spillways of the sluices of North Lake and kingfisher to the diverted stream. Numbers of wildfowl are highest in winter, with mallard, teal, shoveler and tufted duck most numerous (and quite a few Canada geese) but others such as goldeneye, goosander and pochard are regularly seen. In all, 200 species have been recorded. The prize sighting, virtually every year, is the osprey.

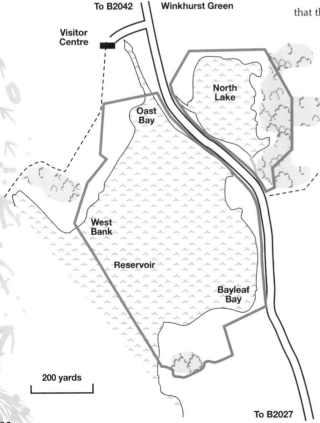

To B2042 | Winkhurst Green

Visitor Centre

North Lake

Oast Bay

West Bank

Reservoir

Bayleaf Bay

N

200 yards

To B2027

— BOUNDARY

WOODLAND

RESERVOIR/LAKE

--- PATH

82

OARE MARSHES

KENT WILDLIFE TRUST

Nearest town: Faversham
OS Map 178 TR 012645

170 acres (67 ha) of grazing marsh with freshwater dykes, sea wall and saltmarsh, part of the Swale SSSI and a Ramsar site. There is a visitor centre and a bird hide.

Location and access: About 2.5 miles (4 km) almost due north of Faversham. The whole reserve may be viewed from the Harty Ferry road and the Saxon Shore Way which runs along the length of the sea wall. Cars may be parked at the northern end of the road (TR 013647).

This is one of the few remaining areas of traditional grazing marsh to be seen in this region, most having been lost to industrial

WILDLIFE FEATURES

Birdlife including birds of prey

building and other uses, or suffering draining and ploughing. There are three main habitat types: the grazing grassland itself, the dykes which drain it and the saltmarsh beyond the sea wall.

The grazing land attracts birds such as the lapwing with its long crest and the redshank, recognised by the white trailing edges of its wings as it flies up. They both nest here, while curlew, wigeon, teal and pintail are among those that winter in the area.

In winter also, the marshes are home to the blackbird-sized merlin, flying low and fast, and the hen harrier with a low hunting glide. The short-eared owl is also seen, hunting low in daylight or at dusk with moth-like wing beats.

The main dykes to the west and across the middle of the eastern section are brackish, the others freshwater (the reedbed in the eastern section is fed by an artesian well). The bittern has been seen here and reed and sedge warblers nest.

The slope of the sea wall and the saltmarsh below carry many attractive flowers. Look for the golden yellow samphire on the summer saltmarsh: a splash of yellow among the purple of the sea-lavender. In autumn the saltmarsh is tinted red by glasswort.

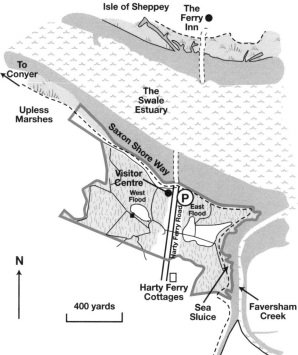

	SALTMARSH		
—	BOUNDARY	- - -	PATH
	GRASSLAND		MUDFLATS
	OPEN WATER	■	HIDE

HOTHFIELD COMMON

KENT WILDLIFE TRUST

Nearest town: Ashford
OS Map 189 TQ 969459

138 acres (56 ha) of heath and lowland bog, an SSSI and Local Nature Reserve.

Location and access: Three miles north-west of Ashford, on the south side of the A20 (about midway between Charing and Ashford). The map shows the parking. Visitors can walk freely along the paths; dogs must be kept under control.

Lowland heaths such as this do not occur naturally; they usually owe their origin to woodland clearance from prehistoric times on, followed by grazing and perhaps firing. Left to themselves they revert back to woodland; invading birch and other trees and bracken must be controlled, as should the gorse (the dwarf gorse is a feature, however). Many heaths have been planted with conifers, or ploughed for farmland in recent decades. This is the last large area of heath and valley bog left in Kent.

With the low shelter and quick warming sandy soil, the heath is a good site for slow-worm, common lizard and grass snake.

What you must do here is inspect the bogs; there are four fingers of it with raised ground .1m between, where a watertight ground forces out springs. Contrary to general belief, a bog is not muddy, nor smelly, but is a very fragile plant community (not to be walked on). The bog mosses form a carpet, and growing in it are flowers such as the

WILDLIFE FEATURES
- **Reptiles**
- **Dragonflies**

yellow asphodel and heath spotted orchid.

Notable insects linked with the bog pools are the dragonflies - birdwatchers' insects! Here the uncommon keeled skimmer dragonfly can be seen.

Another feature of the reserve are the 'tolls' planted with beech, oak and Scots pine. These harbour nuthatch, treecreeper and other birds, while isolated trees on the common are used as song perches by the tree pipit, a summer visitor here.

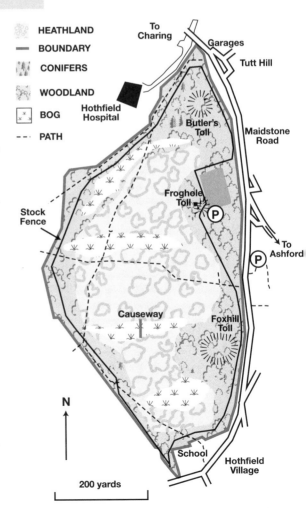

	HEATHLAND
	BOUNDARY
	CONIFERS
	WOODLAND
	BOG
	PATH

To Charing
Garages
Tutt Hill
Hothfield Hospital
Butler's Toll
Maidstone Road
Froghole Toll
Stock Fence
To Ashford
Causeway
Foxhill Toll
N
School
Hothfield Village
200 yards

RECULVER COUNTRY PARK

KENT WILDLIFE TRUST

Nearest town: Herne Bay
OS Map TR 224693

91 acres (37 ha) of clifftop and seashore with cliffs of national geological importance. Most of it is a Local Nature Reserve and a SSSI. The information centre is managed by Kent Wildlife Trust. There are also waymarked trails and country walks.

Location and access: The Country Park is on the north Kent coast, 3 miles (5 km) east of Herne Bay. It is reached from the A299 Thanet Way.

Reculver's 12th century towers can be seen from afar, but also on site are the remains of a Roman fort and an Anglo-Saxon church. Bishopstone Glen in the west is cut into sand and clays laid down more than 50 million years ago. Fossil

WILDLIFE FEATURES
🜋 **Wildfowl**　　🌿 **Grassland**

shells and sharks' teeth washed from the cliffs can be found on the beach at low tide.

The park is home to wildlife throughout the year. The woodland at Bishopstone is a refuge for birds along an almost treeless coast. Along the clifftop skylarks sing from early spring, and in summer butterflies abound. Hundreds of sand martin, their burrows in the cliff face below, feed over the grassland.

The seashore is an exciting place to explore, with animals beneath boulders and sand waiting to be discovered. Brent geese and sanderling are among the winter visitors that feast here, and many migrants pass through in autumn.

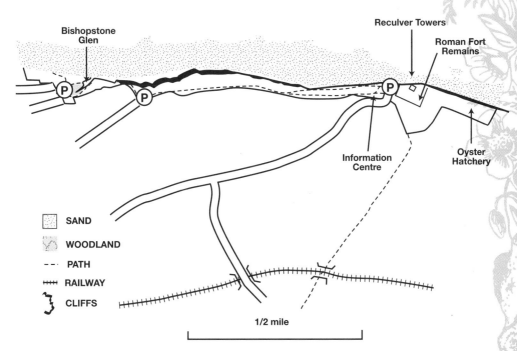

SAND

WOODLAND

PATH

RAILWAY

CLIFFS

1/2 mile

SANDWICH & PEGWELL BAY

KENT WILDLIFE TRUST

Nearest town: Ramsgate
OS Map 179 TR 351620

1,500 acres (610 ha) of coastal reserve with mudflats, saltmarsh, sand dunes and cliff. An SSSI, Ramsar site and Local Nature Reserve. A birdwatching hide overlooks the mudflats.

Location and access: The reserve lies around the mouth of River Stour at Pegwell Bay, south west of Ramsgate. Visitors are asked to avoid the beach at Shellness and the saltmarsh at Stonelees, both sensitive because of roosting and breeding birds. South of the Stour, the reserve can be reached by car along the track (a toll payable), parking just before the golf club gate and walking on. North of the river, there is parking at the main Pegwell Bay car park (fee payable).

One key aspect of this reserve is that it embraces a wonderful combination of different areas: mudflats, saltmarsh, shingle and sand dunes with some rocky cliffs to the north of Pegwell Bay. And apart from its plant interest (in summer the saltmarsh can be alight with sea-lavender, sea aster and other flowers) and its insect interest, the area has long been famous among birdwatchers.

Shelduck (the characteristic duck of mudflats), dunlin, oystercatcher and redshank are joined in winter by nationally important numbers of sanderling and grey plover.

On the rocky shore look for turnstone. There are internationally important numbers of these charming

WILDLIFE FEATURES

🦅 **Waders and wildfowl**
❀ **Saltmarsh plants**

birds along the Thanet coastline.

In summer redshank, shelduck and oyster-catcher stay on to breed, and are joined on the shingle by ringed plover and the rare little tern.

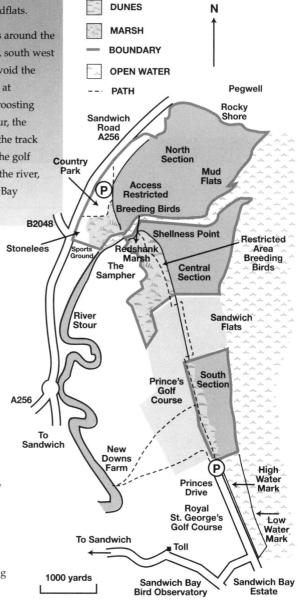

86

GUNNERSBURY TRIANGLE

LONDON WILDLIFE TRUST

Bollo Lane, London W4
Tel: 0181 747 3881

6 acres (2.5 ha) of woodland and grassland.

Location and access: The Triangle lies between two railway lines, north of Chiswick High Road in west London. The entrance is in Bollo Lane opposite Chiswick Park underground station. There is a nature trail and a field studies hut.

A century and a half ago, this area was mainly orchards. The railways now known as the District and North London lines were in place by 1874, followed soon afterwards by a third line along the Triangle's north-eastern side, isolating it from the surrounding area. For some years, gravel was extracted from part of the site, and briefly during the Second World War it was used for allotments. Since then, the woodland has grown up naturally.

In 1984 the land was purchased for nature conservation, and the

WILDLIFE FEATURES
✖ Birdlife

reserve opened in 1985, since when a pond has also been created.

It is the only piece of natural woodland in this part of London, but as well as birch and willow woodland it also offers grassland, marsh and open water.

Many birds are attracted by the woodland, including tawny owl, great spotted woodpecker, redpoll, blackcap and willow warbler.

In the damper areas grow plants which are fairly uncommon locally. They include celery-leaved buttercup, pendulous sedge and hemlock water-dropwort - but they're more for the plant specialist maybe, being difficult to distinguish from close cousins.

These damper areas are also home to frogs and common newts.

There are also several foxes based here.

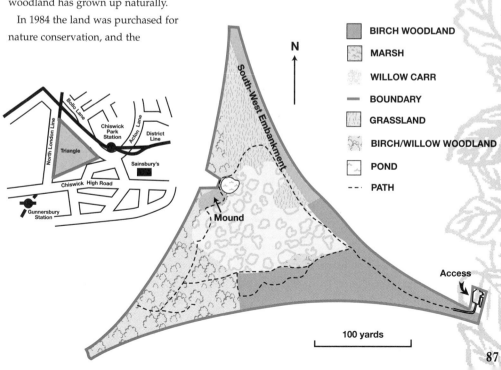

▦	BIRCH WOODLAND
▦	MARSH
▦	WILLOW CARR
▬	BOUNDARY
▦	GRASSLAND
▦	BIRCH/WILLOW WOODLAND
▦	POND
---	PATH

100 yards

CRANE PARK ISLAND

LONDON WILDLIFE TRUST

The Crane Park Island Nature Reserve
Crane Park, Ellerman Avenue
Twickenham, Middx
Tel: 0181 898 9582

A small island in the River Crane in Crane Park

Location and access: Crane Park is near
Whitton, between Great Chertsey Road and
Hanworth Road. Access is via Ellerman Avenue
or Hanworth Road. Follow the path from these
entrances to the prominent Shot Tower - the
reserve is alongside.

There is open access with a disabled path.

The island was formerly part of a gunpowder
mill complex; the explosive was manufactured
here from the late 18th century until 1926. The
old Shot Tower (soon to be a visitor centre) is
still standing on the bank, while on the island
itself there are the ruins of former mill buildings
and large earth mounds (piled to contain acci-
dental explosions) which are now tree-covered
hillocks. A large millpool once occupied much
of the island - this was drained in the 1960s. A
Phragmites reedbed was successfully

WILDLIFE FEATURES
- 🦟 **Dragonflies and damselflies**
- 🐦 **Woodland birds** 🐀 **Water vole**

established in 1996 and now dominates the
former millpond area.

Much of the wildlife value of the island stems
from the variety of habitats. The River Crane
itself, comparatively free from pollution, is a
breeding ground for numerous damselflies and
dragonflies; introduced edible frogs and marsh
frogs are found in the slower reaches; and the
waterways are a favourite hunting ground for
the heron.

Much of the island is woodland, as the map
shows. There are scatters of bluebell, yellow
lesser celandine and other woodland flowers.
Large numbers of woodland birds nest here
(and nest boxes have been added) - tits, robin,
woodpeckers, starling, kestrel and tawny owl
are all regulars, while the chiffchaff sings from
the scrubby areas.

▦	REEDBED
▦	GRASSLAND
▦	WOODLAND
▢	RIVER
▨	SCRUB
⁄⁄⁄	MOUNDS

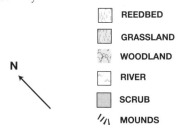

N

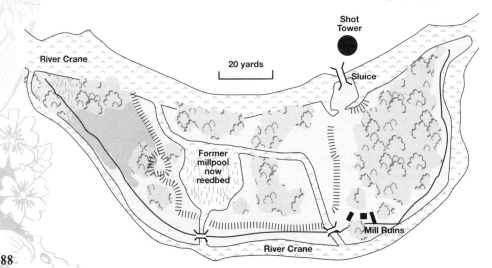

Shot
Tower

River Crane

20 yards

Sluice

Former
millpool
now
reedbed

Mill Ruins

River Crane

CAMLEY STREET

LONDON WILDLIFE TRUST

Camley Street Natural Park
12 Camley Street, London NW1 0PW
Tel: 0171 833 2311

A 2.5 acre (1 ha) ecological park on the site of a former canalside coal depot. It offers a number of habitats and a wide range of wildlife.

Location and access: The directions start from Kings Cross Station (the nearest tube). Drive or walk up Pancras Road between Kings Cross and St Pancras Stations. You reach a road junction under a railway bridge and turn right into Goods Way; Camley Street is about 100 yards on the left. Turn into Camley Street and follow the 'telegraph pole' fence to the large wrought-iron gates.

Opening hours are 0900 -1700 weekdays (closed Fridays) and 1100 -1700 weekends.

The Park is adjacent to the Regent's Canal and occupies what was once a coal depot. In the early 1980s after a period of fly-tipping, the creation of the present-day Park began.

WILDLIFE FEATURES
* 🌼 Meadow flowers and butterflies
* 🦋 Birdlife

A number of habitats are now well established. In summer, the meadow is a mass of oxeye daisies, knapweeds, wild carrot and vetches, with common blue butterflies and grasshoppers among the profuse insect life. The pond, banked by reeds and yellow flag and alight with water lilies, is a magnet for visitors (and pond dipping is available). The marsh is another wetland area, flagged by the vivid yellow of marsh marigold in spring and by water mint in summer. It is a magnet for dragonflies.

The range of birdlife seen here includes mallard, tufted duck and moorhen, with heron too. There may be a pack of house martin swooping overhead, and the kestrel is seen all year round. Visiting birds include siskin, reed warbler and sparrowhawk.

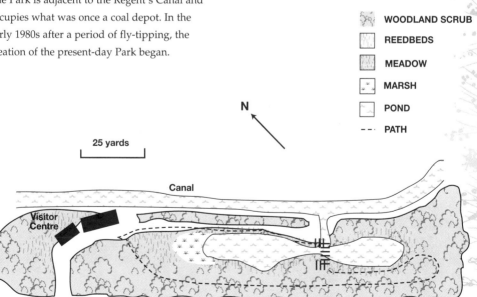

WOODLAND SCRUB
REEDBEDS
MEADOW
MARSH
POND
PATH

25 yards

N

Canal

Visitor Centre

89

SYDENHAM HILL WOOD

LONDON WILDLIFE TRUST

Sydenham Hill, London SE26
Tel 0181 699 5698 (local office), or 0171 261 0447
OS Map TQ 344726

27 acres (11 ha) with some ancient hornbeam
and oak woodland and derelict railway and
gardens, parts of which have become a
secondary woodland of native and exotic trees.

Location and access: Situated on the western
slopes of Sydenham Hill, between Dulwich and
Forest Hill in south London. The main entrance
is from Crescent Wood Road, SE26. The Wood is
open at all times. Cycling is discouraged, and
dogs should be kept under strict control.
Wheelchair access is difficult due to the
topography, but can be arranged by prior
arrangement. Nearest bus stop: route 63 (on
Sydenham Hill, 1 minute away). Information of
the Wood and current events are on notice
boards, or available from the Trust.

The Wood opened as a nature reserve in 1982,
and was declared a statutory LNR in 1990.

WILDLIFE FEATURES
✿ **Woodland flowers**
✘ **Woodland birds**

The ancient oak and hornbeam woodland
supplied smallwood, bark, timber and charcoal
in the coppice-with-standards tradition until the
early 19th century, and this remains as a
patchwork of oak, hazel and hornbeam coppice
together with holly and some large beeches.
However, the relocation of the Crystal Palace to
the nearby hilltop saw the area divided by a
railway in 1865 while housing encroached on
the upper slopes. In 1954 the railway closed,
and later the houses fell derelict and were
demolished, and the gardens became
naturalised. So here you find that a secondary
woodland has developed with native and also
exotic trees such as monkey puzzle and cedar of
Lebanon, bamboo and rhododendron.

There is a marvellous variety of wild flowers
to be seen - bluebell, wild garlic, wood
anemone, Solomon's seal, bugle ... more than
200 species in all. More than 170 species of fungi
have also been recorded.

And there is a rich birdlife. The 70 recorded
species include treecreeper, nuthatch, tawny
owl, all three woodpeckers, chiffchaff, willow
warbler, goldcrest, long-tailed tit, bullfinch, and
in recent years woodcock. The old
railway features,
including a bridge
and tunnel-mouth
(barred-off) are
also of interest,
the latter
may be
providing
a secure
retreat for
pipistrelle
bats.

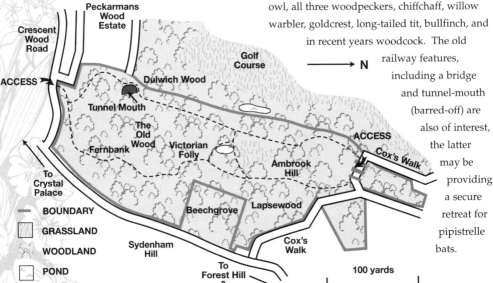

The Millennium Centre, The Chase, Dagenham Rd,
Rush Green, Romford RM7 0SS.
Tel: 0181 593 8096

120 acres (48 ha) of mixed wetland, grassland
and scrub lying within a green corridor running
from the Thames to rural Essex.

Location and access: The reserve is within
walking distance of Dagenham East tube
station, reached via the footpath adjacent to
the Rhône-Poulenc Rorer site or 174 bus from
Dagenham Heathway tube.

Visitors are asked to respect the
wildfowl areas of The Slack and
Curzon Lake.

The reserve dates back to the late
1980s. Gravel was excavated here
until the 1960s, and many pits were
consequently filled with building
rubble. Those that remain have
created a patchwork of wetland and
grassland. Horses graze to create a
short sward over much of the
reserve, but there is a small
woodland which contains the
rare black poplar (often recognised
by the bulbous burrs on its trunk)
while hawthorn and (in wetter areas)
willow create areas of scrub.

The grass sward carries bird's-foot-
trefoil among the plants, while
wetter areas are dominated by lesser
spearwort, gypsywort and rushes,
with water crowfoot in the flood
areas. Grass snakes and dragonflies
haunt these sites.

WILDLIFE FEATURES
🌼 Wild flowers
🐦 Wildfowl and waders

The open water also attracts waterfowl. Duck
such as teal, shoveler and gadwall winter on the
pools, while in spring and autumn wading
birds such as green sandpiper, redshank and
little ringed plover feed along their margins.
Grey heron and snipe may also be seen.
Whitethroat and willow warbler nest in the
scrub. Visiting the reserve a number of times a
year should also bring you sightings of
kingfisher, great spotted woodpecker, lapwing
and reed warbler. In all, 150 different bird
species have been recorded here.

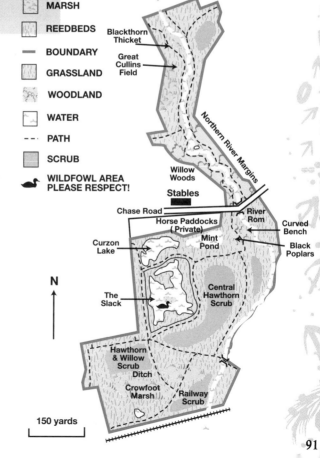

	MARSH
	REEDBEDS
—	BOUNDARY
	GRASSLAND
	WOODLAND
	WATER
---	PATH
	SCRUB
	WILDFOWL AREA PLEASE RESPECT!

N

150 yards

South Midlands

This region takes in the lush rural counties of Herefordshire, Worcestershire and Gloucestershire, as well as the more populated, industrialised Midlands counties. Herefordshire is bordered by hills, with the Black Mountains to the west, and Malvern Hills to the east. The Lugg Meadows on the edge of Hereford are ancient flood meadows on the River Lugg, cut every year for hay. The Lugg eventually flows into the River Wye which, just before it reaches the Severn estuary, rushes through a spectacular limestone gorge containing nationally important woodlands. One of these, Lancaut in Gloucestershire, contains oak, ash, field maple and yew, as well as the small-leaved lime and wild service tree, only found in ancient woodland. In Oxfordshire, as the

Thames dips in the lower Thames basin, the Warburg reserve lies in a winding chalk valley. Fallow, muntjac and roe deer all forage in the woodlands, dormice live in hazel coppice, while grass snakes, adders and common lizards are attracted by two artificial ponds. Farmland and hedgerows still make up much of Warwickshire, and some reserves have been created from areas of sand and gravel extraction. The Warwickshire Wildlife Trust's headquarters at Brandon Marsh are surrounded by pools created by flooded sand and gravel pits which attract exceptional birdlife including great crested and little grebe, tufted duck, and sedge and reed warblers.

SOUTH MIDLANDS

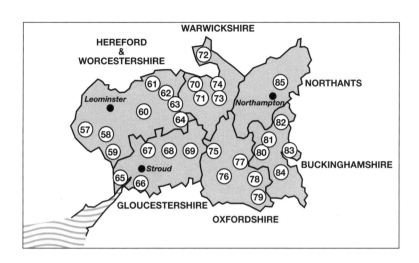

BRILLEY GREEN DINGLE

HEREFORDSHIRE NATURE TRUST

Nearest town: Hay on Wye
OS Map 148 SO 275487

A reserve of 11 acres (4.5 ha), the south-facing side of a steep-sided valley with woodland and a fast flowing stream.

Location and access: The reserve lies less than a mile north of Millhalf, just off the small road leading north from Stowe to Michaelchurch-on-Arrow. A green lane on the left leads off this road westwards and about 100 yards down the lane on the right is a gate and stile leading into the reserve.

The steep-sided valley is cut into hard sandstone, and this rock can be seen exposed at several places along the racing stream. In the 18th century it was part of Brilley Green Common and grazed, though trees remained in the deep side dingles - some of the older trees today may date from that time, as their gnarled bases show that they were once coppiced and one at least was pollarded.

WILDLIFE FEATURES
❁ **Woodland flowers**
🦞 **Crayfish and other stream life**

But by the 19th century the dell was enclosed and planted up with broadleaves at the west and conifers at the east. Most of today's oaks were planted then. Later the conifers were felled and some beech planted.

This has resulted in a mosaic of habitats. Broom, gorse and foxglove flower on the shallow acid soil up the slopes while in the deeper bottom soil you see sheets of bluebell with moschatel, sanicle and other lime-loving flowers. Early purple orchid makes a show in places.

The fast stream has a variety of caddis and other insects, river limpets and crayfish.

The woodland is rich in birdlife with many warblers and tits nesting and also tree pipit, pied flycatcher and woodpeckers. Look out for the occasional dipper along the stream.

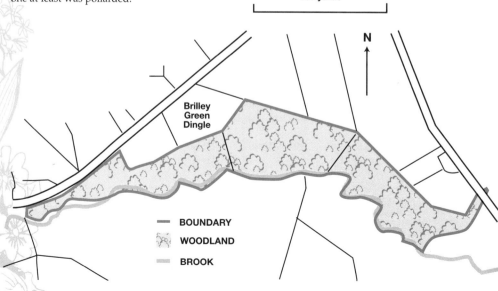

100 yards

N

Brilley Green Dingle

— **BOUNDARY**
🐾 **WOODLAND**
— **BROOK**

94

THE LUGG MEADOWS

HEREFORDSHIRE NATURE TRUST

Nearest town: Hereford
OS Map 149 SO 527411

40 acres (16 ha) of ancient meadowland, it is an SSSI.

Location and access: This reserve is just on the edge of Hereford, down Walney Lane which leads off the A465. Park in the lay-by half way up Aylestone Hill on the east side of the A465, and proceed down Walney Lane on foot.

🌼 **Fritillaries and other meadow flowers**
🦅 **Wildfowl in winter**

fertilisation. This unchanging routine century after century results in a marvellous variety of wild flowers, in part because the sparse fertility does not allow the ranker, hungry grasses to flourish and smother the other plants.

Here we see yellow rattle, oxeye daisy, pepper saxifrage and great burnet. By the river-bank grow purple loosestrife, flowering rush and the true bulrush. The sausage-headed greater reedmace is usually (wrongly) called the bulrush.

The flowering rush is one of our most beautiful wild flowers, but it is matched here in this meadow by the chequered nodding heads of the snake's-head fritillary, out in May; usually dark purple-brown, some of them here are white or pale pink.

Lugg Meadows

— **BOUNDARY**
--- **PATH**

This is classic 'Lammas land'. It is hay meadow which is still owned, in separate strips, by individuals. It is 'shut up' from Candlemas (2nd February) to Lammas Day (1st August) to allow the hay to grow, but after the hay cut it is thrown open to all villagers with commons rights to graze their cattle. The beasts enriched the soil to some extent, and the winter floods brought fresh silt, but there was no heavy

They grew on flood water meadows but such has been the destruction of meadowland by ploughing and draining that they are now rare.

Wildfowl are attracted when the meadows are flooded.

LEEPING STOCKS

HEREFORDSHIRE NATURE TRUST

Nearest town: Monmouth
OS Map 162 SO 549161

A woodland reserve of 19 acres (8 ha). There is a nature trail.

Location and access: The reserve is at Whitchurch-on-Wye, about 3 miles (5 km) north-east of Monmouth on the A40. The reserve entrance is about 160 yards along the lane towards the Doward Heritage Centre. Parking is at the top of the track to the Biblins, but there is room for two cars in the reserve entrance.

The name is an odd one, and has a fascinating interpretation. The word 'Leeping' is said to mean hedges a deer can leap over, while 'Stocks'

WILDLIFE FEATURES
🌸 **Wild flowers**
🍄 **Fungi**

means land with tree stumps left on it after felling. So this was probably once woodland cleared and made into fields, although the landlord kept his rights to hunt deer. The hedges in question, of beech growing on low stone walls and 'laid' (cut and interwoven) at some time in the past, still divide the area into compartments. (The walls are of limestone, which underlies the area.)

During the early 19th century these were ploughed fields, but they went out of cultivation and were invaded by scrub which developed into a mosaic of 'secondary' woodland with fragments of the ancient woodland still to hand.

The Trust management is aimed at retaining the diversity of open and wooded habitat.

The area is rich in wild flowers - more than 130 species have been recorded including white helleborine, deadly nightshade, columbine, bee orchid and meadow saffron. In spring the ancient woodland areas and old boundaries are marked out by sheets of bluebell and wood anemone.

The area is also good for the truffle hound. Well, not that particular fungus, but about 90 species of fungi have also been recorded here.

N

Leeping Stocks

ACCESS

P

BOUNDARY
PATH
WOODLAND

50 yards

A40 / Whitchurch

THE KNAPP & PAPERMILL

WORCESTERSHIRE WILDLIFE TRUST

Nearest town: Worcester
OS Map 150 SO 748522

67 acres (27 ha) of old valley meadows, woodland and orchard. The reserve has an information centre, warden and marked trails.

Location and access: About 7 miles (11 km) west of Worcester. Leave Worcester to the west on the A44, and at the roundabout take the A4103 to the left for Hereford. After about 2 miles take the side road to the north to Leigh and Alfrick. Take the next left to Alfrick and follow the lane for 3 miles. Park in the lay-by on the right before Bridge's Stone bridge.

This reserve in the winding valley of the Leigh Brook is one of the finest in the Midlands. It is delightfully varied.

There's an apple orchard with old lichen-encrusted trees above a pasture with a few wild daffodils. The Leigh Brook has trout, bringing the return of the otter in recent years, and grey wagtail and dipper may be seen here; and a small hide overlooks a bank where the kingfisher nests each year.

There are three separate meadows, all rather different. Big Meadow is a hay meadow with such typical flowers as hay rattle and scatters of green winged and spotted orchids. Papermill Meadow is an old pasture on slightly more acid soil; greater broomrape grows here, a total parasite on plant roots and with no green chlorophyll. Tor Meadow is another small hay meadow with orchids and cowslip.

Butterflies abound in all three meadows, and in the woodland - 30 species in all.

As for the woodland, on the steeper slopes and in patches by the brook, and which

WILDLIFE FEATURES
Otters Wild flowers
Birdlife

occupies half the reserve, most was coppiced until 50 years ago, and coppicing has been resumed to encourage the marvellous carpet of bluebell and other wild flowers. Buzzard and sparrowhawk are among the birds to look out for.

ORCHARD   ROUGH GROUND
BOUNDARY   PATH
WOODLAND   BROOK

MONKWOOD

WORCESTERSHIRE WILDLIFE TRUST

Nearest town: Worcester
OS Map 150 SO 804806

A 150 acre (61 ha) woodland, largely felled 40 or so years ago, but replanted to create a reserve of considerable variety.

Location and access: From Worcester take the A443 north for about 3 miles (5 km). Turn left towards Sinton Green. After 1 mile turn left for Wichenford/Monkwood Green and after 2 miles turn right at Monkwood Green. The road passes through the wood, and on the north side of the road a track leads immediately into a small car park. There is a good system of rides and paths. Please keep dogs under control.

Please avoid areas where foresters are at work, usually in winter.

This was basically a coppice-with-standards ancient woodland, but much of its heart was felled 30-40 years ago and then replanted to produce small round-wood for a brush works. However, this was very like traditional coppicing and favoured the carpets of bluebell, and the wood anemone and other flowers. The wood is very varied with older trees at the boundaries and stands of different ages elsewhere. The Wildlife Trust now coppices some areas, attracting butterflies at first and then warblers and other birds as soon as the shrubs grow.

The open rides, like the newly cut coppice, are good for butterflies - in fact 36 species have been seen here, including the uncommon and delicate wood white; this is

WILDLIFE FEATURES
🦋 **Butterflies**
🐦 **Woodland birds**

its stronghold in Worcestershire. It flies (weakly) in May, laying its eggs on pea-family plants. The white admiral feeding on bramble blossom and the purple hairstreak at the tops of the oak trees (binoculars needed) are two others to be seen here.

The pools attract dragonflies and there is a good bird count in this varied and interesting wood.

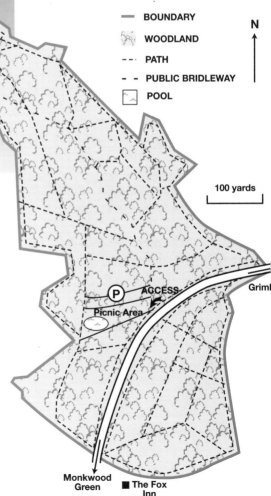

— BOUNDARY
WOODLAND
-·- PATH
- - PUBLIC BRIDLEWAY
POOL

N

100 yards

To Ockeridge

P ACCESS
Picnic Area

Grim

Monkwood Green ■ The Fox Inn

WORCESTERSHIRE WILDLIFE TRUST

Nearest town: Bromsgrove
OS Map 150 SO 936677

The reserve is in two parts, the northern 42 acres (17 ha) of the Moors Pools with surrounding marshes and grasslands and the southern 23 acres (9.5 ha) of the Flash Pools and grasslands. It is an SSSI. There are birdwatching hides.

Location and access: The reserve lies by the A38 at Upton Warren between Droitwich and Bromsgrove. From Bromsgrove take the A38 south towards Droitwich. At Upton Warren, about 2 miles (3 km) from Bromsgrove, an AA phone box stands at the corner of a narrow lane on the left, before you reach the Swan Inn. Turn into the lane and carry on to the car park.

This is Worcestershire's premier birdwatching reserve. The pools have resulted from subsidence following underground brine extraction - and while Moors Pool is a shallow freshwater lake, Flash Pools are salty - forming a unique inland saltmarsh in some places.

Large numbers of any one bird species are unusual - it is the variety that is important here, and virtually any species can turn up - American waders, unusual warblers, surprising ducks and rare gulls and predators. The osprey may be seen on migration, as are sanderling, curlew sandpiper, and bar-tailed godwit. Many warblers nest and big flocks of lapwing and black-headed gull visit the Flash Pools in autumn and

WILDLIFE FEATURES
Birdlife

winter. Flocks of finches can be seen, and the trees and small wooded areas attract tits and woodpeckers.

The water level in the Moors Pools can be manipulated to create good conditions for both winter-feeding duck and summer plants and breeding birds, including sedge warbler. A tern raft has been built in the larger Moors Pool and the common tern has bred.

In addition there are many dragonflies.

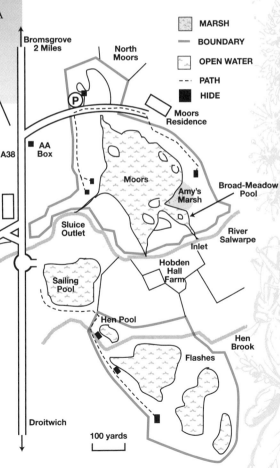

| MARSH |
| BOUNDARY |
| OPEN WATER |
| PATH |
| HIDE |

PIPER'S HILL AND DODDERHILL COMMON

WORCESTERSHIRE WILDLIFE TRUST

Nearest town: Bromsgrove
OS Map 150 SO 960649

A 38 acre (15.5 ha) woodland which started to fill out 150 years ago on what had been wood pasture; it is now well wooded and many of the ancient wood pasture trees survive.
It is an SSSI.

Location and access: The wood is split by the B4091. This road leaves to the south-east from the A38, running south from Bromsgrove to Droitwich. The reserve is about 2 miles (3.25 km) north of Hanbury (it is also known as Dodderhill Common and Hanbury Woods).

WILDLIFE FEATURES
🌲 **Ancient trees**   🦅 **Woodland birds**

Next to coppice-with-standards, wood pasture was the second main use of woodland in the Middle Ages and beyond: the wood was open for grazing by cattle, sheep, maybe pigs and deer. As a result few young saplings survived but existing trees grew on, becoming widely spaced when neighbours died and fell. These remaining trees were often pollarded, de-branched at head height or above (out of reach of grazing animals) to grow a new head of shoots. Being of little timber value, old pollards are among the oldest trees we have.

This wood has developed on old wood pasture and is now well wooded, and the open pasturage gone. Because of its history of grazing and today's deep shade, the wood is not rich in flowers although uncommon species such as bird's-nest orchid can be found. But this common does contain some of the oldest and largest trees in the county. Many are ancient beech and sweet chestnut pollards together with big oaks, believed to be 300-400 years old, with spreading crowns typical of trees which have grown in open conditions.

They are of course ripe for fungi and more than 200 species have been found, including chanterelle (linked with beech and sometimes clustered so that they look like a torn shawl) and beefsteak fungus, a bracket fungus, especially on oak. All three species of woodpecker are attracted by the old trees as well as tits and the nuthatch.

Map legend:
— BOUNDARY
WOODLAND
POND
- - - PATH
TRACK

Stoke Prior

KNOTT'S FARM

WARREN HOUSE

B4091

Tomlins

100 yards

Hanbury

TIDDESLEY WOOD

WORCESTERSHIRE WILDLIFE TRUST

Nearest town: Pershore
OS Map 150 SO 929462

198 acres (80 ha) of ancient woodland, in part coniferised.

Location and access: The north entrance to the wood is about a mile west of Pershore Abbey, the southern tip about a mile north-east of Defford. Take the A44 from Pershore towards Worcester and turn left near the town boundary just before the summit of the hill, into an unclassified road signposted for Besford and Croome. The entrance to the reserve car park is three quarters of a mile (1.3 km) along this road on the left.

There is a military firing range in the south-west corner of the wood, and you must not enter the area marked by red flags when the range is in use or climb the fence into the danger area at any time. Please avoid areas where foresters are working.

This is the Wildlife Trust's largest woodland reserve and it contains a great variety of trees and shrubs: oak, ash, aspen, hazel, guelder rose, spindle, dogwood. Wild service tree and small-leaved lime are indicators that the wood is ancient, though areas have been planted with beech and conifer. Look also for wild pear, crab apple and wild plum - this last is rather like blackthorn (sloe) but more of a tree, and not thorny.

It's a good wood for bluebell, wood anemone and other flowers (the coppicing encourages these) and also for those such as herb Paris and dog's mercury, greater butterfly orchid and tway-blade which can put up with some shade.

WILDLIFE FEATURES
❀ Spring flowers 🦋 Woodland butterflies

Butterflies too are here in numbers, including the white admiral (honeysuckle is the host plant on which they lay their eggs), peacock (nettles) and gatekeeper (grasses). Dragonflies haunt the rides, using them as a hunting ground.

There is, as you'd expect, a vibrant bird population summer and winter.

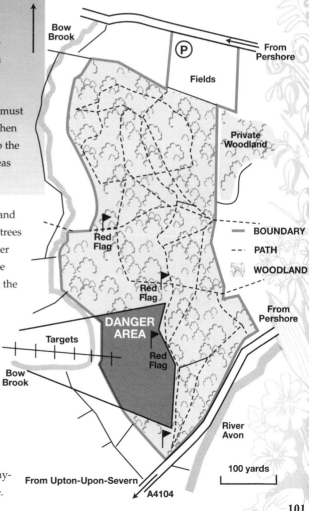

101

LANCAUT

GLOUCESTERSHIRE WILDLIFE TRUST

Nearest town: Chepstow
OS Map 171/172 ST 539966

60 acres (24 ha) of the east bank of the spectacular limestone Wye Gorge, with cliffs and disused quarries, woodland, and saltmarsh. It is a designated SSSI.

Location and access: Take the B4228 heading north from Chepstow, for St Briavels and beyond. Half a mile (0.8 km) north of Woodcroft, Lancaut Lane is signposted to the left. You can park about 250 yards along the lane. The steep access path into the wood is 150 yards further on, on the left. A public footpath runs through the wood from the remains of Lancaut Chapel to below Pen Moel, returning via Offa's Dyke footpath along the cliff top. To minimise erosion, visitors are asked to keep away from the river-bank.

The woodland is marvellous, with oak, ash, field maple and yew. But it also contains small-leaved lime and wild service tree which are found only in ancient woodland, and many rare whitebeams. When sycamore seeds itself in, it is removed as part of the regular management.

There is a luxuriant growth of ferns, and the ground

WILDLIFE FEATURES
🌱 **Wild flowers** 🦋 **Birdlife**

flowers include a fine spring display of primrose, bluebell, dog violet, wood anemone and early purple orchid as well as less common woodland plants such as green hellebore and bird's-nest orchid.

There is also a wealth of wild flowers growing on the rock faces and ledges - hairy violet, red valerian and others. And the saltmarsh sports sea aster, sea milkwort and buck's-horn plantain. In all, 350 or so plants have been found growing in the reserve.

Sparrowhawk, cormorant, shelduck, wood warbler, lapwing and goldcrest are among the wide range of birdlife. Herring gull and raven nest on the cliff faces.

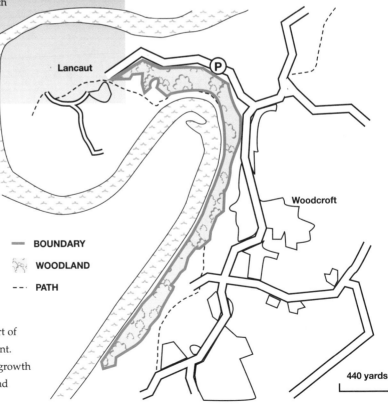

— **BOUNDARY**

🌲 **WOODLAND**

--- **PATH**

LOWER WOODS

GLOUCESTERSHIRE WILDLIFE TRUST

Nearest town: Chipping Sodbury
OS Map 172 ST 743876

700 acres (283 ha) of superb ancient oakwood and grassland. It is an SSSI.

Location and access: From Chipping Sodbury take the B4060 north to Wickwar. Just past the village turn right onto the unclassified road for Hawkesbury Upton. Continue for about 2 miles to Inglestone Farm on the left. The entrance to the woods is on the right, opposite the farm. There is parking within the woods, which are open to the public at all times.

This enormous reserve - one of England's largest ancient woodlands on neutral heavy clay soils - is in fact divided into individual woods separated by 'trenches' (a Norman term), many of which are common land.

Here, wildlife surveys have only recently started, but Lower Wetmoor Wood which has been owned by the Trust since 1967 has been found to have more than 1,000 species living in merely 8 per cent of it - an incredible figure. A rich wildlife results only after

- Woodland birds
- Rare grassland plants

centuries of unchanging management regime: here it has been coppice-with-standards woodland.

Size helps - a large wood will hold stocks of animals and plants ready to recolonise areas which for some reason have suffered setbacks. A large wood is likely to be a more stable wood, in other words. Added to which the lichens and river life show that the area is comparatively unpolluted.

To Wickwar

Inglestone Farm

South Moor Ridings
Stiff's Coppice
Lance Coppice
North Elms Wood
Little Stanley Wood
Crew's Coppice
Spoil Coppice
Sturt Coppice
Margary Hay
West Stanley Wood
East Stanley Wood
Oakhall Coppice
To Hawkesbury Upton
Little Bath Riding
Lower Wetmoor Wood
Shepherd's Knap
Upper Wetmoor
Little Wood
Mossey Wood
Wetmoor
The Grubbings
Bagnel Trench
Common Land
Burnt Wood
Sturgeon Wood
Bay's Wood
Stonybridge Wood

— BOUNDARY
--- PATH
WOODLAND
STREAM

1/2 mile

103

BETTY DAW'S WOOD

GLOUCESTERSHIRE WILDLIFE TRUST

Nearest town: Newent
OS Map 162 SO 696284

22 acres (9 ha) of oak woodland.

Location and access: Newent is about 7 miles (11 km) north west of Gloucester. From the city centre take the A40 (for Ross on Wye) and then turn right onto the B4215. Continue on this road through Newent and take the third turning on the left (about 2 miles past Newent) onto an unclassified road. Continue for about 1.5 miles. A path on the left gives access to the wood.

The wood can be reached from Junction 3 of the M50. Take the B4221 to Gorsley Common and take the first turn on the left, onto an unclassified road described above.

The wood is open to the public all year.

This is a superb example of an ancient sessile oak wood which has escaped coniferisation, the fate of many.

The sessile oak is the one of our two native oaks which favours rather acid soils, and is usually found, for example, on the poorer hill soils of north and west Britain. Its leaves are shallowly lobed with a longish stalk; the leaves run smoothly to the stalk and the acorns have no, or a short, stalk. The other, the common oak, has lobes at the base of its leaf and acorns on a long stalk. However, there is variation, and the two do cross to produced trees of mixed character.

The large oaks here date from about 1850. Those in Colonel's Grove were felled in 1920 and this part of the wood replanted with ash and beech.

WILDLIFE FEATURES
* Ancient sessile oak woodland
* Wild daffodil   Woodland birds

As well as oaks, Betty Daw's wood also contains wild cherry and ash, and some wild service tree and small-leaved lime - these last two are indicators of ancient woodland. There is hazel coppice.

But the reserve is best known for its spectacular show of wild daffodil, accompanied by wood anemone and bluebell, and primrose. They have recently flourished, thanks to coppicing of the hazel and ride-widening, which have let sunlight down to the woodland floor.

The wood has a good bird count, in part the result of a nest box scheme. Pied and spotted flycatchers, nuthatch, wren, treecreeper and marsh tit are among the birds using the boxes. Other birds nesting here include dunnock, song thrush and garden warbler, while the nightingale can sometimes be heard. You also have a good chance of seeing many woodland butterflies, notably white admiral, wood white and silver-washed fritillary.

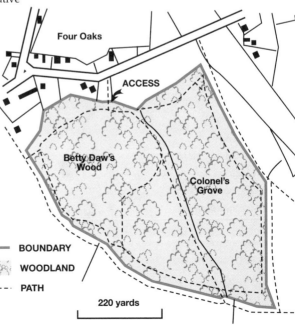

BOUNDARY
WOODLAND
PATH

220 yards

ASHLEWORTH HAM & MEEREND THICKET

GLOUCESTERSHIRE WILDLIFE TRUST

Nearest town: Gloucester
OS Map 162 SO 830265

101 acres (40.9 ha) of meadow (the Ham) and a steep wooded bank (the Thicket) which was the former high boundary of the River Severn. The meadow is part of a larger SSSI. There are bird-watching hides in Meerend Thicket.

Location and access: From Gloucester take the A417 north to Hartpury, about 3 miles. Turn right onto the unclassified road for Ashleworth. From Ashleworth take the road for Hasfield (north-east); the site is about a mile from Ashleworth, with the wet meadow to the right of the road and Meerend Thicket to the left. Access to Ashleworth Ham is restricted in winter (contact the Wildlife Trust) but Meerend Thicket is open all year for bird-watching from the hides.

The Ham lies in the flood plain of the Severn and is a remnant of much wider areas of old meadow-land, now destroyed by drainage and ploughing.

The reserve is renowned for its wintering wildfowl. Up to 4,000 wigeon, 1,500 teal and 1,000 mallard can be seen here, with small numbers of pintail and shoveler. Tufted duck, pochard, goldeneye and great crested and little grebes are amongst the diving birds. Bewick swan are regular visitors and some white-fronted geese are seen.

WILDLIFE FEATURES
🦆 **Wildfowl** ❀ **Meadow plants**

Nesting birds are also of interest - mallard, lapwing, snipe, curlew and redshank breed here while redstart, sedge and grasshopper warblers, yellow wagtail and reed bunting also nest.

Passage migrants also drop by to feed - snipe are commonest. Up to 4,000 fieldfare flock here in some winters - often hunted by peregrine.

To maintain the wetland, two sluices were installed and a wader scrape was dug at the same time. The reserve is grazed only after the young birds have fledged.

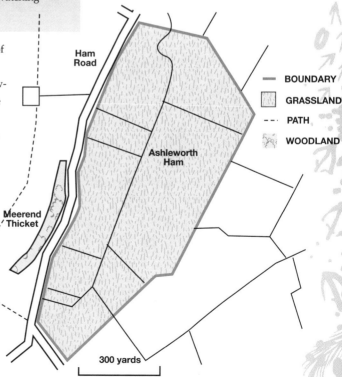

Ham Road

Ashleworth Ham

Meerend Thicket

— BOUNDARY
▒ GRASSLAND
--- PATH
🌳 WOODLAND

300 yards

WHELFORD POOLS

GLOUCESTERSHIRE WILDLIFE TRUST

Nearest town: Fairford
OS Map 164 SU 174205

31 acres (12.3 ha) forming part of the Cotswold Water Park marl lake system, the largest in Britain, created by digging the limestone gravel. There are two bird hides.

Location and access: Lechlade is about 11 miles north of Swindon on the A361. From Lechlade take the A417 west (to Fairford). After about 2 miles, turn left onto the unclassified road, for Whelford. Drive down this road for 1 mile. The entrance to the reserve is on the left. The reserve is open to the public all year.

The lakes of the Cotswold Water Park were created by gravel digging and have become popular for water skiing and other activities -

WILDLIFE FEATURES
 Winter wildfowl   **Dragonflies**

which underlines the importance of Whelford Pools for wildlife.

The narrowly separated pools drain southwards to the Rivers Thames and Coln, and are of major importance for wintering wildfowl. However, in addition to the two main lakes there are three small pools favoured by dragonflies: the blue bodied emperor (a 4-inch wingspan, truly a bird watcher's insect) breeds here as does the red-eyed damselfly - 11 species breed in all.

As for the birds, good numbers of tufted duck, pochard, coot, mallard and Canada geese come here in winter, with rather fewer wigeon, great crested grebe, mute swan and shoveler; while red-crested pochard and ruddy duck are among the more unusual visitors. The kingfisher is one of the many birds to nest here.

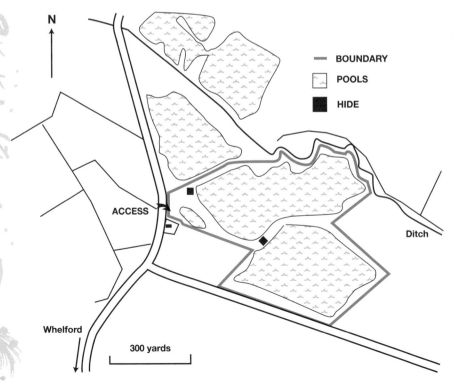

N

BOUNDARY
POOLS
HIDE

ACCESS

Ditch

Whelford

300 yards

CLOWES WOOD & NEW FALLINGS COPPICE

WARWICKSHIRE WILDLIFE TRUST

Nearest town: Solihull
OS Map 139 SP 101743

108 acres (44 ha) of woodland, but also with some heathland, a damp meadow and ditches, streams and ponds, all part of a larger SSSI. There is a nature trail.

Location and access: From Solihull take the B4102 south to Earlswood. At Earlswood turn right off this B road into an unclassified road, and you pass Earlswood Lake on the left. Just past this, take the turning to the left (Wood Lane). There is car parking down this lane. The railway must be crossed by the footbridge.

WILDLIFE FEATURES

 Wild flowers

The oak-birch woodland is typical of the area and there is a great deal of it in Little Clowes Wood. Rowan is frequent throughout and there are some stands of beech in Little Clowes Wood which were planted at the beginning of this century - they're around 100 years old, in other words.

Clowes Wood is one of the few places in Warwickshire where lily-of-the-valley grows wild - it is more familiar from gardens. Other flowers to be seen include bluebell and wood anemone, wood sage and common cow-wheat. The use of the word 'cow' is held to mean second rate. Cow-wheat bears no resemblance to wheat (it has lipped anaemic yellow flowers). It does have large seeds though.

The heathland, with heather and bilberry is a rare sight in this county.

The wet alder woodland is small but does contain a variety of plants - look for wood horsetail, for example, a feathery looking member of the prehistoric horsetail tribe. The meadow is a marshy grassland on what was an old hay meadow.

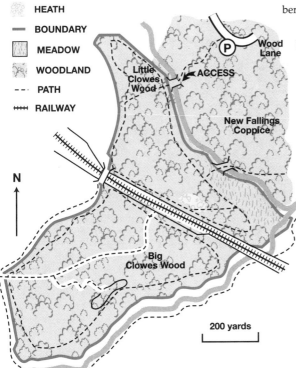

HEATH

BOUNDARY

MEADOW

WOODLAND

PATH

RAILWAY

N

Wood Lane

P

Little Clowes Wood

ACCESS

New Fallings Coppice

Big Clowes Wood

200 yards

SNITTERFIELD BUSHES

WARWICKSHIRE WILDLIFE TRUST

Nearest town: Stratford upon Avon
OS Map 151 SP 200604

A 124 acre (50 ha) woodland area, of SSSI status.

Location and access: From the western edge of Stratford upon Avon take the A46 north towards Warwick. Snitterfield is about 5 miles (8 km) from Stratford. At Snitterfield you want the A3400 to Bearley. The reserve is about 1 mile along this road, on both sides of the road. The car park is on the left.

Snitterfield Bushes was once part of an extensive area of old broadleaved woodland which stretched as far as Bearley. The central

WILDLIFE FEATURES
Butterflies　　**Wild flowers**
Woodland birds

area was cleared for an airfield in the Second World War, leaving a legacy of concrete tracks through the wood. The reserve consists today of even-aged ash and silver birch with occasional tall oaks. Below this, the shrub layer is mainly hazel, but with field maple, wayfaring tree, guelder rose and dogwood - all of which like a lime-rich soil. There are bluebell in late spring, but also early purple orchid, greater butterfly orchid and broad-leaved helleborine. This combination underlines the point that despite its wartime history, this woodland is of ancient origin.

Twenty-six butterfly species have been seen here, including purple hairstreak which flies high in the oak trees, white admiral which you will probably see taking nectar from bramble flowers in the sunshine of a path or glade and marbled white.

There are also plenty of the common woodland birds. The nightingale has occasionally nested in recent years, but this far north is approaching the edge of its range. Coppicing is being re-introduced, however, which creates the dense low cover which this bird likes.

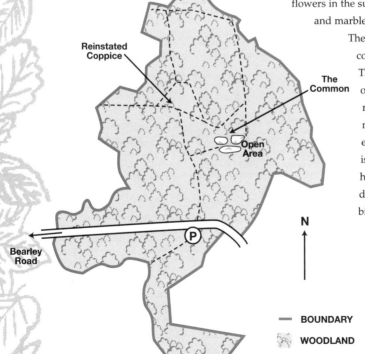

Reinstated Coppice

The Common

Open Area

N

Bearley Road

P

— BOUNDARY
WOODLAND
--- CONCRETE TRACK
POND

200 yards

ALVECOTE POOLS

WARWICKSHIRE WILDLIFE TRUST

Nearest town: Tamworth
OS Map 139 SK 255046

An SSSI of pools and wetland. There is a nature trail.

Location and access: From Tamworth town centre take the B5000 towards Polesworth. About 2 miles from the centre, before reaching the M42 motorway, turn left into Robeys Lane, signposted for Alvecote. Follow this road for about half a mile; the car park for the reserve is on the right, just before a railway bridge.

The site can also be accessed from Junction 10 of the M42. There is public access to the nature trail; additional pools can be seen from nearby roads and footpaths.

WILDLIFE FEATURES
➤ Wildfowl and other birds

The reserve forms part of the extensive Alvecote Pools SSSI. The pools are mainly about 50 years old, formed as a result of mining subsidence, with the River Anker flowing through the three largest. For more than 40 years it was comprehensively monitored by two brothers, Maurice and George Arnold, making it one of the most thoroughly recorded nature reserves in England. There are interesting examples of the way that species have adapted to local conditions, the stunted oak trees are one example, and the black wolf spiders which live on the coal tip another.

The wetland and marsh plants are many and varied, and include a large colony of marsh orchid.

The butterfly population includes small copper, purple hairstreak, and the ringlet, which is locally scarce.

But the reserve gained its SSSI status because of the wetland birds it attracts. Nesting birds include great crested grebe, pochard, tufted duck, little ringed plover, snipe and redshank. They are regulars, but oystercatcher and common tern are also known to have nested. In addition, there is an impressive list of wintering wildfowl and passage birds.

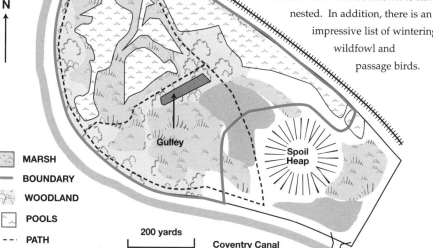

Robeys Lane

ACCESS

Ⓟ

N

Gulley

Spoil Heap

- MARSH
- BOUNDARY
- WOODLAND
- POOLS
- PATH

200 yards

Coventry Canal

UFTON FIELDS

WARWICKSHIRE WILDLIFE TRUST

Nearest town: Leamington Spa
OS Map 139 SP 378615

Limestone grassland, pools and woodland, an SSSI and LNR of 77 acres (32 ha). There is a nature trail and bird hides.

Location and access: From Leamington Spa take the A425 east and continue on this road until the village of Ufton. At Ufton, take the first right unclassified road (Ufton Fields Lane) signposted for Harbury. The entrance to the reserve, with car park, is about a quarter of a mile on the left.

Paths allow wheelchair access around the nature trail.

The reserve is managed in partnership with Warwickshire County Council.

This site was worked for limestone in the years 1952-54, and then abandoned. The spoil heaps form many ridges covering half the site and creating rainwater pools; there are also six larger pools.

WILDLIFE FEATURES
🌼 Wild flowers 🦋 Birdlife

Colonisation of the abandoned workings has now been taking place for more than 40 years - and would still continue with invading hawthorn, bramble and rank grasses moving in. But as the early colonisers included six species of orchid, management involves making sure that they survive, together with typical lime-loving plants such as yellow-wort and common centaury. The former is rather a handsome flower with an unusual arrangement of joined-up pairs of leaves, forming rings up the stem.

More than 130 species of birds have been seen here - they include willow tit, goldcrest, reed bunting and bullfinch. The green woodpecker and little grebe regularly nest here. Unexpected sightings include crossbill and great grey shrike.

There is also good butterfly count - dingy and grizzled skippers and marbled white among them.

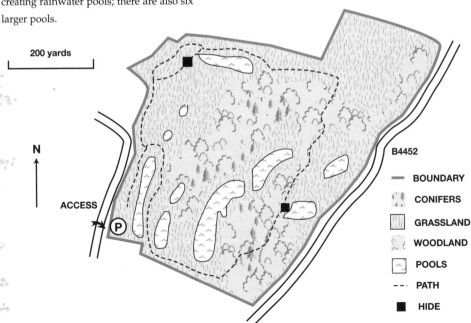

▬	BOUNDARY
▨	CONIFERS
▥	GRASSLAND
▨	WOODLAND
⬠	POOLS
- - -	PATH
■	HIDE

200 yards

N

ACCESS

P

B4452

BRANDON MARSH

WARWICKSHIRE WILDLIFE TRUST

Nearest town: Coventry
OS Map 139 SP 386761

A wetland reserve of 228 acres (92 ha) leased from Redland Aggregates and Coventry City Council. An SSSI, the reserve has a nature trail, a visitor centre and bird hides.

Location and access: From Coventry centre take the A428 east (towards Rugby). Turn right down the A46 Eastern Bypass and at the next (Tollbar Island) roundabout turn left and just past the Shell garage turn left onto Brandon Lane. The reserve is on this road, down a track on the right. There is a signposted car park. The reserve is open 0900-1700 Monday-Friday and 1000-1700 at weekends. There is disabled access from the nature centre.

WILDLIFE FEATURES
✕ Birdlife

This reserve has 10 main pools - 30 acres of open water in all, surrounded by wetland vegetation - alongside the River Avon. Some pools are flooded sand and gravel pits, others created when the river flooded into mining subsidence, but five small ones have been specially constructed for dragonflies.

Although 387 species of plants have been recorded and new ones found every year, and dragonflies and butterflies are well represented, it is the birdlife here which is exceptional. More than 210 species have been recorded with 70 nesting. The latter include great crested and little grebes, coot, moorhen and tufted duck while the reedbeds attract sedge and reed warblers and reed bunting and the drier grassland areas grasshopper warblers, and yellowhammer and skylark.

The two small woods harbour different birds - song thrush, black-cap, whitethroats (both common and lesser) and garden warbler.

In addition spring and autumn bring passage migrants, especially waders!

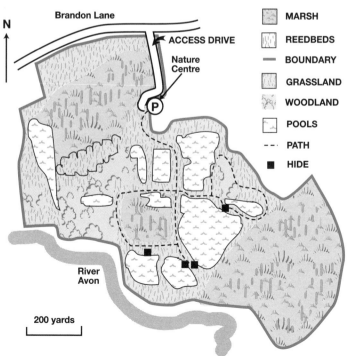

MARSH	
REEDBEDS	
— BOUNDARY	
GRASSLAND	
WOODLAND	
POOLS	
- - PATH	
■ HIDE	

N

Brandon Lane

ACCESS DRIVE

Nature Centre

P

River Avon

200 yards

FOXHOLES

**BBONT - THE WILDLIFE TRUST
FOR BERKS, BUCKS & OXON**

Nearest town: Burford
OS Map 163 SP 254206

A reserve of 158 acres (64 ha), mainly woodland but with a variety of habitats including a wet meadow. Much of it is SSSI status.

Location and access: Burford is about 19 miles west of Oxford, just off the A40. From Burford take the A424 north, towards Stow-on-the-Wold. About 3 miles (5 km) from Burford turn right into a lane signposted for Bruern Abbey and continue on this road until just before the abbey, when you turn left onto a rough track. Continue for half a mile to the car park (on right). The track may be unsuitable for cars in some weathers.

The public footpaths and bridleways are open to the public.

WILDLIFE FEATURES
❀ **Woodland flowers**   ✹ **Butterflies**
✹ **Woodland birds**

The woodland here is a remnant of the ancient Wychwood Forest, sloping gently from higher ground with acidic soil across base-rich (alkaline) soils down to the River Evenlode. Soil and use have created a variety of habitats. For example, in the area of the reserve next to Cocksmoor Wood two different kinds of wet ash-maple woodland can be recognised; one with primrose, early purple orchid and wild angelica, the other (which has oak and ash standard trees) with sanicle, goldilocks butter-cup and herb Paris, none of them common elsewhere in the wood.

Elsewhere there are a few mature oaks, and beech, larch and hornbeam have been planted. The woodland is excellent for fungi.

Away from the trees, in the open rides on acid soil there are patches of bog moss, while in the wet meadow along the river, great burnet and devil's-bit scabious flower. The reserve is excellent for butterflies - 20 species including the white admiral. Both the grass snake and adder are common, though the last is now in decline. And there is abundant birdlife!

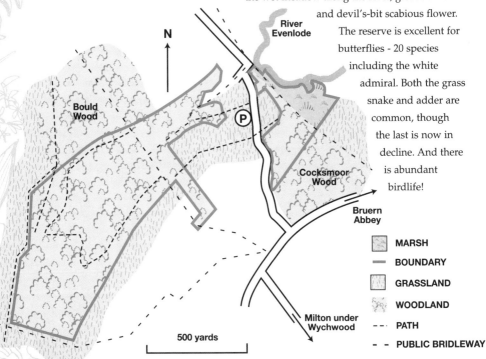

▨	MARSH
▬	BOUNDARY
▧	GRASSLAND
▨	WOODLAND
- - -	PATH
- -	PUBLIC BRIDLEWAY

DRY SANDFORD PIT

Nearest town: Abingdon
OS Map 164 SU 467997

An old stone and sand quarry reserve, 20 acres (8 ha) in area, part of which is an ecological and geological SSSI.

Location and access: This reserve lies in Cothill village, 2 miles (3 km) north-west of Abingdon. It is best approached by turning off the Wootton Road (B4017) almost directly opposite the garage which marks its junction with the Boars Hill/Foxcombe Hill road. Very soon after entering Cothill, turn left beyond the Dry Sandford turning, into a lay-by which leads up a slope to a small car park. The reserve is in front of you over a stile. The fen area is fragile and should be avoided. Keep dogs on a lead when sheep are grazing.

This reserve is one of a number in this locality, known jointly as the Cothill Reserves. It is largely an old sand and stone quarry, partly filled in, but low cliffs remain to the north-east. These make it one of Britain's best sites for burrowing bees and wasps.

Springs feed part of the old quarry floor and create shallow open water here surrounded by fen, running on into Sandford Brook. The area next to the brook is mainly woodland, the rest mainly grassland with some trees and scrub.

WILDLIFE FEATURES
🦋 **Birdlife**   ❀ **Wild flowers**
🦟 **Insects**

Orchids seen in the fen area include early marsh orchid, common spotted orchid and a large colony of marsh helleborine. The kingfisher is seen here and the wet is also a magnet for frog, toad and newt - and grass snake which hunts them. Dragonflies and damselflies are common.

The turf areas carry many wild flowers, while on the bare rock and sandy soil below the cliff there is a 'heath' of lichens.

The glow worm is seen on summer nights, and the penetrating song of the great green bush cricket is something to listen for.

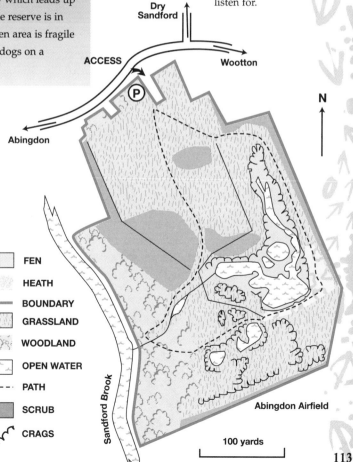

Dry Sandford

ACCESS   **Wootton**

Ⓟ

Abingdon

N

	FEN
	HEATH
—	BOUNDARY
	GRASSLAND
	WOODLAND
	OPEN WATER
- - -	PATH
	SCRUB
	CRAGS

Sandford Brook

Abingdon Airfield

100 yards

113

SYDLINGS COPSE & COLLEGE POND

**BBONT - THE WILDLIFE TRUST
FOR BERKS, BUCKS & OXON**

Nearest town: Oxford

OS Map 164; SP 559096

A varied reserve of 42 acres (16.8 ha), with a wetland enclosed in a steep-sided valley together with broadleaved and conifer woodland, heath and open grassland. The whole site is part of a larger SSSI. There is a wildlife trail.

Location and access: From the Headington roundabout on the ring road proceed northwards past the crematorium until the B4027 is reached. Turn left and drive about 700 yards, to the Royal Oak farmhouse on the right. Cars can be parked on the grass verge.

Turn left onto a bridlepath and walk about 600 yards, past two pieces of woodland on the right. Just past the second wood, Sydlings Copse lies one field away on the right (on some maps it is labelled Wick Copse). Note that there is no clear path from Sydlings Copse to College Pond. The wildlife walk goes past the eastern end of College Pond but the footpath at the western end does not link up with Sydlings Copse. Please keep dogs on a lead when entering grazed areas.

Relatively small, but crammed, is this reserve. In the steep-sided valley are a reedbed, fen, wet 'carr' woodland, a stream, broadleaved and conifer woodland and heath. Some of the grassland is on acid soil (marked by bracken and gorse), some limy. The wild flower count here is high and so the insect life is particularly good, with 28 species of butterfly including the

WILDLIFE FEATURES

 **Wild flowers** **Birdlife**

marbled white and dark green fritillary (not in fact green, but with patches of dark green scales on the back underwings). Look out for burnet - a day flying, gaudy red and black moth.

In Sydlings Copse look for wild liquorice, a sprawling plant with zig-zag stems and greenish yellow vetch-like pea flowers and inch-long curved pods in August. It has nothing to do with the plant which provides liquorice!

Birdlife is abundant, with all three species of woodpecker.

The heath is now grazed by Hebridean sheep.

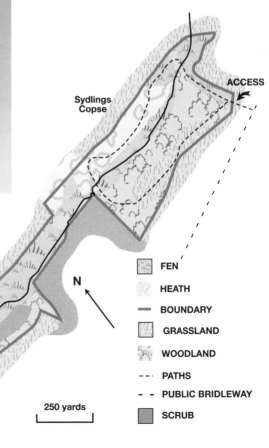

Sydlings Copse

College Pond

ACCESS

N

250 yards

	FEN
	HEATH
	BOUNDARY
	GRASSLAND
	WOODLAND
	PATHS
	PUBLIC BRIDLEWAY
	SCRUB

CHINNOR HILL

**BBONT - THE WILDLIFE TRUST
FOR BERKS, BUCKS & OXON**

Nearest town: Chinnor (south-east of Thame)
OS Map 165 SP 766002

A reserve of 70 acres (28 ha) of chalk slope, with woodland, scrub and grassland. It is an SSSI, and in addition to its wildlife interest, there are two Bronze Age burial mounds and ancient sunken tracks down the slopes.

Location and access: Chinnor is off the A40, about 4 miles (6 km) south-east of Thame.

Entering Chinnor from the west, turn right at the crossroads into an unclassified road. Drive up this road (up the scarp) and take the first left, back towards Bledlow Ridge. As the road curves to the right, turn left into Hill Top Lane; the car park is at the end of this lane. Dogs should be kept on a lead within the grassland when sheep are grazing.

This reserve on the Chiltern scarp has two kinds of soil, clay-with-flints at the top and shallow, quickly draining chalky soil on the slopes. There is an area of woodland with oak and ash and small areas of mature open-floored beech woodland at the top of the hill. These apart, the whole area was once open grazing, with juniper growing on the steep slopes.

Earlier this century, stock grazing ceased but rabbits took over. However, when they were wiped out by disease in the 1950s, a scrub of hawthorn, wild privet, spindle and other woody plants grew up, smothering and killing some (not all) of the juniper. Some of this scrub is being cleared and the Trust has sheep grazing to maintain the open grassland.

There are wild roses here - dog rose and sweet briar with apple scented leaves, to the south of the Icknield Way.

The open chalk grassland is scattered with flowers such as rockrose and thyme (with purplish flowers in August). Look also for the very prickly, straw-coloured carline thistle.

The scrub is alive with birdsong in spring; while in winter flocks of redwing and fieldfare scavenge the berries.

WILDLIFE FEATURES
❀ Wild flowers ✘ Birdlife

Stepping Hill Field

Chalk Pit

Tumuli

N

Chinnor

Upper Icknield Way

P

Hill Top Lane

Radnage

Bledlow Ridge

BOUNDARY
GRASSLAND
WOODLAND
PATH
PUBLIC BRIDLEWAY
SCRUB
GRASSLAND RESTORATION

400 yards

115

THE WARBURG RESERVE

BBONT - THE WILDLIFE TRUST
FOR BERKS, BUCKS & OXON

Nearest town: Henley on Thames
OS Map 175 SU 720879

270 acres (107 ha) of woodland and grassland. It is an SSSI. There is a visitor centre and a warden.

Location and Access: From Henley on Thames take the A4130 for Nettlebed and Wallingford. At the village of Bix, about 3 miles (5 km) from Henley, turn right into a marked access road.

This magnificent reserve extends across a winding chalk valley with a complex mosaic of woodland, scrub and grassland. Much of it is mixed woodland of oak, ash, beech, field maple, yew (and some conifers from previous plantings) with carpets of wood anemone and bluebell. The glades are good spots for sighting classic woodland

WILDLIFE FEATURES
🌼 **Wild flowers**   🦋 **Butterflies**
🐦 **Birdlife**

butterflies such as purple emperor, white admiral and silver-washed fritillary. There are also stands of shady beech woodland with violet and narrow-lipped helleborines, and remnant patches of conifer plantation which support goldcrest and crossbill in the winter months.

Classic chalk-loving flowers such as the Chiltern gentian grow in the older grassland areas, while the reserve's flock of sheep keeps scrub and coarser grasses under control by grazing, allowing a whole suite of chalk grassland plants to flourish, including pyramidal orchid and wild marjoram.

Two artificial ponds attract amphibians and reptiles such as grass snakes, while adders, slow worms and common lizards are all found here. In winter you can watch marsh tit and redpoll from the pond hide, while nesting birds include sparrowhawk and woodpeckers, and in spring the rides are the place to try and spot woodcock. Rabbits are common, but look out too for hares on open ground near woodland. Fallow, muntjac and roe deer also forage through the woodlands, and there are dormice too, in areas of hazel coppice.

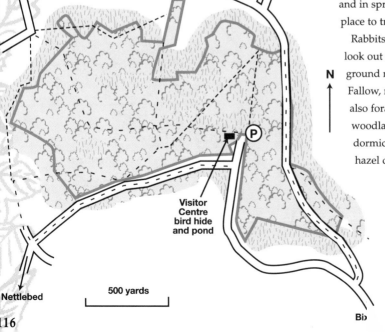

Maidensgrove

N

Visitor Centre bird hide and pond

Nettlebed

500 yards

Bix

— **BOUNDARY**

▦ **GRASSLAND**

🌳 **WOODLAND**

--- **PATH**

- - **PUBLIC BRIDLEWAY**

116

RUSHBEDS WOOD & LAPLAND FARM

**BBONT - THE WILDLIFE TRUST
FOR BERKS, BUCKS & OXON**

Nearest towns: Aylesbury and Bicester
OS Maps 164 & 165 SP 672154

111 acres (45 ha) of woodland and 6 acres (2.5 ha) of meadow and the 27 acre (11 ha) Lapland Farm. The reserve is an SSSI.

Location and access: From Aylesbury, take the A41 north (towards Bicester) for about 9 miles, to Kingswood. At Kingswood turn left onto the unclassified road south-westwards and continue for about 2 miles to a T-junction. For Rushbeds Wood turn left and drive for about a quarter of a mile, turning right into a track just before the next T-junction. Continue through the gateway and over the railway bridge; cars can be parked on the left. Please close the gate.

For Lapland Farm drive straight over the first T-junction, and ahead up the track, cross the railway bridge, and park on the hard standing.

The public has access to the wood along the rides. There is a public footpath across the farm; please keep to it in the growing season and keep dogs under strict control.

Rushbeds Wood is an ancient woodland which appears on a map of 1590 as part of the Forest of Bernwood. Most of the trees were felled in the 1940s and part is being coppiced again, the rest being left to develop into wildwood. There is continuity - more than 200 species of flowering plants have

WILDLIFE FEATURES

🌼 **Woodland and meadow flowers**

🦋 **Butterflies**

been recorded, and the woodland butterflies seen include white admiral, purple emperor and a colony of the rare black hairstreak. The large amount of dead wood attracts numerous beetles and other insects which in turn attract woodpeckers.

The two meadows of Lapland Farm have 'indicator' flowers of ancient grassland such as greater burnet with reddish 'bottle brush' flowers. Have a look at the two narrow meadows south of the wood - they provide sheltered feeding sites for summer butterflies - you should see abundant marbled white, meadow brown and common blue butterflies.

🔲 POND	──	MAIN TRAILS
--- PATHS	▬	BOUNDARY
- - PUBLIC BRIDLEWAY	▨	GRASSLAND
▨ SCRUB	▨	WOODLAND

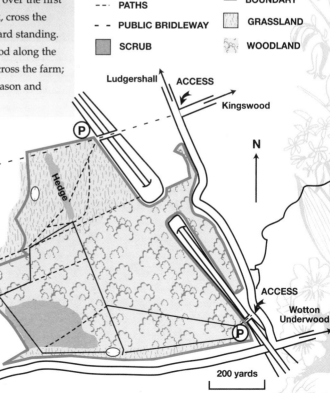

FINEMERE WOOD

BBONT - THE WILDLIFE TRUST FOR BERKS, BUCKS & OXON

Nearest town: Aylesbury

OS Map 165 SP 721215

An ancient woodland of 109 acres (40.3 ha) with some adjoining grassland and scrub. It is SSSI status. There are interpretative boards and a circular wildlife walk.

Location and access: From Aylesbury take the A41 north-westerly (towards Bicester) for about 5 miles (8 km) to Waddesdon, then turn right onto the unclassified road, signposted for Quainton. At the crossroads (about 1 mile) continue straight ahead for a further mile and turn left onto the Quainton-Edgcott road and at a T-junction signposted to Edgcott turn left again. After about three quarters of a mile, there is a graded track to the right; cars can be parked on the verge nearby. The wood is a further 5 minute walk.

WILDLIFE FEATURES
Butterflies
Birdlife

This wood was part of the Great Forest of Bernwood, but felled and replanted in the 1950s and 60s.

There is a mosaic of habitats. A central area has now been cleared where there was an old meadow - many meadow plants remain here. Two streams run through the wood. There are planted Scots pine and Norway spruce (our Christmas tree) and where planting failed the habitat varies from dwarf conifers to scrub. There are fragments of the original woodland which, because unmanaged for decades, have developed a into a high forest of oak over hazel coppice, with blackthorn brakes and aspen groves marking damp ground. Giant ash and maple coppice stools survive in the drier north-western reaches of the wood.

Some 200 species of flowering plants have been found growing here, but the wood is really exceptional for butterflies with the white admiral (a truly woodland species) and the black hairstreak (linked with the blackthorn) among the 20 species recorded. Woodcock and all three British woodpeckers are seen (or heard) - and there are lizard and grass snake.

Finemerehill House

N

River Ray

Woodland Farm

To Edgcott

— NEW PATHS
▬ BOUNDARY
▨ MEADOW
▨ WOODLAND
- - - PATH
╫╫╫ RAILWAY
▨ RIVER

500 yards

Ⓟ

118

STONY STRATFORD

**BBONT - THE WILDLIFE TRUST
FOR BERKS, BUCKS & OXON**

Nearest town: Milton Keynes
OS Map 152 SP 785412

57 acres (23 ha) of reinstated gravel workings.
There are bird hides.

Location and access: From central Milton
Keynes take the new A5 north to the roundabout and turn south towards Stony Stratford,
but then left along the bypass loop road and
take first left before you reach the first roundabout. The public have access to the northern
part of the reserve and the path to the public
bird hide. The reserve is a sanctuary for wildfowl and access to the fenced area is restricted.

Looking in parts like an ancient mere, with a
rich population of geese, ducks and waders, it is
the kind of place where Sir Peter Scott might
have propped his easel. Yet a photo taken a few
years ago shows an open meadow where
redshank nested. The gravel under the grass
was dug, ideal for the new bypass, but the
planners made the leap of imagination
necessary to envisage a prize nature reserve
within the boundaries of Milton Keynes.
So the gravel was dug to a sculpted design
which, when flooded, would produce a
purpose-built wetland with lagoons of
varying depth and nesting islands.

Even before the last of the machinery
left the site, waders, duck, geese, swans
and grebes had moved in. And now an
artificial bank even houses a thriving
colony of sand martin.

At the start, diaries show that on one
single day 1,000 flowering rushes, 25
bulrushes and 100 yellow iris were
planted by volunteers. The instant
maturity not only satisfied the birdlife

WILDLIFE FEATURES
🦅 **Wildfowl and waders**

but also local residents, who were then willing
to give their support.

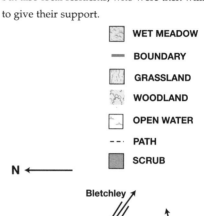

▨	WET MEADOW
▬	BOUNDARY
▨	GRASSLAND
▨	WOODLAND
▢	OPEN WATER
---	PATH
▉	SCRUB

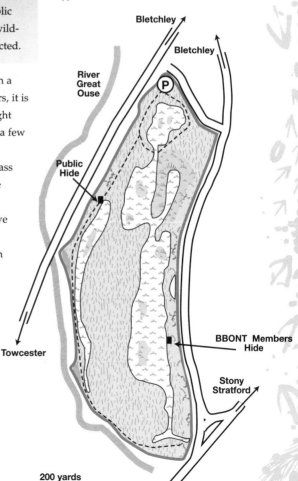

200 yards

119

COLLEGE LAKE WILDLIFE CENTRE

**BBONT - THE WILDLIFE TRUST
FOR BERKS, BUCKS & OXON**

WILDLIFE FEATURES
🐦 **Wildfowl and other birds**

Nearest town: Tring
OS Map 165 SP 933139

A worked out chalk quarry restored for wildlife, with a visitor centre and bird hides (most are accessible in wheelchairs). It extends over 100 acres (40 ha), with some grassland, woodland and a 25 acre lake. Part of the quarry is a geological SSSI.

Location and access: From the roundabout on the A41 just to the west of Tring, take the B488 north and carry on to Bulborne (about 2.5 miles). Cross the canal bridge and carry on for a further 275 yards to the reserve entrance on the left hand side. The car park and warden's office are by the entrance.

The site is open daily from 1000 to 1700. Visitors must have a permit, obtainable from the warden's office.

This worked-out chalk quarry restored as a wildlife centre is a super example of creative conservation. The project (which began in 1985) now has a lake, several large islands, shingle beaches and floating nest rafts.

Having been shaped out while the quarry was still being worked, the lake filled up naturally and the islands were created using hundreds of tons of shingle. Thousands of native trees and shrubs have also been planted.

The reserve is particularly interesting for its birdlife, and is an addition to the famous bird-watching Tring reservoirs. Here at College Lake a variety of waders, terns and other species are regularly seen on passage, while breeding birds include lapwing, redshank and little ringed plover.

Warden's Bank near the entrance has an unusual history - the ancient flowery turf was at Pitstone Hill and threatened by quarrying: it was cut into blocks and brought here. It is thriving, with cowslip and other flowers, and even the anthills are still in business!

Railway Cutting

N

Visitors Centre

Warden's Bank

Warden's Office

Ivinghoe

ACCESS

Grand Union Canal

Bulbourne

300 yards

Tring B488

MARSH
GRASSLAND
WOODLAND
OPEN WATER
PATH
HIDE

DANCERSEND & THE CRONG MEADOW

**BBONT - THE WILDLIFE TRUST
FOR BERKS, BUCKS & OXON**

Nearest towns: Wendover and Tring

OS Map 165 SP 900095 (Dancersend)

SP 904088 (The Crong Meadow)

82 acres (33 ha) of woodland, grassland and scrub with the additional 2.6 acres (1 ha) of Crong Meadow. The whole reserve is part of a larger SSSI.

Location and access: From Wendover take the A4011 northwards towards Tring for 3 miles. Just before this road meets the A41, turn sharp right onto the unclassified road for St Leonards and continue for 1.5 miles. At the sharp left-hand bend, by the pond, park on the right-hand verge opposite the pond or in the pull-in on the left. Walk up the track opposite the bend to reach the reserve.

The Crong Meadow is 1 mile further along the road, on the right. Cars can be parked in the yard behind the Waterworks building on the left.

Dogs are not allowed into the meadow when livestock are grazing.

Dancersend has a range of Chiltern habitats on the slopes of two dry valleys, and soil and management differences have created a rich variety, with a tally of more than 290 different plants.

Most of the woodlands used to be beech with oak, but these were felled in the Second World War and scrub then colonised. In the 1950s most of the area was replanted with beech with larch and spruce as nurse trees - the conifers are now gradually being removed to reveal a remarkable number of plants

WILDLIFE FEATURES

🦋 **Butterflies** 🌼 **Wild flowers**

surviving from the original woodland, such as stinking hellebore and Solomon's seal.

The woodlands are home to a variety of birds, including nuthatch and green and great spotted woodpecker.

The jewel of Dancersend is the small area of 'meadow plots' - chalk grassland saved from scrub. This grassland area is now alight with orchids and other wild flowers and butterflies such as the Duke of Burgundy fritillary. The Crong meadow also carries a large variety of grassland wild flowers - more than 130 have been recorded.

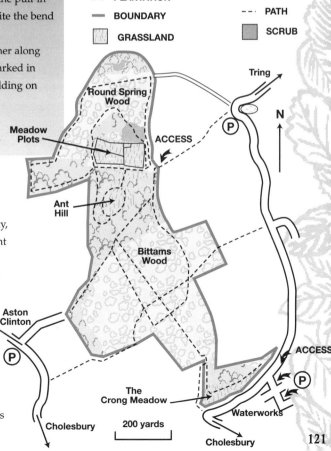

FORESTRY COMMISSION PLANTATION

WOODLAND

— BOUNDARY

- - - PATH

GRASSLAND

SCRUB

Round Spring Wood

Tring

N

ACCESS

Meadow Plots

Ant Hill

Bittams Wood

Aston Clinton

ACCESS

The Crong Meadow

Waterworks

Cholesbury

200 yards

Cholesbury

PITSFORD NATURE RESERVE

THE WILDLIFE TRUST FOR BEDS, CAMBS, NORTHANTS AND PETERBOROUGH

Nearest town: Northampton
OS Map 141 SP 780708

480 acres (194 ha) of wetland, woodland and grassland surrounding part of a reservoir. There are bird hides and there is a warden. Because of the large numbers of wintering wildfowl, the whole reservoir has SSSI status.

Location and access: From Northampton, take the A43 north (towards Kettering). After about 6 miles (10 km), turn left onto an unclassified road for Holcot. Continue on this road through the village. The reserve is about half a mile further on; the road gives access to the parking area at the western end of the causeway and continues on to Brixworth. Brixworth is reached from Northampton by the A508.

Permits are needed for visits (from the Fishing Lodge at the Holcot end of the causeway) and dogs are not allowed in. Otherwise, good views of the birds can be had from the causeway.

WILDLIFE FEATURES

🦅 **Breeding and migrant wildfowl and waders**

Pitsford Reservoir supplies household water and because of the pattern of demand, water levels are relatively higher in winter, lower in summer, creating ideal conditions for the many water and water-associated birds. As well as the open water and its mud margin, there is willow and other scrub, young oak woodland and conifer plantation, while grassland is maintained by sheep grazing and haycutting on the western side of the reserve to produce suitable feeding conditions for wigeon and geese.

Pitsford provides a safe winter haven for up to 10,000 ducks - wigeon, gadwall, teal, mallard, pintail, shoveler, pochard, tufted duck, goldeneye, goosander and ruddy duck form the regulars and they may be joined by others - as well as three species of divers and five of grebes. Swans are also seen.

In winter, flocks of fieldfare, redwing and blackbird feed on the berried shrubs and groups of goldcrest and tits forage in the plantation trees.

Birds apart, the great range of habitats allows a tremendous variety of wildlife, including a number of mammals, amphibians, reptiles, butterflies and dragonflies and 97 species (so far counted) of spiders.

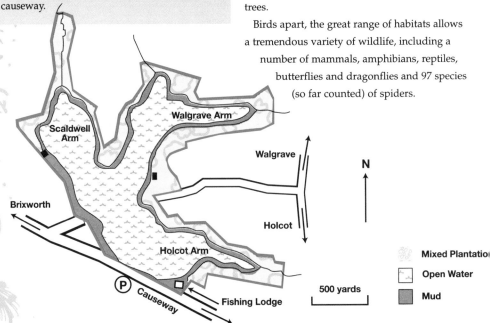

Walgrave Arm

Scaldwell Arm

Walgrave

Brixworth

Holcot

N

Holcot Arm

P Causeway

Fishing Lodge

500 yards

Holcot

Mixed Plantation

Open Water

Mud

Eastern England

Many of the vast, sweeping counties of eastern England are characterised by dunes, saltmarsh, broads, estuaries, marshes and mudflats, while further inland, Hertfordshire supports deciduous woodlands and chalk streams flanked by ancient meadows. The sweeping east coast takes in reserves stretching from Far Ings, flooded clay pits and reedbeds on the bank of the Humber, to Fingringhoe Wick, a magnificent Essex Wildlife Trust reserve on the River Colne estuary. On Norfolk's coast is Cley Marshes, Britain's first nature reserve, and one of the best for bird-watching. One of Britain's rarest birds, the bittern, breeds there, as well as avocet, and many other species including spotted redshank, sedge, reed and grasshopper warblers. On the border of Norfolk and Suffolk, Redgrave and Lopham Fen is a restored tract of peat fen, home to the fen raft spider, Britain's largest and rarest spider. Also in Suffolk is Bradfield Woods, ancient woodland still managed as coppice today. More than 350 plant species have been recorded there including bluebell, herb Paris and early purple orchid, attracting no less than 15 butterfly species.

EASTERN ENGLAND

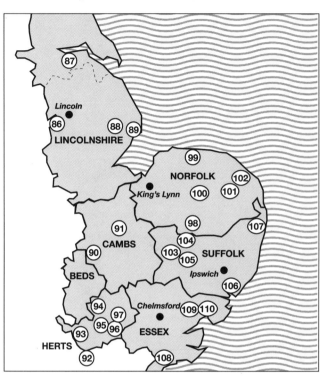

WHISBY NATURE PARK

LINCOLNSHIRE TRUST FOR NATURE CONSERVATION

Nearest town: Lincoln

OS Map 121 SK 914661

205 acres (83 ha) of flooded gravel pits and their surroundings which have become a public wildlife amenity. The nature park has a visitor centre, wardens, waymarked walks and trail guides and birdwatching hides.

Location and access: The nature park lies to the west of the Lincoln relief road. From the round-about on the A46 at the southern end of the relief road take the first turning to the left (or if travelling south turn right after passing over the railway) into Moor Lane. The main entrance to the car park and visitor centre is on the right after a quarter of a mile. There are toilets here.

WILDLIFE FEATURES

- ▼ **Winter wildfowl and other birdlife**
- ❀ **Wild flowers**
- ✳ **Insects/invertebrates**

and in winter also teal, pochard and goldeneye while other birds seen in summer around the lakes include common tern, reed warbler and sand martin. The kingfisher is frequently seen and nightingale and other songsters sing from the scrub.

It is full of delightful corners, however. Apart from the bird life, there is the orchid glade to visit - the southern marsh orchid and the common spotted orchid often flower in large numbers. There is also 'Little Heath', a patch of heathland, once part of the large Whisby Moor. Heathland flowers include sky blue harebell and yellow tormentil. In all around 300 different species of flowering plants are to be found in this wonderful refuge.

Because so many ponds, marshes and other wetland habitats in the wider countryside have been drained or simply dried up, wildlife areas such as this nature park are becoming increasingly important to wildlife, even if artificial. The wildfowl, best seen from the hides, include great crested grebe and tufted duck,

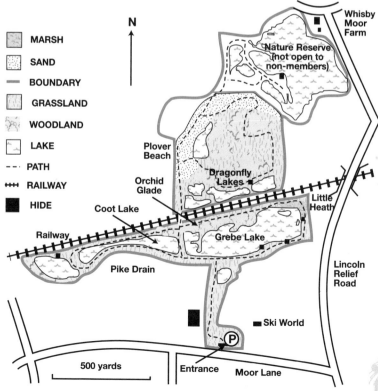

MARSH

SAND

BOUNDARY

GRASSLAND

WOODLAND

LAKE

PATH

RAILWAY

HIDE

N

Whisby Moor Farm

Nature Reserve (not open to non-members)

Plover Beach

Orchid Glade

Dragonfly Lakes

Coot Lake

Little Heath

Railway

Grebe Lake

Pike Drain

Lincoln Relief Road

Ski World

500 yards

Entrance   Moor Lane

FAR INGS

LINCOLNSHIRE TRUST FOR
NATURE CONSERVATION

Nearest towns: Scunthorpe and Hull

OS Map 112 TA 011229

A 135 acre (55 ha) area of flooded clay pits and reedbeds along the bank of the Humber. It is an SSSI. A visitor centre is at the entrance and there are birdwatching hides.

Location and access: The reserve is a short distance west of the Humber Bridge. Starting at the A15 bridge junction on the south bank of the Humber (just west of Barton on Humber), take the A1077 Ferriby road westwards, and then the first turning right (north). Continue to the T-junction and turn left. The reserve and visitor centre with parking and toilets (some disabled facilities) are a short distance to the right. (The adjoining Barton Reedbeds nature reserve is to the right at the T-junction, but can be reached on a path along the river bank from the reserve.)

The visitor centre is staffed Saturday and Sunday in summer and Sunday afternoons in winter, and on bank holidays.

No dogs please.

WILDLIFE FEATURES
✖ Birdlife

The flooded clay pits along the Humber are the result of an old brick and tile industry. To the legacy of open water, reedbed, grassland (dotted with the yellow, blue and white of a variety of wild flowers in May), hedgerow and scrub have recently been added the 'scrapes' where the topsoil has been removed to leave shallow water and islands which attract greenshank, green sandpiper and other waders on migration. Redshank and lapwing also nest here.

Birds are in fact the outstanding attraction of the reserve: heron, grebes and kingfisher are seen and many duck nest on the water margins. There are also abundant scrub and reedbed birds - a survey of a few years back found no fewer than 46 pairs of reed and 32 pairs of sedge warblers nesting, with a lesser number of blackcap and whitethroat. It is hoped that the bittern will return to breed.

There are also a good many sheltered corners for butterflies.

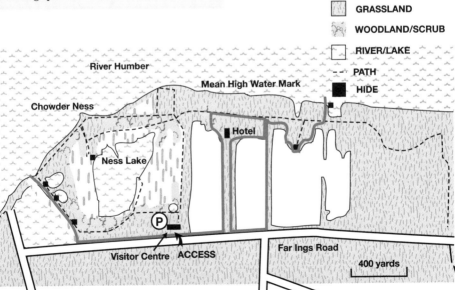

REEDBEDS
— BOUNDARY
GRASSLAND
WOODLAND/SCRUB
RIVER/LAKE
PATH
HIDE

River Humber
Mean High Water Mark
Chowder Ness
Hotel
Ness Lake
P
Visitor Centre   ACCESS
Far Ings Road
400 yards

SNIPE DALES

LINCOLNSHIRE TRUST FOR
NATURE CONSERVATION

Nearest town: Horncastle, south of Louth

OS Map 122 TF 319683 (nature reserve);
TF 330682 (country park)

A 121 acre (48 ha) nature reserve and 90 acre (36 ha) country park. The nature reserve consists of two stream-fretted valleys mainly open but with some woodland; the country park is mainly conifer woodland. There are interpretation boards and waymarked trails.

Location and access: The nature reserve and country park have separate car parks a mile (1.6 km) apart, but both off the B1195 Horncastle-Spilsby road. The nature reserve is about 5 miles east of Horncastle on the B1195, close to the hamlet of Winceby. The country park is also well signposted from the A158 Skegness-Lincoln road. There are picnic tables and toilets (including disabled) at the country park.

The country park offers attractive walks through mainly Corsican pine, but there is some

WILDLIFE FEATURES
✗ Birdlife ❀ Plant interest

beech along the southern edge and the wide ride which runs to the north-east corner has some magnificent mature ash trees. As areas of pines are thinned, native trees are replacing them, while nine new ponds already attract toads and dragonflies and passing waders and wildfowl. Chaffinch, redpoll, willow warbler and tits are characteristic birds of the pines, and siskin are often common here in winter.

In the nature reserve, the drier higher slopes are largely grassland, but below the spring line and along the stream can be dense with tall meadowsweet and great willowherb in summer, together with great horsetail. On the higher slopes, oak and ash are being planted to restore former woodland - bluebell and primrose signal these areas. Much of the open area is rough grassland which is managed by cattle grazing.

There is an interesting birdlife. On the slopes near the viewpoint for example whitethroat, willow warbler and linnet sing, while the yellowhammer and the grasshopper warbler can both be heard.

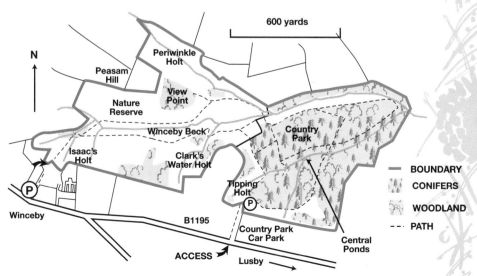

127

GIBRALTAR POINT

LINCOLNSHIRE TRUST FOR NATURE CONSERVATION

Nearest town: Skegness
OS Map 122 TF 556581

Extensive sand dunes, saltmarsh, and fresh-water marsh, a magnificent example of natural habitat development. It is a National Nature Reserve of 1,080 acres (437 ha), an SSSI of course. The reserve is equipped with a visitor centre, hides, interpretation boards, etc.

Location and access: The reserve lies 3 miles (5 km) south of Skegness. The access points are at Seacroft Esplanade at the southern end of Skegness and from the two car parks on Gibraltar Road, for which there is a small charge.

The visitor centre is normally open daily May-October and at weekends otherwise. The Trust maintains the field station nearby. Certain areas are no-go designated sanctuaries.

Gibraltar Point, situated at the western edge of the Wash, is a wonderfully breezy place with a rich variety of coastal habitats including dune, scrub and grassland, saltmarsh, freshwater marsh, meres and foreshore. The West Dunes are the oldest of the dunes (being shown on maps of 1825) and carry well-estab-lished colourful grassland and also sea buck-thorn scrub in places (popular with whitethroat and other songbirds). A second ridge 500 yards seawards began fixing 100 years ago, while past it a third is now building up. Look here for the early colonisers - such as the pink-flowered sea rocket, somewhat succulent as a defence against the salt, and the beautiful sea holly.

The sand and mudflats south of the dunes are some of the most extensive in Britain and therefore attract huge numbers of wintering wildfowl of international importance. At migration time, large numbers of birds are

WILDLIFE FEATURES
🦋 **Birdlife**   ❀ **Wild flowers**
✳ **Insect/invertebrates**

present and can include extreme rarities. The saltmarsh which eventually develops on the sheltered mud can be quite attactive with flowers such as sea-lavender, and busy with many insects.

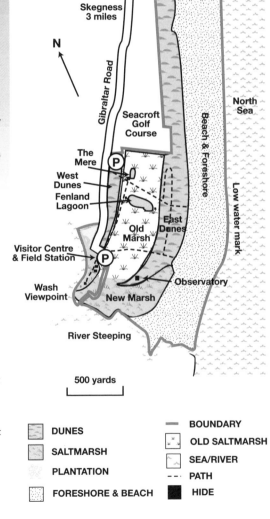

Skegness 3 miles

N

North Sea

Gibraltar Road

Seacroft Golf Course

Beach & Foreshore

Low water mark

The Mere P

West Dunes

Fenland Lagoon

East Dunes

Old Marsh

Visitor Centre & Field Station P

Observatory

Wash Viewpoint

New Marsh

River Steeping

500 yards

DUNES — BOUNDARY

SALTMARSH — OLD SALTMARSH

PLANTATION — SEA/RIVER

FORESHORE & BEACH — PATH

HIDE

GRAFHAM WATER

WILDLIFE TRUST FOR BEDS, CAMBS, NORTHANTS AND PETERBOROUGH

Nearest town: Huntingdon
OS Map 153 TL 143671

370 acres (149 ha) of grassland, scrub and woodland and open water. There is an information centre and warden, and there are bird-watching hides and nature trails.

Location and access: Grafham Water is between Huntingdon and St Neots. Leave the A1 for the B661 at Buckden or the A14 (old A604) at Ellington, and follow the signs for Grafham Water. There are three car parks round the reservoir (Anglian Water charge for their use). Mander car park near West Perry is the closest to the reserve, information centre and hides. Nature trails start at this car park. A 10 mile surfaced track circles the reservoir and runs through the reserve which is suitable for cycles and, in part, wheelchairs.

WILDLIFE FEATURES
✸ Birdlife including wildfowl

The reservoir is huge (1,550 acres) so binoculars are useful! This large reservoir had creeks (which would offer seclusion from boats and fishermen) and other wildlife habitats planned in when it was opened in the 1960s and they now see a variety of wildlife. Blackcap, garden warbler and nightingale sing in the spring woods, while in winter the reservoir itself becomes the focus of attention. It usually remains ice-free, attracting gadwall, wigeon, shoveler, goldeneye and goosander as well as nationally important numbers of great crested grebe - and many more arrive when local gravel pits freeze up. There are often several thousand lapwing on the ploughed fields alongside. Passage waders also drop in during the spring and autumn and include common sandpiper and greenshank.

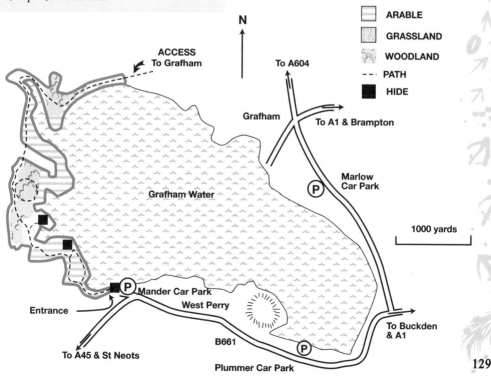

	BOUNDARY
	ARABLE
	GRASSLAND
	WOODLAND
---	PATH
■	HIDE

129

THE OUSE WASHES

WILDLIFE TRUST FOR BEDS, CAMBS, NORTHANTS AND PETERBOROUGH

Nearest towns: March, Chatteris or Ely

OS Map 143 TL 470860

The Ouse Washes are a 20 mile (32 km) strip of wet grassland, half a mile broad, which become flooded in winter. It is one of the most important places for wildfowl in Britain, managed jointly with the RSPB and the Wildfowl and Wetlands Trust. The 455 acre (182 ha) Wildlife Trust reserve covers the central stretch and is an SSSI and Ramsar site.

Location and access: From March take the A141 towards Chatteris, and at Wimblington take the B1093 to Manea. From the village follow the signs to the RSPB reserve at Welches Dam, and park in the RSPB car park. A footpath runs along the base of the bank to the hides. Please stay on the lower path to avoid disturbing the birds (and dogs are not welcome for the same reason). The visitor centre is open 0900-1700 daily. Between September 1st and January 31st, there may be shooting on private washes nearby which may cause disturbance.

WILDLIFE FEATURES
🦆 **Wildfowl**　❀ **Wild flowers**

At times of high water the banked rivers are allowed to flood the Washes rather than the surrounding farmland (and villages), and they are transformed in winter not least by the sheer number of birds. The vast variable-depth lake attracts a host of wildfowl. In summer too the wet conditions attract many birds to nest. The winter tally, of international importance, includes large numbers of teal, pintail, wigeon, shoveler, pochard and Bewick's swan.

In summer ruff, black-tailed godwit, lapwing, redshank and snipe may nest in the rough grassland and nine species of duck nest in the dykes between the fields. The meadows are rich in plants; yellow fringed water lily and other fenland relic water plants can be seen in the rivers and dykes (and these are also good for dragonflies).

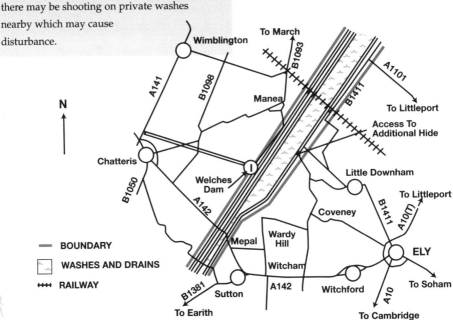

- **—** BOUNDARY
- **▨** WASHES AND DRAINS
- **+++** RAILWAY

OLD PARK WOOD

HERTS & MIDDLESEX WILDLIFE TRUST

Nearest town: Harefield
OS Map 176 TQ 049913

19 acres (7.7 ha) of possibly the most varied piece of woodland in Middlesex, teeming with wildlife; an SSSI.

Location and access: The wood is behind Harefield Hospital. From Harefield Village (which lies between the A412 and the A404/4180 south of Rickmansworth) take the Rickmansworth road, turning left into Hill End Road and left again through the hospital gates. Keep to the right around the hospital road until arriving at a fence where there is a small parking area. Follow the waymark down the slope, go through the gate and follow the field edge into the wood.

The changes in character of this wood as you walk through it, reflect changes in the soil.

WILDLIFE FEATURES
❀ **Spring flowers**   ✖ **Woodland birds**

Birch and oak at the top, for example, give way to oak and hornbeam, with oak and ash at the bottom of the hill.

The highlight here is the abundant show of wild flowers in spring. Glossy yellow lesser celandine usually leads the way, and wood anemone follows while somewhat later the bluebell forms a stunning carpet. When these last two are together in the same wood it is a clue that it is an old wood. You can also see yellow archangel and the uncommon coralroot bittercress, with its wonderful display of brief pink flowers in April.

Golden saxifrage and handsome glossy marsh marigold flower on the stream banks and around the pond. This pond is also important for dragonflies, frogs and newts.

As for the rest of the wildlife, the wood often rings with birdsong, while all three British species of woodpeckers are here.

Most of the wood is being left to develop naturally but some open areas are being created and managed as paths and glades.

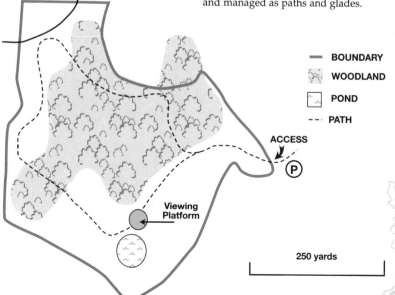

BOUNDARY
WOODLAND
POND
PATH

ACCESS

Viewing Platform

250 yards

FROGMORE MEADOW

HERTS & MIDDLESEX WILDLIFE TRUST

Nearest town: Chorleywood
OS Map 176 TQ 022988

7.5 acres (3 ha) of old marshy flower-rich meadow in a tranquil river valley.
  The reserve is an SSSI.

Location and access: From Chorleywood use or cross the A404 towards Chesham, going north on a side road. Pass through Chenies, a village about 2 miles north-west of the centre of Chorleywood, and take the immediate right into Doddsmill Lane towards Flaunden. Park on the roadside near Mill Farm and walk along the road for about 15 yards. On the right is a footpath across fields. Follow this until you reach Limeshill Wood, where you bear right through a gate into the reserve.

WILDLIFE FEATURES
✿ Meadow flowers

This meadow lies beside the River Chess; with a mosaic of damp and dry areas, signposted by the flowers. In the wetter parts you can see the glorious marsh marigold in early spring, greater birds-foot-trefoil with yellow pea flowers, rose-red ragged robin and also the rare marsh valerian. This last is a white relation of the more familiar red valerian seen growing on old walls and such places. There are many sedges here (triangular stems!)

Drier, more acid soil away from the river is marked by such flowers as purple betony, yellow tormentil and heath bedstraw. Along by the river, however, there are tall fen plants, such as the great willowherb with purple-pink flowers, a close relative of the familiar rosebay willowherb, often seen on derelict town sites.

There are old hedgerows around the meadow, with plenty of nesting birds.

Cattle are grazed, but not intensively, to keep down the space-greedy coarse grasses and prevent scrub encroaching.

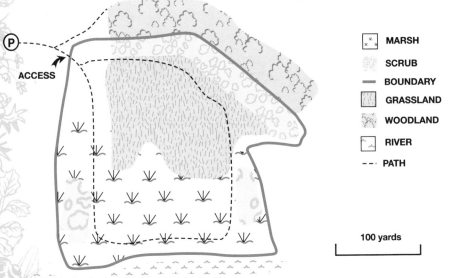

ACCESS

MARSH
SCRUB
BOUNDARY
GRASSLAND
WOODLAND
RIVER
PATH

100 yards

River Chess

TELEGRAPH HILL

HERTS & MIDDLESEX WILDLIFE TRUST

Nearest town: Hitchin
OS Map 166 TL 117288

7.5 acres (3 ha) of chalk grassland and scrub fringed by old beech trees. There are two dewponds. The ancient Icknield Way trackway passes through the reserve.

Location and access: The reserve is located via the village of Lilley, about 4 miles north-east of Luton centre, just to the west of the A505 between Luton and Hitchin. Pass through Lilley westwards on the road for Hexton, and about halfway there (about 1.5 miles, 2.5 km) turn right into Tresure's Grove car park, where the road is crossed by the Icknield Way. The reserve lies about half a mile along the track.

This is a magic place, steeped in history. The woodland on the north side of the reserve contains some fine old beech trees, underneath which the elegant white helleborine orchid flowers in summer. Further up on the hill itself the steep rutted banks caused by centuries of

WILDLIFE FEATURES
❀ **Downland flowers** ✖ **Birdlife**

cattle and cart traffic carry a rich array of chalk grassland flowers, among them being horseshoe vetch, rockrose, milkwort (all yellow), sky blue harebell and the handsome mauve devil's-bit scabious. These plants are host to the chalkhill blue, green hairstreak and small heath butterflies.

On this hill you can see what happens if grazing stops. First of all scrub invades, and then trees seed in - it can take about 50 years to go from open grassland to young woodland which is recognisably woodland. To preserve the grassland flowers, the grassland here is mown and the scrub cleared.

The changes attract birds, which respond to the structure of the place - the scrub (and the small area of hazel coppice) attracts white-throats and many other birds.

At the far end of the reserve, within the mature scrub, are two dew ponds - their aquatic life is certainly surprising to find at the top of a chalk hill!

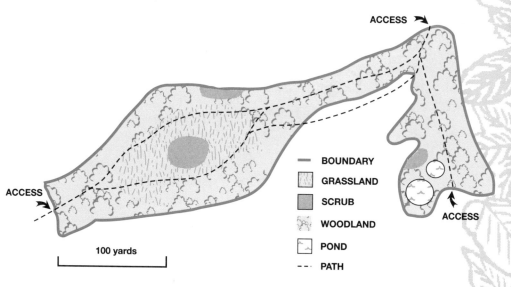

ACCESS

ACCESS

ACCESS

— BOUNDARY
▨ GRASSLAND
▪ SCRUB
▨ WOODLAND
▱ POND
--- PATH

100 yards

133

BROAD COLNEY LAKES

HERTS & MIDDLESEX
WILDLIFE TRUST

Nearest town: St Albans
OS Map 166 TL 177034

A 27 acre (10.9 ha) reserve comprising three lakes, the result of gravel diggings in the 1920s. They each have a different character and the range of habitats runs from open water, through wet woodland to dry pasture. There are paths suitable for the disabled and waterbird viewing areas.

Location and access: This reserve lies south of London Colney, which is about 3 miles (5 km) south-east of the centre of St Albans. On the B5378 (Shenley Lane) running south from London Colney to Shenley, turn left into the car park just before the British Legion huts.

These three lakes each have their own character: one is fed by the River Colne, one is relatively still and deep and the smallest has partly developed into marshy woodland with alder and willow.

WILDLIFE FEATURES
⟁ Wildfowl

It is a marvellous place for birds: great crested grebe can be seen on the open water (they nest in the 'bulrush' reedswamp), along with tufted duck, moorhen, coot and mallard.

In the winter months, in the alder trees, flocks of siskin can be seen feeding with willow tit and long-tailed tit.

The small lake is changing into a reedmace and reed sweet-grass marsh, with brooklime and celery-leaved buttercup along its edges. Flowering rush, purple loosestrife and some less common sedges grow on the western edge of the long lake. On its open water grow fringed water lily and other aquatics.

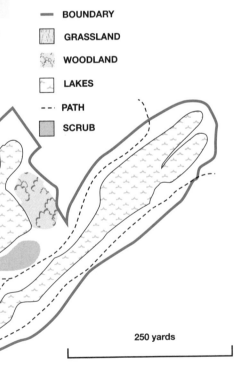

— BOUNDARY

▨ GRASSLAND

▧ WOODLAND

▢ LAKES

--- PATH

▨ SCRUB

ACCESS

250 yards

FIR & POND WOODS

HERTS & MIDDLESEX WILDLIFE TRUST

Nearest town: Potters Bar
OS Map 166 TL 276011

68 acres (28 ha) of varied woodland, meadow and wetland, a relic of the ancient Enfield Chase.

Location and access: Go north along Potters Bar High Street (the A1000) and after about half a mile (1 km) fork right on the B156 towards Northaw and Cuffley. After about another half mile turn right into Coopers Lane Road and the reserve is about half a mile (1 km) on the right. There is a lay-by opposite the entrance to the Oshwal Centre; enter the reserve here.

This is the best remaining part of the ancient Enfield Chase; a chase was a lesser hunting preserve, held by a magnate, unlike the royal 'forest'. Like a forest, a chase could include open land.

Here there are two main areas of woodland, primarily oak and hornbeam with some beech, rowan and silver birch.

This woodland is rich in birdlife, with warblers and woodpeckers. February and March are the best months to hear the drumming of the woodpeckers - this, like birdsong in fact, is a territorial signal. You might also see a sparrowhawk coursing the woodland margins.

At the southern end of Pond Wood is an ancient meadow with woodland on three sides and Turkey Brook on the fourth. It is studded with old anthills, a sign that it has never been ploughed, but embraced by woodland as it is, it is threatened by invading scrub and trees and so badger-faced Welsh mountain sheep (which can happily munch scrub) are being grazed

WILDLIFE FEATURES
- **ᕽ Woodland birds**
- **ᙡ Butterflies & other meadow invertebrates**

here. This meadow is a lovely butterfly and grasshopper haven, best in late summer.

The lake at the southern end of the reserve is gradually being colonised by reedmace ('bulrush') and gipsywort (rather nettle-like but with whorls of smallish white-purple flowers). There are numerous dragonflies here - bird-watchers' insects!

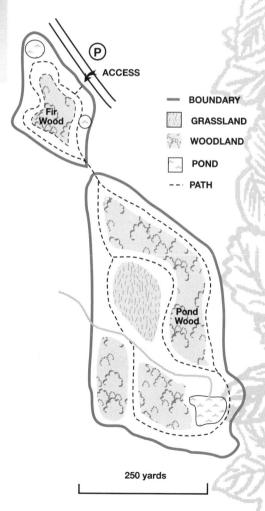

━━	BOUNDARY
	GRASSLAND
	WOODLAND
	POND
- - -	PATH

250 yards

HERTFORD HEATH

HERTS & MIDDLESEX WILDLIFE TRUST

Nearest town: Hertford

OS Map TL 350106/354111

62 acres (25 ha) of open heathland with woodland, two large ponds and several smaller bog pools. It is an SSSI.

Location and access: The reserve is in two parts, on either side of the B1197 in Hertford Heath Village, south-east of Hertford. You leave Hertford eastwards on the A414, then turn south on the B1197 towards Hoddesdon to reach it. In the village, turn into Roundings Road adjacent to the East India College Arms pub. The entrance is a short way down on the right.

The other area of the reserve is at the end of Heath Lane which is opposite the pub, or it can be reached from Mount Pleasant in Hertford Heath Village.

The woodland holds mature hornbeam coppice, quite old, and secondary oak and birch woodland; there is also a scatter of hazel, holly, blackthorn and hawthorn. On the open heathland areas grow heather, heath bedstraw, tormentil and petty whin (the last three with

WILDLIFE FEATURES

❀ **Late summer heather**   ✕ **Woodland birds**
❀ **Wetland flowers**   ✺ **Dragonflies**

yellow flowers). They are spreading healthily since the Wildlife Trust took the invasive scrub and trees in hand. (Although seeming 'wild' and permanent, heathland quickly scrubs up and reverts to woodland if it is not grazed or otherwise managed.)

Being a damp heathland there are a number of pools with sphagnum mosses and rushes; these are the special habitat for dragonflies and damselflies. The large woodland pool provides a fine show of yellow flag (iris) and the delicately flowering water violet - nothing like a violet, but with narrow leaflets and a tall spike of pink flowers in midsummer.

Birds commonly seen here include little owl, long tailed tit, nuthatch, tree creeper and lesser spotted woodpecker

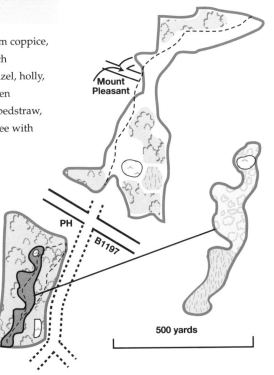

⸬	HEATHLAND
—	BOUNDARY
⸬	WOODLAND
▦	GRASSLAND
☐	POND
--	PATH

Mount Pleasant

PH

B1197

500 yards

EAST WRETHAM HEATH

NORFOLK WILDLIFE TRUST

Nearest town: Thetford
OS Map 144 TL 913887

An area of Breckland heath with an ancient Scots pine plantation as an additional habitat, as well as two remarkable meres.

Location and access: The reserve is 4 miles (7 km) north-east of Thetford on the A1075, before you reach East Wretham. The A1075 leaves the A11 Thetford to Norwich road 2 miles out of Thetford. There is a car park. The reserve is open daily 0800 to dusk.

This heath lies at the heart of Breckland, but despite its name it contains little heather. Instead much of it is fine grassland or turf speckled with flowers - forget-me-not, lady's bedstraw, viper's bugloss and the delicate sky blue harebell provide a colourful welcome in their season. Centuries of close grazing and a

WILDLIFE FEATURES
* Wild flowers ✿ Wildfowl
* Birdlife

rather extreme dry climate of hot summers and cold winters has also encouraged miniature plants together with insects rarely found elsewhere.

Also unusual are the crumbling remains of the Second World War runways from the time when this was part of a bomber base. Miniature gardens of lichens and mosses have developed, with carpets of biting stonecrop (yellow flowers, fleshy leaves) in places.

This reserve is also remarkable for the two meres, natural lakes. They are fed by ground water so that their levels change over the year, being highest in summer and lowest in winter after the summer drought (and sometimes they dry up altogether). They attract waders such as green sandpiper, ringed plover, curlew and snipe to feed on the mud, and wildfowl such as mallard, gadwall and teal.

The gnarled Scots pines were planted at the time of the Battle of Waterloo. The tawny owl nests here, along with redstart, crossbill and goldcrest, and the great spotted woodpecker.

East Wretham Village
Private House
ACCESS
Langmere
Drove Road
Public Footpath
Ringmere
A1075

BOUNDARY
CONIFERS
GRASSLAND
WOODLAND
MERE
PATH

N

500 yards

CLEY MARSHES

NORFOLK WILDLIFE TRUST

Nearest town: Sheringham
OS Map 133 TG 054451

A coastal reserve with foreshore, salt and freshwater marsh, pools and scrapes, large areas of reedbed and grazing marsh. There is a visitor centre and warden and bird hides with wheelchair access. There are toilets at the centre.

Location and access: The reserve is alongside the village of Cley-next-the-Sea, about 6 miles (9 km) west of Sheringham on the A149. There is a car park. The reserve is closed Mondays, except bank holidays; the visitor centre is open April-October 1000-1700.

There is an entry charge to assist with the upkeep that this special reserve needs.

Permits are available from visitor centre.
Norfolk Wildlife Trust members free.

This is a special reserve in more than one way. It was (in 1926) Britain's first county nature reserve, starting the movement which has today more than 2,300 nature reserves across Britain,

WILDLIFE FEATURES
🦅 Wildfowl, waders and other species

in the care of The Wildlife Trusts.

It is also one of Britain's leading nature reserves for bird watching. The many thatched hides give spectacular views over the specially made pools and scrapes which attract thousands of water birds. During the spring, the pools fill with waders such as spotted redshank on their way to their Arctic breeding grounds. Sedge, reed and grasshopper warblers can be seen and heard in the reedbeds. The summer brings a range of birds to breed, including the elegant avocet with its striking black and white plumage and long curved beak. Cley is also one of the handful of places in Britain where the bittern breeds - the males' foghorn-like 'boom' can be heard in the early morning or evening.

Throughout August and September, waders break their southward journey to feed around the pools. Throughout the autumn there is a good chance of seeing rarities which have strayed off course - Cley is one of the best places for seeing rare birds. Winter sees large numbers of wigeon, teal, shoveler and other wildfowl.

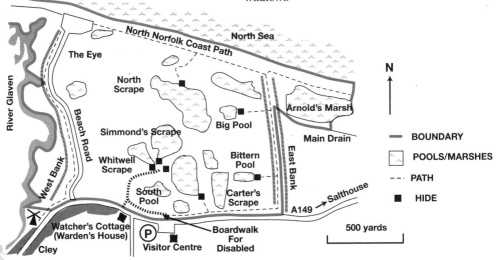

138

FOXLEY WOOD

NORFOLK WILDLIFE TRUST

Nearest town: Norwich
OS Map 133 TG 049229

300 acres (121 ha) of ancient woodland, the largest remaining block of ancient woodland in Norfolk, although earlier this century it became neglected and large areas were planted with conifers in the 1960s. There are waymarked trails.

Location and access: Foxley is a village about 12 miles (19 km) north-west of Norwich on the A1067 to Fakenham. The entrance and car park are off the side road from Foxley to Themelthorpe. The reserve is open daily (except Thursdays) 1000-1700. No dogs please.

WILDLIFE FEATURES
✤ Woodland flowers ✕ Woodland birds

In spring, the wood is speckled with colour - yellow primrose lines the rides, violets flower in the newly coppiced areas, there's a scatter of the drooping orange-pink flowers of water avens and sheets of bluebell carpet the ground in places. Herb Paris can also be seen (often hidden among the dog's mercury) - a clue to an old wood.

The Wildlife Trust programme includes removing most of the conifer trees and restarting coppicing (the coppice here is mainly ash and hazel with some field maple and small-leaved lime - this last being another indicator of the age of the wood). The tall 'standard' trees are mainly oak and ash.

That work will improve the 'body' of the wood for birds; nevertheless it is already lively with birdsong when blackcap and willow and garden warblers arrive in late spring. The laughing call (yaffle) of the green woodpecker and the drumming of the great spotted woodpecker are also heard. The woodcock is more often seen flying its territorial 'roding' flight when the branches are still bare in late winter. On warm sunny summer days there are thousands of meadow butterflies in the rides, and look out for the white admiral butterfly near a sunny bramble patch.

Themelthorpe

ACCESS

Car Park

West Ride

Bluebell Trail

Hunter's Ride

Church Ride

Foxley Village

500 yards

— BOUNDARY
WOODLAND
--- PATH

139

RANWORTH BROAD

NORFOLK WILDLIFE TRUST

Nearest town: Norwich
OS Map 134 TG 357149

A Norfolk broad undisturbed by boat traffic. There is a floating conservation centre, nature trail and the possibility of guided boat trips.

Location and access: As the crow flies, the reserve is about 9 miles (14 km) in a north-easterly direction from the centre of Norwich. Ranworth is signposted to the left (north) of the B1140 road from Norwich to Acle. Use the Norfolk Wildlife Trust car park in the village as there is no parking at the reserve entrance. Following signs from the staithe, it is a 5 minute walk to the reserve; the floating display centre (with shop and refreshments) is reached via a boardwalk and is open April-October 1000-1700. Binoculars and telescopes are provided for bird watching. No dogs please.

The Broads are victim to their own popularity; however, Ranworth is free from boat traffic and is a refuge for wildlife. A boardwalk allows visitors to walk deep into its natural delights.

There is some mature oakwood by the reserve entrance (listen for the tapping of woodpeckers) but alder and sallow take over when the ground becomes softer and wetter, with clumps of tussock sedge and strings of wild hop and honeysuckle. The rare royal fern grows in this 'carr' woodland.

In the shallows there are reedbeds and fen, with flowers such as meadowsweet and milk parsley. This last is one of the cow parsley tribe and host plant of the rare yellow and black swallowtail butterfly, seen here between May and August. Dragonflies are another of this broad's attractions. As for the birds, great

WILDLIFE FEATURES
- Swallowtail butterfly
- Cormorants and other birdlife
- Wildfowl

crested grebe nest here, as does the common tern; while in winter teal, wigeon, shoveler and pochard feed - and up to 400 cormorants roost!

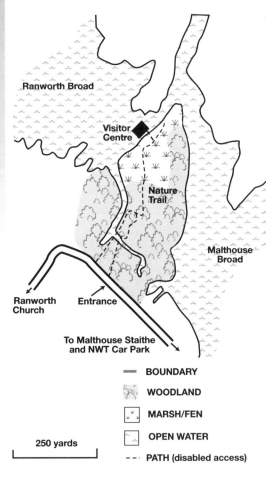

	BOUNDARY
	WOODLAND
	MARSH/FEN
	OPEN WATER
	PATH (disabled access)

250 yards

140

HICKLING BROAD

NORFOLK WILDLIFE TRUST

Nearest town: Acle
OS Map 133/134 TG 427222

A corner of one of the oldest and largest areas of open water in southern Britain, with pools and ditches, reedbeds, fen and grazing marsh and woodland. There is a visitor centre open 1000-1700, a warden and waymarked trails with disabled access and toilets.

Location and access: There are toilets. From Hickling village follow brown 'duck' tourist signs, turn into Stubb Road at the Greyhound Inn. Take the first turning left to follow Stubb Road for another mile. Turn right at the sign for the car park and visitor centre. No dogs please.

There is an entry charge to assist with the upkeep that this special reserve needs. Norfolk Trust members free.

The Broads are shallow, flooded medieval peat diggings, and the three Hickling walks show the variety of habitats which have since evolved here. The shortest winds through woodland and fen, on to a dragonfly pool and back. Usually in spring and early summer there are early marsh and spotted orchids among the flowers to be seen.

The second walk is at first along a boardwalk path through extensive reedbeds. This is a wonderful chance to see and hear warblers and buntings flitting between the densely ranked stems, while you may spot a marsh harrier circling overhead. This is where you will also have a chance of seeing the rare swallowtail butterfly in summer - with large (about 3 inches span) bright black and yellow wings. Its host plant is milk parsley, a finely leaved relative of the cow parsley, a fenland plant. This walk continues with a grassy path along the edge of the broad before returning.

WILDLIFE FEATURES
🦋 **Swallowtail butterfly**
🐦 **Birdlife**

A third walk passes through the grazing marshes which provide nest sites for skylark and yellow wagtail and others. These marshes demand traditional working by grazing and cutting to preserve their character.

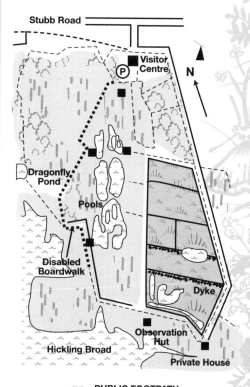

- `- -` **PUBLIC FOOTPATH**
- **GRAZING MARSH**
- **FEN**
- **REEDBEDS**
- **WOODLAND**
- **POND/OPEN WATER**
- `- -·` **PATH**

250 yards

141

LACKFORD WILDFOWL RESERVE

SUFFOLK WILDLIFE TRUST

Nearest town: Bury St Edmunds
OS Map 155 TL 800708

An area of more than 100 acres (42 ha) created from flooded gravel workings (other pits are used as a sailing lake and for fishing). The site was set up due to the generosity of local member Bernard Tickner, and is managed by the Trust in conjunction with Atlas Aggregates. It is an SSSI. There is an information hut and bird hides.

Location and access: The reserve is alongside the A1101 running north-west from Bury St Edmunds to Mildenhall. Lackford is about 5 miles from Bury, the reserve being north of the A1101, just west of the turning for West Stow. It is in the Lark valley with the West Stow Country Park beyond it. The information hut is manned most weekends. No dogs please.

This is a prime site for bird-watching. Even the sailing lake to the left as you cross the causeway to the reserve has, in winter, large numbers of tufted duck, pochard and gadwall with perhaps

WILDLIFE FEATURES
↣ Wildfowl and waders

shoveler, goldeneye and goosander and occasional rarities such as divers and ruddy duck.

Bill's Hide (no.1) is the best place in Suffolk to see the kingfisher and also nesting great crested grebe. Look for summer dragonflies and butterflies on the way from here. Little ringed plover nests on the islands in the small pond; and redshank and shelduck. The shelduck regularly accept the artificial nest sites provided (pipes in mounds of sand!). Sallow and reeds edge the water and here you look out for sedge, reed and willow warblers and water rail where the plants are densest.

Sparrowhawk and occasionally goshawk are hunting incomers, and on summer evenings a hobby is often seen chasing the sand martins and dragonflies. The osprey has also become a regular visitor while on migration. The list of potential sightings really is never ending - even Caspian tern, hoopoe and red necked grebe have been seen at this marvellous site.

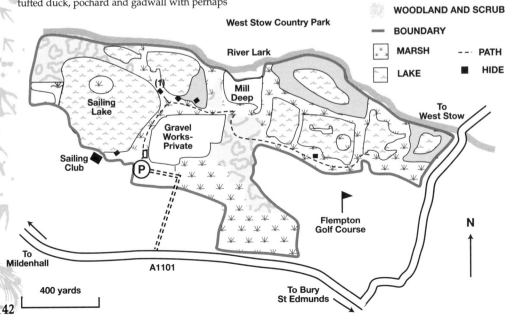

WOODLAND AND SCRUB
— **BOUNDARY**
MARSH --- **PATH**
LAKE ■ **HIDE**

West Stow Country Park
River Lark
Mill Deep
To West Stow
Sailing Lake
Gravel Works- Private
Sailing Club
P
To Mildenhall
A1101
Flempton Golf Course
N
To Bury St Edmunds

400 yards

142

REDGRAVE & LOPHAM FEN

SUFFOLK WILDLIFE TRUST

Nearest town: Diss
OS Map 144 TM 046797

306 acres (124 ha) of open water, wetland, heath and woodland, with the largest remaining tract of valley fen in England. It is an SSSI, a Ramsar site and a National Nature Reserve.

Location and access: Take the A1066 Thetford road from Diss, and after about 5 miles you reach South Lopham. Take the B1113 south towards Redgrave. After a mile, take the side road to the left, continue for 1 mile and turn right into the car park and visitor centre. Dogs on leads only.

This relic tract of peat fen provides a refuge for many now rare plants and animals. A nearby borehole lowers the ground-water and threatens the site, but it is hoped that this will be moved by summer 1999 as part of a restoration programme.

As soon as you leave the car park, you will, in spring and summer, be greeted by birdsong - blackcap and willow warbler and also maybe the nightingale. Walk west to reach the bridges past which lies Little Fen with sedge, reed and grasshopper warblers nesting along the ditches. At its far end an

WILDLIFE FEATURES
❀ **Fen communities**   ✕ **Birdlife**
✳ **The rare fen raft spider**

area of thin peat over waterlogged sandy soil creates a wet heath, rare in the lowlands, flagged by cotton grass. The natural source of the River Waveney is nearby.

Eastwards past the bridges (watch out for the blue flash of a kingfisher) you arrive at a boardwalk skirting some small peaty pools. These are the haunt of the fen raft spider, Britain's largest and rarest spider. It is one inch long and sleekly black with (usually but not always) broad rally stripes along each side. It waits on floating leaves, ready to run out to seize even sticklebacks. It stretches its legs fully out to be supported by the surface film, a raft-like appearance.

Eastwards lie Middle and Great Fens, usually with plenty of dragonflies on the wing in summer, and maybe snipe and water rail also to be seen. The reserve is grazed by Polish tarpan ponies.

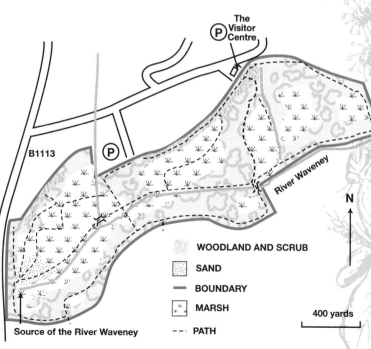

Source of the River Waveney

WOODLAND AND SCRUB
SAND
BOUNDARY
MARSH
PATH

B1113

The Visitor Centre

River Waveney

N

400 yards

143

BRADFIELD WOODS NATIONAL NATURE RESERVE

SUFFOLK WILDLIFE TRUST

Nearest town: Bury St Edmunds
OS Map 155 TL 935581

180 acres (72 ha) of ancient woodland, one of the best sites for woodland flowers in Britain. It is an SSSI. There is an information centre and there are wardens.

Location and access: The reserve is about 7 miles (11 km) due south-east of Bury St Edmunds. Leave the town southwards on the A134 for Sudbury and after about 3 miles you arrive in Sicklesmere. There is a side road to the left; take it, to pass through Little Welnetham, and Bradfield St George after which the car park and information centre are to the right. Dogs on leads only.

The best way to enjoy these woods is to wander freely along the many open rides.

The wood has been worked as coppice-with-standards for centuries. The enormous ash coppice stools must date back to the Middle

WILDLIFE FEATURES
❀ **Woodland flowers**
🦋 **Butterflies** 🐦 **Woodland birds**

Ages. Coppicing continues, bringing a healthy income for maintenance from the sale of material used for thatching, tool handles, rustic poles and firewood. This regular opening of the woodland floor stimulates the plant life - more than 350 species have been recorded here, a total only bettered in a couple of woods elsewhere in Britain.

So wander - and look out for spectacular spreads of ramsons, bluebell and oxlip in spring; and herb Paris and early purple orchid...

This plant diversity underpins the summer butterfly tally of 15 different species.

As for the birdlife, the nightingale is vociferous as are blackcap, garden and willow warbler and whitethroat - all with liquid song - and chiffchaff. All three woodpeckers can be seen or heard, and woodcock, willow tit and sparrowhawk also nest here.

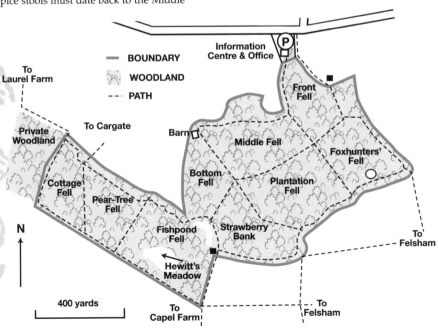

144

TRIMLEY MARSHES

SUFFOLK WILDLIFE TRUST

Nearest town: Felixstowe
OS Map 169 TM 258355

A series of wet meadows and freshwater lagoons, totalling 205 acres (83 ha). There is a visitor centre and five hides.

Location and access: The reserve was created beside new port facilities. There is parking at the top of Cordy's Lane, Trimley St Mary, just outside Felixstowe. Walk down Cordy's Lane, and turn right at the bottom alongside warehouses, past a landscaped earth mound to the river wall. You soon reach the first hide overlooking a wet meadow, and after that the visitor centre and a hide overlooking a large reservoir. More hides are further on.

You can also reach the reserve from Levington, along a footpath, a distance of about 3 miles. Unfortunately, dogs are not allowed on this reserve.

WILDLIFE FEATURES
🐦 Wildfowl and waders

This is a very new reserve, created as a result of the battle to stop the enlargement of Felixstowe Docks. It is already attracting exciting numbers of birds. The geography includes grazing wet meadows, a summer and a winter flood meadow and two permanent freshwater lagoons. The smaller of these has a series of islands, with one covered in shingle to encourage common tern, ringed plover and avocet to nest here.

From the first hide, overlooking a wet meadow, when partly flooded in winter and early spring, you can see wigeon, brent goose and snipe and in summer lapwing and redshank. A second hide overlooks the lagoon with its islands: spring and summer sightings include avocet, oystercatcher, black-tailed godwit and little tern. A third hide overlooks the summer flood with large numbers of feeding waders - and this is the best area to look for scarcer passage migrants such as wood sandpiper and little stint.

A fourth hide overlooks the winter flood with dabbling ducks, while the northern reservoir is deep enough for divers and grebes.

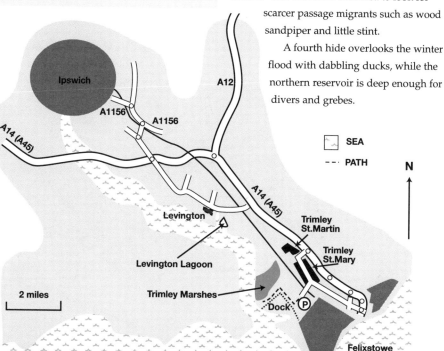

145

CARLTON MARSHES

SUFFOLK WILDLIFE TRUST

Nearest town: Lowestoft
OS Map 134 TM 508920

More than 100 acres (40 ha) of grazing marsh, fen and peat pools. An SSSI. There is an information centre.

Location and access: The reserve is at the western end of Oulton Broad, a busy boating and holiday venue. Leaving Lowestoft, you join the A1117 which crosses a wing of Oulton Broad, and take it south for a short distance before going right (westwards) on the A146 Beccles road. You pass an Esso garage on the right and shortly afterwards take a lane on the right which crosses the railway line to take you to the car park at the information centre, as shown on the map.

This reserve is actually at the end of the popular and busy Oulton Broad, part of what was once

WILDLIFE FEATURES
🐾 Broadland in miniature
🦋 Dragonflies

a huge estuary. Today it echoes the different habitats to be found in the Broads in quite a small area. The plant-rich cattle-grazed marshes are chosen by waders for example, and are worth scanning, particularly in winter, for short-eared and barn owls and hen harrier. The marsh dykes have the now-rare water soldier, a plant with spiny leaves (like an aloe) which sinks weighted by chalk to escape the winter ice. These dykes are also prime for dragonflies, including the rare Norfolk hawker - brown bodied with green eyes.

Bogbean, one of our handsomest wild flowers, is seen around Sprats Water, also a favourite haunt of the kingfisher.

If you follow the marsh track between the grazing marshes, you pass on the right the reedbeds known as Whitecast Marshes. The marsh harrier sometimes nests here and you may see the hen bird fly up to take food from the male. Happily this bird is now on the increase - in 1971 only one nest was known in Britain, but those you see here are among the 30 or so pairs in Suffolk alone.

REEDBEDS

SCRUB

BOUNDARY

GRAZING MARSH

PATH

RAILWAY

PUBLIC BRIDLEWAY

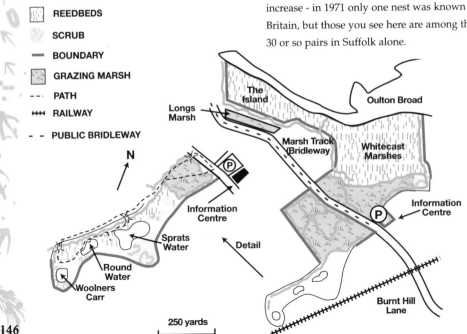

N

Longs Marsh

The Island

Oulton Broad

Marsh Track (Bridleway)

Whitecast Marshes

Information Centre

Information Centre

Sprats Water

Detail

Round Water

Woolners Carr

Burnt Hill Lane

250 yards

LANGDON

ESSEX WILDLIFE TRUST

Nearest towns: Basildon
OS Map 177 TQ 659874 / 683873 (main entrances).

441 acres (186 ha) of meadows, woods, ponds, plantations and scrub. There are nature trails and a visitor centre.

Location and access: The reserve is to the south-west of Basildon New Town, 4.5 miles east of junction 29 on the M25, between the A127 and the A13. It comprises four areas, as the map shows.

Parking is as follows: for Dunton - the new Centre; for Lincewood - Langdon Hills recreation ground TQ 674876; for Marks Hill - in Delmores off Langdon Hills High Road TQ 683873; for Willow Park - Lee Chapel Lane TO 676872.

This is Essex Wildlife Trust's largest inland reserve. Its value lies in its variety and the abundance of species once common in the countryside. The meadows have not been artificially 'improved' with fertilisers and so wild orchids can be counted in thousands.

WILDLIFE FEATURES
Butterflies
Wild flowers

Three hundred and fifty different species of flowering plants grow here.

Each of the four areas has its own character. Dunton has relic 1930s 'plotland' homes and gardens (rather like allotments with houses) now largely scrubbed up and with old orchards of damsons and other fruit. Lizards are often seen.

Lincewood has some ancient woodland on high ground (with later woodland lower) and on the recreation ground you can see thousands of the pink flowered green winged orchid in May-June. Lincewood also has a riot of old roses, peas and other garden escapes. There are three ponds that are home to frogs and toads and great crested newts.

Marks Hill has a patchwork of old and recent woodland, meadows and abandoned plotland. It is noted for its spring flowers - bluebell and wood anemone in the woodland, orchids in the grass, while Willow Park alongside is an ancient deer park with hay meadows, some woodland and seven ponds. Again, this is a super place for wild flowers and butterflies.

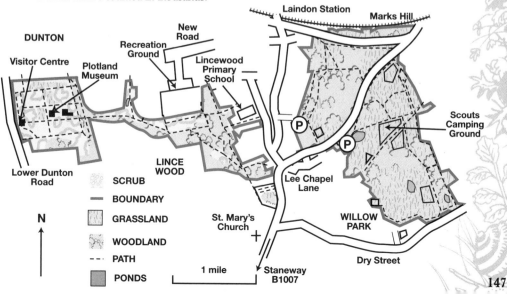

147

ABBERTON

ESSEX WILDLIFE TRUST

Nearest town: Colchester
OS Map 168 TL 963185

9 acres (3.6 ha) of SSSI at the head of a well protected bay of the 1,200 acre Abberton Reservoir. It is a man-made reserve with planted trees etc. The site has a visitor centre and bird hides.

Location and access: Abberton reservoir lies 6 miles (9.5 km) south-west of Colchester on the B1026 road to Maldon. It is just outside the village of Layer-de-la-Haye. Brown and white 'Wildfowl Centre' signs identify it. The Centre, shop and nature reserve are open 0900-1700 daily except Mondays and Christmas Day and Boxing Day. There are disabled facilities. Dogs are not allowed in the Centre or reserve.

WILDLIFE FEATURES
✈ Wildfowl and waders   ❀ Wild flowers

For reason of its wild duck, swans and other water birds, whether resident, passing through on migration, or over-wintering, this reservoir is one of Europe's most renowned wetland sites. In addition, recent dry winters have caused water levels to fall, exposing large areas of mud which attract flocks of waders from the coast. Among the highlights are common tern nesting on the raft and a colony of cormorant nesting in trees (a rare sight in Britain) and up to 500 mute swan finding refuge during the flightless summer moult.

Following the digging of the large pond, wildfowl now nest on it in some numbers, including mute swan, Canada goose, mallard and moorhen. Hedges and thickets were planted and warblers and finches now also nest (with yellowhammer and linnet in the gorse). There are nooky grassland corners for butterflies, small copper, common blue and small skipper among them.

The panoramic windows of the visitor centre give a front seat view of the wildfowl spectacles on reservoir and pond.

ACCESS
N
To Colchester
To Maldon B1026
Board Walk
Hide
Tern Raft
Abberton Reservoir
Visitor Centre and Parking For Disabled
Hide
Hide
New Boardwalk
Peninsular Trail
P
Hide
Peninsular Trail

— BOUNDARY
WOODLAND/SCRUB
WATER
--- PATH
HIDE

200 yards

FINGRINGHOE WICK

ESSEX WILDLIFE TRUST

Nearest town: Colchester
OS Map 168 TM 041195

A magnificently varied reserve, the Trust's flagship. 125 acres (51 ha) of grassland, woodland, gorse heathland, ponds and a lake and saltmarsh panoramas on the west shore of the River Colne estuary. It is an SSSI. There are a visitor centre (and the Trust HQ) and eight birdwatching hides and nature trails.

Location and access: The reserve lies 3 miles (5 km) south-east of Colchester. It is signposted from Colchester with brown and white nature reserve signs. Take the B1025 from Colchester towards Mersea for 3 miles. Having crossed the Roman River, turn left at the next sign and follow the signs to the reserve; the lanes are narrow. There is a 10 mph limit on the reserve: a tarmac road leads to the centre car park.

The centre is open 0900-1800 and the reserve 0900-1900 daily except Mondays, Christmas Day and Boxing Day. Visitors to the reserve are required to obtain a day permit from the centre. There are facilities for the disabled.

WILDLIFE FEATURES
**✕ Birdlife ❀ Wild flowers
❦ Butterflies**

This reserve has been created from disused gravel workings. Or rather, evolved, because when digging ceased nature took over, seeding itself in to create the mosaic we see today. The disturbed landscape is now virtually buried in woodland and thicket, with a mixed plantation of trees, though there is some grassland too.

The wild flowers can be spectacular, with orchids among them. The ponds are a vital wildlife feature (thirteen of the dragonfly clan are seen; and the great crested newt); and to all this is added the river frontage with saltmarsh and mudflats to attract wintering avocets and other waders and the flocks of Brent geese. There cannot be many places where you can watch curlew while a nightingale sings nearby, but that is a daily delight here in May. Whatever the season, you can expect to notch up 50 bird species on a decent day. Mammals are more reclusive of course, but look out for common seal in the estuary.

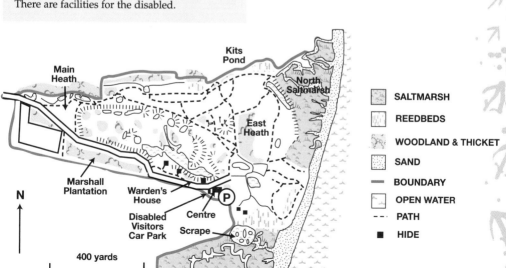

SALTMARSH
REEDBEDS
WOODLAND & THICKET
SAND
BOUNDARY
OPEN WATER
PATH
HIDE

N

400 yards

North Midlands

The only thing most of the counties in this varied region have in common is that they are landlocked, with the exception of Cheshire. While much of Leicestershire and Nottinghamshire are given over to agriculture and industry, Derbyshire and Staffordshire have wild areas of moorland and uplands. A few remaining peat bogs are still found in Shropshire, including Wem Moss, a lowland raised bog where mosses and wetland plants have built up layers of peat into a low dome, like a giant sponge. The attractive yellow bog asphodel is found there, as well as cotton grass, aromatic bog myrtle and the insectivorous sundew. To the north, Red Rock Marsh borders the Dee estuary in Cheshire. An area of sand dunes and brackish lagoons, it is home to a rare colony of natterjack toads, as well as spectacular numbers of waders in the winter. To the east, Leicestershire has Rutland Water, internationally important for birds. The Reserve is taking part in a programme to reintroduce breeding osprey to England and is also a prime site for breeding tree sparrows.

A good example of close partnership between industry and conservation can be seen at Duke's Wood in Nottinghamshire. The ancient woodland was the site of the UK's first onshore oilfield and some early 'nodding donkeys' can still be seen .

NORTH MIDLANDS

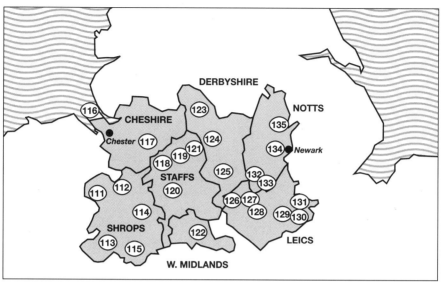

LLYNCLYS HILL

SHROPSHIRE WILDLIFE TRUST

Nearest town: Oswestry
OS Map 126 SJ 275239

101 acres (41 ha) of common, a limestone sward now with some scrub and woodland. There is a small pond. It is an SSSI. It is now grazed by sheep and ponies.

Location and access: Head south from Oswestry on the A483 to Llynclys and turn right onto the A495 at the crossroads by the White Lion. Approach the reserve via Turners Lane, the first road off the A495, but leave your car in the lay-by on the south side of the main road (at SJ 278241). Walk up the lane for 100 yards and then fork right up the bridleway onto the common. After about 200 yards fork uphill to the left to reach the main part of the common.

Please do not drive up Turners Lane.

WILDLIFE FEATURES
✿ **Orchids and other flowers**
✄ **Birdlife**

Set among extensive woodlands, numerous small meadows and limestone quarries, the common provides a varied area of scrub and woodland (on the steep west slope), with yew, spurge laurel and spindle, and areas of flower-rich grassland.

On this grassland, you will find two types of plant community. Where the soil is thin, there grow the typical plants of limestone: rockrose, common centaury, wild thyme and quaking grass. There are also orchids: early purple, common spotted, fragrant, pyramidal, and greater butterfly orchid and the distinctively two-leaved twayblade. In places you can also find the two ferns of old grassland: adder's-tongue and moonwort.

On the deeper soils, rain has washed much of the lime from the surface and there is a more heath-like community, but this still includes primrose and cowslip in spring followed by lady's bedstraw, bird's-foot-trefoil and knapweed. In high summer there is plenty of agrimony with spikes of small yellow flowers. Common blue, small copper and gatekeeper are among the butterflies you should see.

Although the scrub shades out these flowers, it does attract nesting warblers and other birds.

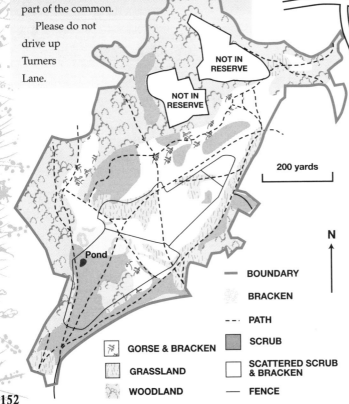

NOT IN RESERVE

NOT IN RESERVE

Turner's Lane

200 yards

Pond

N

BOUNDARY
BRACKEN
PATH
SCRUB
SCATTERED SCRUB & BRACKEN
FENCE
GORSE & BRACKEN
GRASSLAND
WOODLAND

WEM MOSS

SHROPSHIRE WILDLIFE TRUST

Nearest town: Wem
OS Map 126 SJ 473342

61 acres (28 ha) of lowland raised bog, retaining all the natural features of this increasingly rare habitat. It is a Ramsar site and NNR.

Location and access: The bog is near the village of Northwood, about 4 miles (6 km) due east of Ellesmere. From Whitchurch take the A485 south-west for Ellesmere, and after about 8 miles there is a side road left (the B5063) for Northwood. A public footpath skirts the site, reached along a track (no cars) from Northwood. There is very limited car parking space on the roadside around Northwood village. Walking on the reserve is difficult.

WILDLIFE FEATURES

🦎 **Lizards and other reptiles**
✿ **Bog plants**

This is a superb natural 'wilderness' in the intensively farmed landscape - a raised bog with its centre slightly higher than its margins. But there are a number of distinct habitats to be found.

Along the eastern side, which still receives mineral-rich ground water, a wet fen 'carr' with alder, willow and alder buckthorn (food plant of the brimstone butterfly) has developed. Projecting westwards from this wood, a tongue of slightly raised land is marked out by purple moor grass, whose flower heads give it a purple sheen (and the handsome yellow bog asphodel also flowers here). There is plentiful cross-leaved heath and heather, the former on wetter ground, which is also marked by the white heads of cotton grass, and throughout the moss you find aromatic bog myrtle. Cranberry straggles the surface of the bog moss, and there are patches of sundews, with sticky red hairs to trap flies.

There is a good deal of interesting animal life - adders and snipe and other birds. Snipe are likely to take you by surprise, flushed from the concealing heather with a fast erratic flight.

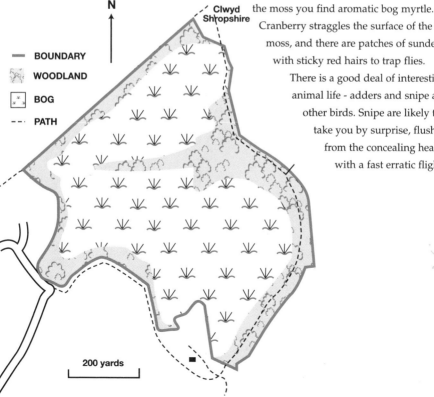

BOUNDARY
WOODLAND
BOG
PATH

N

Clwyd
Shropshire

200 yards

153

CLUNTON COPPICE

SHROPSHIRE WILDLIFE TRUST

Nearest town: Bishop's Castle
OS Map 137 SO 343806

56 acres (23 ha) of broadleaved coppice woodland on the steep south flank of the Clun valley. It is a scheduled SSSI.

Location and access: Take the B4385 south from Bishop's Castle, and about 2 miles (3 km) from the town, the road turns sharply left. Continue straight ahead on the road for Brockton, Lower Down and finally Clunton (Clunton is on the B4368 road west from Craven Arms to Newtown).

Turn south in the middle of Clunton village beside The Crown Inn over a bridge and steeply uphill to the centre of an unfenced area of woodland. There is limited parking in the small quarry entrance on the right; or park opposite The Crown in Clunton and walk up.

This is a sessile oak coppice woodland, with scattered birch, hazel, holly and yew. This oak is typical of the thin acid soils of upland Britain. It is less spreading than common or pedunculate oak, and its woodlands tend to be airier, with a light forest floor carpeted with delicate wavy hair grass, perhaps scattered with the pale yellow flowers of cow-wheat, and with clumps of greater woodrush in damper areas. The bilberry is quite sturdy too, growing to a good height; all this because the wood is not heavily grazed by sheep, the fate of many such places (if they haven't been felled and coniferised). It is also good for ferns, mosses and fungi. The hard fern is one

of the easier ferns to identify, with spore-bearing fronds which resemble a fish backbone rising erect from a rosette of green sterile fronds.

The coppice is particularly attractive in late spring, with the songs of wood warbler, pied flycatcher and other summer visitors, the drumming of woodpeckers and the mewing call of buzzards overhead.

WILDLIFE FEATURES
❀ Fens   ✖ Woodland birds

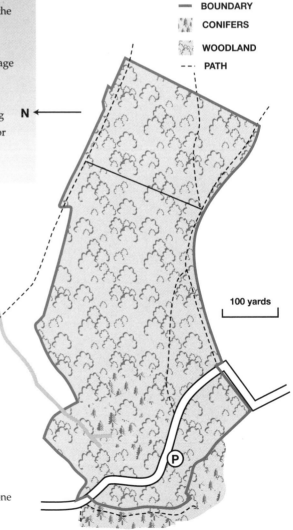

BOUNDARY
CONIFERS
WOODLAND
PATH

N ←

100 yards

P

GRANVILLE COUNTRY PARK

SHROPSHIRE WILDLIFE TRUST

Nearest town: Telford
OS Map 127 SJ 720125

An extensive necklace of reclaimed industrial areas, including colliery waste mounds, and old canal and iron works sites. One area, Muxton Marsh, is an SSSI.

Location and access: This country park is on the eastern edge of Telford. Follow the road signs from the B5060 (Redhill Way or Donnington Wood Way) which runs up the western side, or off Wellington Road in Muxton to the north. A car park at the end of Muxton Lane serves the northern and eastern parts, and car parks along Granville Road give access to the central and southern sections.

The half dozen blocks which together make up the country park are connected by well-surfaced paths, many of which are suitable for wheelchairs.

Much of the park has evolved from industrial dereliction: the hills, looking like natural wooded or heathy knolls, are old colliery mounds, for example. On some you can see the first stages of this colonisation, with annual 'weeds' leading the way, and the heather is a surprise in such an urban setting. But in time these pioneers are followed by birch and then oak. Some of the oaks on the older pit mounds of the Muxton Bridge and Freehold collieries to the north form mini-woods, with yellow archangel, stitchwort and wood anemone as the 'woodland' flowers.

WILDLIFE FEATURES
❀ **Wetland flowers**   ✤ **Dragonflies**

There are two important wet areas. On the north-west side is Muxton Marsh, an SSSI, a damp meadow which became wetter as the colliery mound impeded its drainage, and part of it to the left of the path has developed as 'carr', a wet woodland with alder and willow; while to the right an open marsh remains, with marsh orchid and other special plants. The second site is the old canal basin by Lodge Furnaces, which still holds water and has dragonflies and other wildlife.

155

CRAMER GUTTER

SHROPSHIRE WILDLIFE TRUST

Nearest town: Ludlow
OS Map 138 SO 648794

11 acres (4.1 ha) of unimproved damp pasture running down to a brook. It is an SSSI.

Location and access: The reserve is about 9 miles (14 km) east-north-east of Ludlow, between the villages of Oreton and Catherton. Take the A4117 east from Ludlow and turn left at Foxwood at the top of Hopton Bank and then after 2 miles turn right at the crossroads after "The Gate Hangs Well" to cross the north-east side of Catherton Common. Park on the edge of the common. There is a walk of about 800 yards to the reserve.

At first glance, there may seem little of wildlife interest here, on this piece of wet pasture, but botanically it is one of the richest fields in the whole of Shropshire, with more than 100 flowering plants recorded.

WILDLIFE FEATURES
❀ A colony of marsh gentian and other flowers

The plant pattern is determined mainly by the water seepages. The heathers give the first clue, with cross-leaved heath in the wetter and heather in the drier areas together with bell heather. The wetter areas also have bog pimpernel, bog asphodel and some patches of cranberry.

There are many species of sedges (recognised as a group by their triangular stems) - two of the best known are common cotton grass and hare's-tail cotton grass (yes, sedges despite their names).

Plants apart, you may well hear the bubbling call of the curlew and on hot summer days the song of the skylark overhead. The magnificent golden ringed dragonfly may be seen along the stream and two less common butterflies to look out for are the green hairstreak and the small pearl-bordered fritillary.

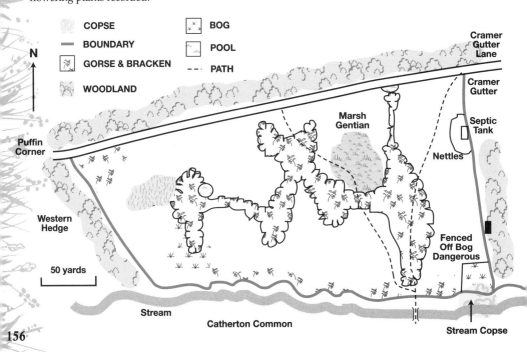

COPSE
BOUNDARY
GORSE & BRACKEN
WOODLAND
BOG
POOL
PATH

N

Cramer Gutter Lane
Cramer Gutter
Marsh Gentian
Septic Tank
Nettles
Puffin Corner
Western Hedge
50 yards
Fenced Off Bog Dangerous
Stream
Catherton Common
Stream Copse

RED ROCK MARSH

CHESHIRE WILDLIFE TRUST

Nearest town: Birkenhead
OS Map 108 SJ 206880

10 acres (4 ha) of sand dunes with brackish and freshwater marsh.

It is an SSSI. The spectacular bird sites of the Dee estuary and Hilbre islands are alongside.

Location and access: The reserve can be reached on foot from the West Kirby promenade or Stanley Road, Hoylake, where cars can be parked.

This is a naturally evolving sand dune system with, apart from the dunes themselves, brackish slacks or lagoons, a freshwater marsh and a large reedbed. The marsh lies between dune ridges - to seaward they are being constantly eroded and rebuilt while to landward they merge with the golf links (the word 'link' in fact is a Scottish term for a dune grassland, ideal for golf!).

Marram grass with its web of hidden stems binds and stabilises the loose sand, where wild asparagus and various orchids are among the plants that can grow. The reedbed is largely common reed with areas of sea club rush. This last enthuses only the botanist, perhaps, but for the others among us, the ground-down shells give the sand a limy flavour which encourages flowering plants and the margins of the reedbed are richest with more than 50 species. One to look for is parsley piert, like a miniature lady's-mantle; also look for quaking grass, usually noticed on chalk downland.

But a main interest of the reserve is that it is home to the only breeding colony of natterjack toad on the Wirral. Natterjacks are slightly smaller then common toads, with a smoother skin with a yellow line down the spine. Usually

WILDLIFE FEATURES

- Wild orchids and other flowers
- Natterjack toad
- Wintering wildfowl and waders

active at night, they crawl rather than hop. Following severe losses, the Trust has reintroduced them here in recent years.

And of course there are the massed winter flocks of waders of the Dee estuary - regularly 100,000 strong. The estuary also serves as a pit stop for migrating birds.

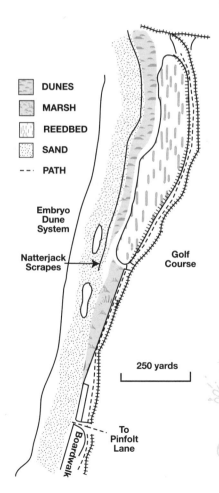

DUNES
MARSH
REEDBED
SAND
--- PATH

Embryo Dune System

Natterjack Scrapes

Golf Course

250 yards

Boardwalk

To Pinfolt Lane

THE QUINTA

CHESHIRE WILDLIFE TRUST

Nearest town: Congleton
OS Map 129 SJ 801671

This is an unusual 36 acre (14.5 ha) reserve, consisting of an arboretum, new plantation woodland, ancient woodland, old meadows and water features. It is an SSSI and SBI (Site of Biological Importance).

Location and access: The reserve is on the western edge of the village of Swettenham, about 6 miles (10 km) north-west of Congleton. Swettenham is easiest reached from the A535 between Wilmslow and Middlewich, taking the side road just north of Holmes Chapel. Once in the village, the reserve is well signposted. There is a car park within the grounds. The area is open during daylight hours, every day except Christmas.

WILDLIFE FEATURES
- 🌲 **5,000 species of trees and shrubs**
- ❀ **Grassland flowers**
- 🦅 **Birdlife**

Following on from the arboretum walk, however, are two areas of newly created woodland, with mainly native trees - oak, ash, rowan, field maple and alder (and also Norway maple). There are two areas of sloping hay meadow nearby.

The southern slopes of open grassland south of the plantation are part of the 4 mile SSSI along the River Dane valley.

Reached by 39 steps is the Clough, a Site of Biological Interest - half the site is ancient woodland, half a steep grassland with a good many wild flowers.

While here, look out for the kingfisher near the water. There are woodpeckers and flycatchers also to be seen, and the nuthatch. The hare too is often seen.

This is an unusual nature reserve - and popular. Around 5,000 people a year visit it; however, most of them come not for its wildlife interest, but for its trees. The arboretum contains between four and five thousand species of trees and shrubs. Some of them are in formal plantings - the Reith Avenue has red-twigged lime, for example.

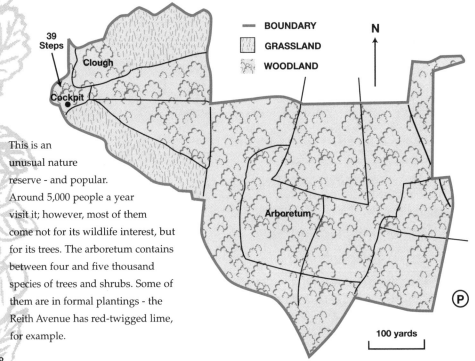

158

HEM HEATH WOOD

STAFFORDSHIRE WILDLIFE TRUST

Nearest town: Stoke on Trent
OS Map 118 SJ 885412

21 acres (8.5 ha), part of a much larger block of woodland extending for three quarters of a mile beside the London-Stoke railway line. There are interpretation boards and a nature trail.

Location and access: This reserve is just to the south of Stoke on Trent, reached via the A5035 road between Longton and Trentham. The small parking area indicated on the map is opposite the entrance to Old Trentham Colliery.

Old maps show that this wood is around 150 years old and planted (so the straight rides suggest) for timber, but it was only felled once. The main trees are oak, beech, sycamore and ash. Beech would not be growing naturally so far north. Notice the wild privet (post 2); this and the sanicle suggest that the soil is less acid here than elsewhere - the bank is of spoil dug when the railway was built. There are horse chestnuts at post 3, and fine willow and alder trees at post 4 where the ground is damper. The pond has stands of greater reedmace ('bulrush') and water horsetail. Look for the marsh cinquefoil, with purplish flowers - it's rather localised in Staffordshire. Sycamore has been cleared from the south and flowers such as bluebell flourish in the new light.

There are wild cherry trees in several parts of the wood, but the largest are on the east side around post 6.

All the familiar woodland birds nest here - great and blue tits, chaffinch etc - and the woodpeckers, but the bottom of the wood is not really dense enough yet (the Trust's plans

WILDLIFE FEATURES
- Bats
- Autumn fungi
- Birdlife

include planting a shrub layer beneath the trees) for warblers, although chiffchaff, willow and wood warblers are heard each year - the thinnish ground cover suits the last. Coot and mallard are lured by the pond.

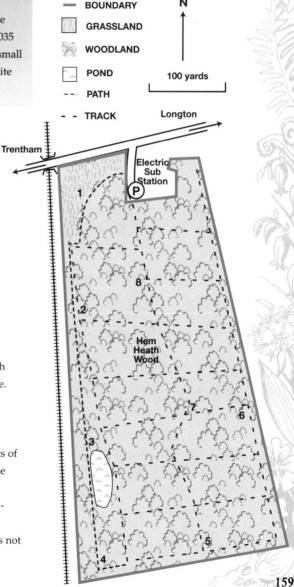

KEY
- — BOUNDARY
- GRASSLAND
- WOODLAND
- POND
- --- PATH
- - - TRACK

N

100 yards

Longton

Trentham

Electric Sub Station

P

1

8

2

Hem Heath Wood

7

6

3

5

4

ROD WOOD

STAFFORDSHIRE WILDLIFE TRUST

Nearest town: Leek
OS Map 118 SJ 997529

Despite its name, this hilltop reserve consists mainly of fields, grazed or cut for hay, although there are several patches of woodland and scrub. There is a stream bordered by marshy ground.

Location and access: The reserve is on a minor road midway between the A520 at Cheddleton and the A523 near Bradnop. There is a fingerpost by the roadside directing visitors to the car park.

Given that the soil here (derived from Millstone Grit rock) is acid in nature, there is a rich plant tally, including some rare in Staffordshire - adder's-tongue fern, early purple orchid and dyer's greenweed are three of these. Others are uncommon in the county - look for the twayblade orchid and the unmistakable greater tussock sedge at one of the marshy areas.

WILDLIFE FEATURES
- Wild flowers
- Woodland birds

There is a wet flush in A and much of field B north of the wood is marsh. On drier ground - in C for example - there are areas of hay rattle, a good indicator of old grassland. Field F is quite different however, with bracken, rosebay willowherb and areas of heather and bilberry.

This good plant diversity is helped by the management regime: the two bottom fields are lightly grazed by cattle from September on, the two top are grazed only after they have been cut for late hay (and when the wild flowers have seeded).

The woodland has oak, ash, downy birch (with downy twigs and often brownish bark) and wild cherry and others. There are quite a few flowers here - bluebell, broad-leaved helleborine and moschatel, for example.

As for birds, 32 species have been counted including redstart, treecreeper and curlew.

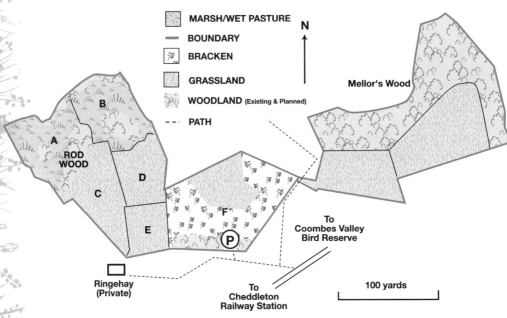

MARSH/WET PASTURE
BOUNDARY
BRACKEN
GRASSLAND
WOODLAND (Existing & Planned)
PATH

N

Mellor's Wood

ROD WOOD

B
A
D
C
E
F
P

To
Coombes Valley
Bird Reserve

Ringehay
(Private)

To
Cheddleton
Railway Station

100 yards

DOXEY MARSHES

STAFFORDSHIRE WILDLIFE TRUST

Nearest town: Stafford
OS Map 127 SJ 915239

This is one of Staffordshire Trust's largest and best known reserves, consisting of 360 acres (145 ha) of marsh, wetland and lowland grassland. Much of it is designated SSSI. There are interpretation boards, three nature trails and a bird observation platform.

Location and access: There is car parking at the end of Wootton Drive off Creswell Farm Drive off the A5013 Eccleshall road. Other access is as shown, plus a path along the River Sow from Sainsbury's in Stafford.

To avoid disturbance to the nesting birds please keep dogs on leads from March to June and keep to the marked paths.

The reserve supports a rich diversity of wildlife, especially birds - more than 150 species have been seen here - largely a result of the diversity of habitats in the River Sow floodplain. Here we have the open water of large pools, swampy areas and wet grassland. They are a marvellous place for wintering waders such as snipe, redshank, lapwing and golden plover. In spring and autumn, migrating waders following the river valley tend to drop in to feed - such as oystercatcher, common sandpiper and black-tailed godwit - but in fact almost any species can turn up.

Passage birds apart, the conditions attract many to nest here - kingfisher and yellow wagtail, with reed bunting among the reeds, while the reserve is especially important for breeding redshank, snipe and sedge warbler. These marshy areas can be alight with yellow flag iris and marsh marigold. Look out for

WILDLIFE FEATURES
❀ **Fenland flowers**
✖ **Birdlife including wildfowl and waders**

angelica (a cow parsley relative growing to head height with purplish stems). Dragonflies also patrol these wet areas, with butterflies on the drier ground, especially along the old railway - large and small skippers, small copper, common blue and others.

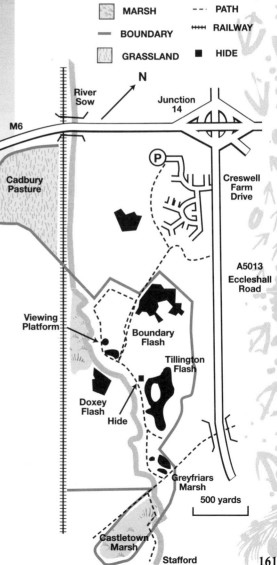

CASTERN WOOD

STAFFORDSHIRE WILDLIFE TRUST

Nearest town: Ashbourne
OS Map 119 SK 119537

51 acres (20.5 ha) of woodland, scrub and grassland in a steep-sided limestone valley sloping down to a meander of the River Manifold. A reserve of SSSI status. There are interpretation boards and a nature trail.

Location and access: The starting point is Wetton, 7 miles north-west of Ashbourne and reached by minor roads. Castern Wood is approached by the unclassified road running due south-east from Wetton. This continues almost straight for 1.5 miles over a small crossroads. At the end of the lane, turn right by a tall public footpath sign, through a gate and into a field. Follow the track to a small parking area at its end.

Please close gates and keep dogs on leads. Keep to the marked trail to avoid damaging vegetation.

This area has been mined for lead, and the spoil heaps and adits (tunnels) remain. In spring the grassland is studded with cowslip and primrose together with, interestingly, some false oxlip, a hybrid between them. Later in the year harebell can be seen and other flowers include early purple orchid, carline thistle and tormentil. Exmoor ponies are let in to graze only when most of these have seeded. Look at what grows on the spoil heaps - here you should find rockrose, wild thyme and biting stonecrop.

WILDLIFE FEATURES

🌾 **Wild flowers** 🦋 **Uncommon butterflies**
🦇 **Bats**

The woodland is mainly on the steep scree slopes, with ash, invasive sycamore, and a few field maple and lime; the diseased and dead wych elm is suckering in some places. It is rather open woodland, with a sparse shrub layer and dog's mercury carpets much of it.

The animal life relates mainly with the open ground (there are many butterflies and day-flying burnet moths and chimney sweep. Birds include tawny owl, woodpeckers, pied flycatcher and redstart. The adits however are used by four or five species of hibernating bat (the grills prevent disturbance).

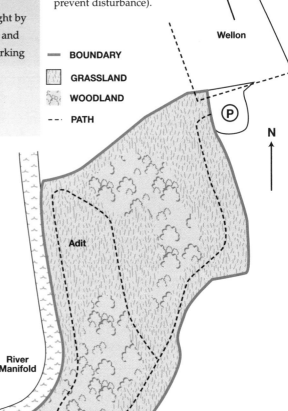

BOUNDARY

GRASSLAND

WOODLAND

PATH

Wellon

P

N

Adit

River Manifold

100 yards

162

BIRMINGHAM ECOPARK

THE WILDLIFE TRUST FOR BIRMINGHAM AND THE BLACK COUNTRY

258A Hob Moor Road, Small Heath, Birmingham B10 9HH (adjacent to Starbant School annexe).

The EcoPark is a working organic nursery surrounded by demonstrations of wildlife gardening, habitat creation and sustainable growing. The EcoPark uses the techniques of 'permaculture' to meet the requirements of crops and maximise the use of space, for example by natural recycling of nutrients and the use of layered and companion planting.

The site includes new woodland, ponds and a meadow and formal plantings of native species and horticultural varieties which encourage wildlife. A demonstration garden takes all the features used in the EcoPark and reproduces

them on a scale appropriate for a typical small or medium garden.

The Plant Biodiversity Bank is another exciting project which is helping to maintain locally distinctive populations of some of the Midland's rarest plants.

The EcoPark promotes the practical recycling of natural resources. Water used on the site is cleaned by a natural reedbed system and collected, together with rainwater, in a large wildlife pond, where it can be stored before being re-used. The site also operates a community compost scheme, producing large quantities of compost for use on the site.

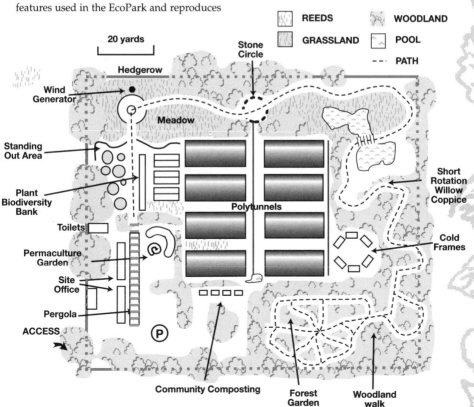

163

MILLERS DALE RESERVE

DERBYSHIRE WILDLIFE TRUST

Nearest town: Bakewell
OS Map 129 SK 140731

Millers Dale is one of three neighbouring reserves of SSSI status. 60 acres (24 ha) in area, it has disused limestone quarries and large spoil heaps.

Priestcliffe Lees (99 acres/44 ha) lies alongside, a north-facing slope with grasslands and woodland, while Chee Dale (60 acres/24 ha), separately to the west, is a craggy steep-sloped ash woodland.

Location and access: The B6049 leaves the A6 Bakewell-Buxton road a mile west of Taddington. It runs through Blackwell, and Millers Dale station is a mile further on. Park in the car park here. Access to Millers Dale reserve is via the Monsal Trail over the viaduct or via the Wormhill road down to the eastern point.

Priestcliffe Lees is reached eastwards along the Monsal Trail. Chee Dale is just over a mile along the A6 to the west. Leaflets on these two, with access details, are available from the Wildlife Trust for an sae.

WILDLIFE FEATURES
 Ash woodland
Orchids and other wild flowers
Woodland birds

The quarry floors of Millers Dale are noted for fragrant, bee and common spotted orchids, carline thistle and other lime lovers, with thyme and marjoram among those on the waste heaps.

The woodland (which is being cleared of sycamore) has mainly ash trees, but look also for wych elm and bird cherry.

There is a good deal of birdlife in these two reserves: redstart, tree creeper and great spotted woodpecker all occur, with woodcock too; and the jackdaw nests on the quarry faces. Look out for kingfisher and dipper along the river.

Chee Dale also has a rich ash woodland with a marvellously mixed shrub layer. Here yew and rock whitebeam are a striking feature of the cliff edges. There is also some grassland.

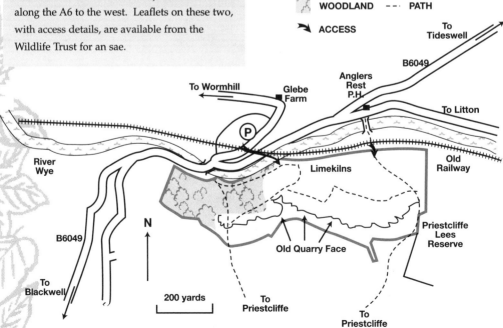

164

DERWENTSIDE & CROMFORD CANAL

DERBYSHIRE WILDLIFE TRUST

Nearest town: Matlock
OS Map 119 SK 316556 and 348519

Derwentside **1** is a 17.5 acre (7 ha) length of rough meadow, woodland and disused sewage beds, while Cromford Canal **2** (now classified as an SSSI and LNR) is a 13 acre (5 ha) length of canal, with its banks and towpath, part of which is a Trust reserve.

Location and access: These two reserves run alongside the A6 south of Matlock, Derwentside starting about 1.5 miles (2.5 km) south of Cromford. There is no access to the Derwentside Reserve itself, but it can be seen from the canal towpath which can be reached at various points along the A6 south of Whatstandwell. The Trust's canal reserve does not link directly with Derwentside, but is a separate section to the south.

The Derbyshire CC car park attached to the High Peak Junction visitor centre to the north of Derwentside is recommended; it gives access to the towpath.

The snaking reserve of Derwentside has old sludge beds colonised by nutrient-greedy nettles, rough meadowland and woodland. The grassland has butterbur, meadow cranesbill and other flowers. The woodland has a varied make-up: with alder on the river bank and also in wetter places within the wood, but oak and sycamore dominate other areas. The dead elms and other trees attract woodpeckers and tree creeper.

There are daffodil, wood anemone and other woodland flowers. The wild daffodils, the main reason for designating

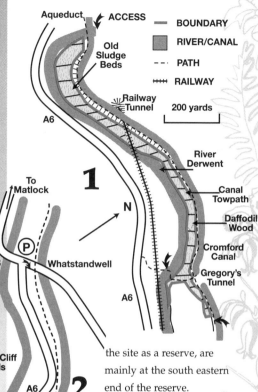

WILDLIFE FEATURES
❀ **Wild daffodils**   🐀 **Water vole**

the site as a reserve, are mainly at the south eastern end of the reserve.

Cromford Canal is an SSSI for its plant interest. It crosses a variety of soils. 250 species have been logged, and some are locally rare or uncommon - flowering rush, perhaps our most handsome wild flower (and anything but a rush), sweet flag and arrowhead.

There is a goodbird-life, with kingfisher and (in winter) siskin and redpoll among others. Water voles may be seen all along the canal.

HILTON RESERVE

DERBYSHIRE WILDLIFE TRUST

Nearest town: Derby
OS Map 128 SK 249315

A reserve of 74 acres (29 ha) of worked-out gravel pits, with open water, marsh, carr and other woodland, including pine plantations. It is an SSSI.

Location and access: The reserve lies south-west of Derby, just off the A516 where it is cut by the new A564 Derby-Stoke dual carriageway. The map shows the parking. There is good access for the disabled at the south-west end.

This splendidly diverse site has a plant tally of no fewer than 250 species. Some of the crack willows which dominate the woodland are very

WILDLIFE FEATURES
❀ **Wetland plants**
🦆 **Wildfowl and other birdlife**

large, and there are a couple of good sized black poplars to be seen (one of Britain's rarest natives in the wild, with rugged black bark often with large trunk burrs). Of key interest are the sedimentation lagoons which have developed good populations of spotted and southern marsh orchids and hybrids between the two.

To match the plant tally, more than 120 species of birds have been seen here. In winter the water attracts a variety of waterfowl, including pochard, tufted and ruddy duck. In summer, the little grebe and great crested grebe nest in the shallows among the reeds and the rafts have encouraged the common tern to nest. The scrub and woodland attract warblers and tits and all three woodpeckers.

The smaller ponds attract frog, common toad and the endangered great crested newt, as well as the smooth newt. Nine species of dragonfly have been recorded including the emperor and the ruddy darter; unlike the ceaselessly patrolling (and better known) hawkers, the darters spend much time perched, darting off to chase other insects on the wing. Speckled wood and brimstone are among the variety of butterflies to be seen.

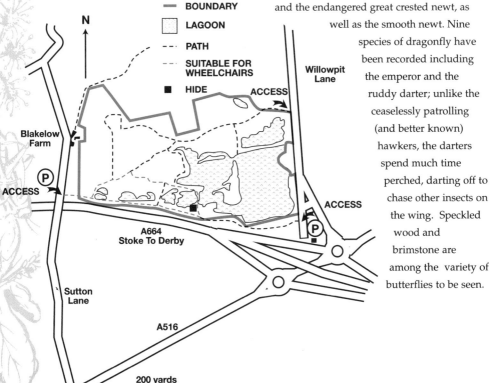

BOUNDARY
LAGOON
PATH
SUITABLE FOR WHEELCHAIRS
HIDE

N

Willowpit Lane

ACCESS

Blakelow Farm

ACCESS
(P)

A664
Stoke To Derby

ACCESS
(P)

Sutton Lane

A516

200 yards

CLOUD WOOD

LEICESTERSHIRE & RUTLAND WILDLIFE TRUST

Nearest town: Ashby-de-la-Zouch
OS Map 129 SK 417214

81 acres (33 ha) of ancient woodland, part of an SSSI.

Location and access: The reserve is in the parish of Breedon on the Hill, on the A453 running south from Nottingham to Ashby-de-la-Zouch. It lies about 1 mile (1.5 km) south-east of Breedon village, alongside the A447 running south to Coalville. Cars should be parked in the lay-bys shown on the map. You should be aware and careful when near the quarry.

This ancient woodland is known as one of the best sites in Leicestershire for flowering plants.

It had long been coppiced in the traditional way, which encourages the wild flowers, but this ceased earlier this century. Around the time of the Second World War, it was clear felled and its timber removed but, instead of being replanted with conifers as was usual, it was allowed to regenerate. The wood was given to the Trust in 1993, since when coppicing has been restarted in some areas, others being left to develop naturally into high forest. The rides are being cleared of scrub and widened and glades cut at the ride junctions.

More than 220 species of ferns and flowering plants have been found growing here. In spring, the woodland floor is carpeted with wood anemone, bluebell, primrose and many others, but there are some rarities too, such as violet helleborine, greater butterfly and bee orchids and the colourless bird's-nest orchid. Look for Solomon's seal, thought to be native here; it's a distinctive plant, with white flowers hanging from arching stems. And, unusually,

WILDLIFE FEATURES
❁ **Woodland ferns and flowers**
🦋 **Butterflies**

there is the cottony, straw-coloured carline thistle to be found in the open rides.

Birds are attracted by the structure of a wood, so that bird life is not at present diverse, but it should improve when the results of the new management become apparent. Fallow deer have been seen here.

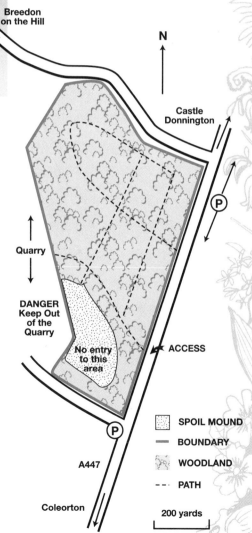

Breedon on the Hill

N

Castle Donnington

Quarry

DANGER Keep Out of the Quarry

No entry to this area

ACCESS

P

A447

Coleorton

SPOIL MOUND
BOUNDARY
WOODLAND
PATH

200 yards

167

ULVERSCROFT

LEICESTERSHIRE & RUTLAND WILDLIFE TRUST

Nearest town: Coalville
OS Map 129 SK 490124

148 acres (60 ha) of a whole range of habitats from hilltop to valley bottom - with mature planted woodland, recent plantation, overgrown heathland, scrubbed-up grassland and old meadowland, much of it lying within an SSSI. There is a nature trail.

Location and access: The reserve is about a third of a mile (0.5 km) east of Copt Oak in Charnwood Forest. Access is from Whitcroft's Lane, which leaves the B5350 Copt Oak to Loughborough road 300 yards north of Copt Oak. There is limited parking along Whitcroft's Lane adjacent to the reserve. Please stay on the footpath when crossing from Poultney Wood to Herbert's Meadow, and keep to the drier ground on the edge of the fields in spring and early summer when the grassland is sensitive to trampling. Cattle may be grazing in Herbert's Meadow.

This is a complex reserve to get to know, as the map shows, with a muddled history - Fox Covert for example had been farmland and Poultney Wood old woodland but both were replanted with conifers and hardwoods in the 1960s. There is quite a rich bird life in the oak and beech woodland with treecreeper, nuthatch, green and great spotted woodpeckers. The

areas of heathland and grassland were grazed until the 1950s but have become scrubbed up since with gorse, bramble and others, but tree pipit use the isolated trees here. Butterflies such as large and small skippers, small copper, common blue and meadow brown find nooky corners within the scrubbed up grassland.

The most interesting area botanically is Herbert's Meadow. The plants reflect the varied soils - fragrant orchid and devil's-bit scabious on alkaline, meadow vetchling on neutral and heath spotted orchid and tormentil on acid. The wet areas are flagged by marsh thistle in profusion.

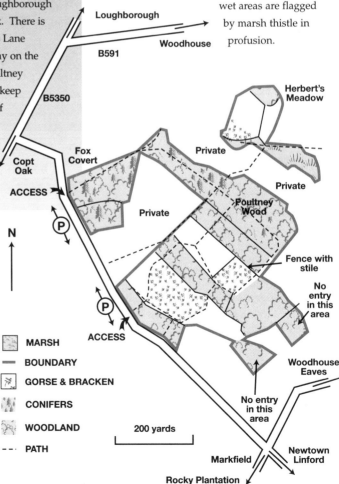

MARSH

BOUNDARY

GORSE & BRACKEN

CONIFERS

WOODLAND

PATH

200 yards

LEA MEADOWS

LEICESTERSHIRE & RUTLAND WILDLIFE TRUST

Nearest town: Leicester
OS Map 129 SK 506115

29 acres (12 ha) of ancient meadowland together with a stream. The reserve forms part of an SSSI.

Location and access: The reserve is about 6 miles north-west of Leicester. Coming from Leicester, drive through Anstey (just past the A46) and then Newtown Linford village and take the left-hand fork down Ulverscroft Lane, by Bradgate Woods woodyard. Carry on for 1.25 miles (2 km) along Ulverscroft Lane. The reserve entrance is opposite Blakeshay Farm by a public footpath sign. Cars should be parked on Ulverscroft Lane. The stile by a green gate is the entrance to the reserve. Carry on down the 'green lane' to a gate which forms part of a cattle pen. To the right is a stile into the meadows. There may be shooting on winter Saturdays on the reserve boundary, and May to October there may be cattle plus bull grazing.

Remnants of a medieval bank can be seen along the eastern boundary, there are signs of ridge and furrow in some areas and the mounds and hollows of an old settlement. They show that the soil has escaped deep ploughing and should be rich in flowers.

And so it is. The large undulating meadow

WILDLIFE FEATURES
❀ **Grassland flowers** ✺ **Butterflies**
✕ **Birdlife**

stretching from the entrance stile carries drifts of pignut, while later in the summer the medley of betony, harebell and devil's-bit scabious spreads out like a mauve quilt among the grasses, sedges and rushes. There are marshy places, another clue that it is 'unimproved', and in the wetter places you can expect to see common and heath spotted orchids, with great burnet one of the flowers flagging the drier areas.

Snipe, and kingfisher at the stream, are among the 76 species of birds seen here; the stream itself is marvellously clean and has crayfish, bullhead, minnow, brook lamprey and three-spined stickleback.

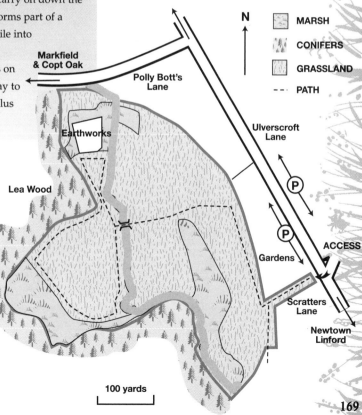

N

MARSH
CONIFERS
GRASSLAND
- - - PATH

Markfield & Copt Oak

Polly Bott's Lane

Ulverscroft Lane

Earthworks

Lea Wood

P

P

Gardens

ACCESS

Scratters Lane

Newtown Linford

100 yards

169

PRIOR'S COPPICE

LEICESTERSHIRE & RUTLAND WILDLIFE TRUST

Nearest town: Oakham

OS Map 141 SK 834052

A 71 acre (29 ha) ancient ash wood on a steep north-facing slope. An SSSI.

Location and access: The reserve is south of the village of Braunston, south-west of Oakham. From Braunston take the road towards Leighfield (Brooke). After a sharp left-hand bend at the top of the hill take the next right turn, signposted to Leighfield Lodge. Proceed another 800 or so yards and you will see the reserve car park on the right, just before a gate across the road.

This is an ancient fragment of the ash-maple and wych elm wildwood which once clothed Leicestershire before being cleared by the first farming communities. Difficult to clear because of the heavy clay soil and the steep slope, it was worked as coppice - and there are giant coppice stools to be seen here. Some are more than 3 yards across, and must be several hundreds of years old.

WILDLIFE FEATURES

❀ **Woodland flowers** 🦋 **Butterflies**
🦅**Woodland birds**

By regularly flooding the soil with light after the cut but not disturbing it, coppicing encourages woodland flowers. There are large populations of wood anemone, early purple orchid, wood forget-me-not and wood sorrel (with clover-like leaves which droop at night). Rarer, but also to be seen here, are violet helleborine, greater butterfly orchid and herb Paris.

More than 40 different birds nest in Prior's Coppice - nuthatch, blackcap, garden warbler and others - while the lesser-spotted woodpecker is often seen. Rare visitors have included the endangered stone curlew.

The sparrowhawk is also regularly seen darting down the rides. These rides, by the way, contain good areas of woodland grassland, increasingly difficult to find in the Midlands. They are mown each year and the cuttings removed.

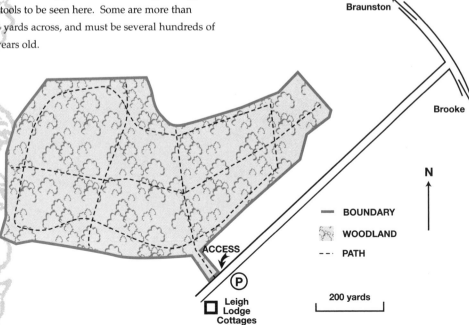

170

CRIBBS MEADOW

LEICESTERSHIRE & RUTLAND WILDLIFE TRUST

Nearest town: Melton Mowbray

OS Map 130 SK 899188

Two fields of 12 acres (5 ha), an SSSI consisting of old grassland and two ponds and a disused railway line.

Location and access: The reserve lies about 3 miles (5 km) east of the village of Wymondham on the Leicestershire-Lincolnshire border. Take the minor road east out of Wymondham towards South Witham and Thistleton. After 3 miles (5 km) turn right towards Thistleton and park on the right hand verge between the junction and the site of the former railway bridge. Access is by the gate to the north field, then over the railway line to the south field. Please close gates after use.

WILDLIFE FEATURES

- ❀ **Hay meadow flowers**
- 🦋 **Meadow butterflies**

These are enclosure fields, dating back to the 16th century, on boulder clay, a heavy 'blue' clay containing fragmented chalk and limestone. They offer a heritage of beautiful old meadow flowers. Notable in spring and early summer are the green-winged orchid and the common spotted-orchid and plentiful cowslip. Later in the year, bird's-foot-trefoil spreads across the meadows. Look also for the adder's-tongue fern, rather resembling cuckoo-pint. It can grow up to 8 inches tall.

Later in the year agrimony, great burnet (with dull red 'sausage' flower-heads) and yellow rattle are seen. When ripe, the seeds of this last do rattle in the dried bladder-like seed-head. It's a classic indicator of old hay meadows; its rattle a signal that the hay was ripe and ready for making.

This grassland is good for butterflies, and the scrubbed-up railway line provides good cover for yellowhammer and many different warblers.

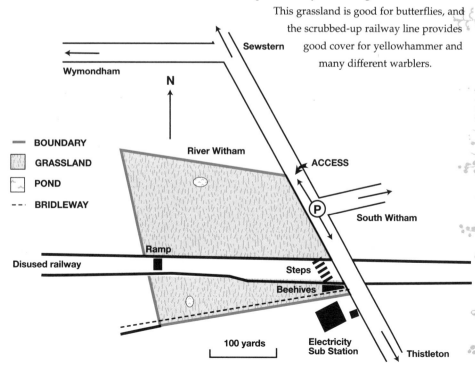

171

RUTLAND WATER

LEICESTERSHIRE & RUTLAND WILDLIFE TRUST

Nearest town: Oakham
OS Map 141 SK 880070

A narrow strip totalling 500 acres (202 ha) around the western end of Rutland Water. Two sections of the reserve are open to visitors. Lyndon has a visitor centre, wildlife trail and birdwatching hides, two with wheelchair access. Egleton has a birdwatching centre and 13 hides. The nature reserve and the reservoir itself are of SSSI status, a Ramsar site and Special Protection Area. Habitat improvements, which include the formation of three large lagoons at Egleton, continue.

Location and access: Egleton Reserve, reached via the A6003, is 1 mile south-east of Oakham. Follow the signs for the Birdwatching Centre. It is open daily 0900-1700 (1600 November-April).

Lyndon Reserve is on the south shore a mile east of the village of Manton and is open 1000am to 1600 weekends and bank holidays November-May and daily except Mondays May-October.

Visitor permits for both must be purchased, to help with some of the costs of creating and maintaining the reserves and their facilities. Dogs are not allowed at Egleton.

Rutland Water is one of the most important wildfowl sanctuaries in Britain. It is also home to the annual British Birdwatching Fair. Up to 21,500 wildfowl have

WILDLIFE FEATURES
🐦 Wildfowl, waders and other species

been recorded in a single day during the winter months, and in all more than 240 species have now been seen here. It regularly holds populations in excess of 10,000 birds and is of international importance for gadwall, for example. One of the initiatives concerns the osprey, one of the most popular, yet rare, birds of Britain. Rutland Water is on its migration route and there is a programme to introduce a breeding population (transferring young birds from the thriving population in Scotland). If successful, it will mean that the osprey will breed in England for the first time in 150 years. Rutland is also a prime site for tree sparrows.

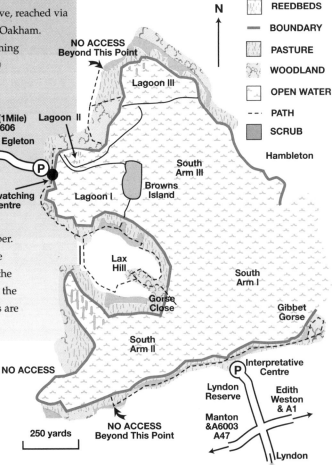

N

REEDBEDS
BOUNDARY
PASTURE
WOODLAND
OPEN WATER
PATH
SCRUB

NO ACCESS Beyond This Point

Lagoon III

Oakham (1Mile) A1 & A606

Lagoon II

Egleton

A6003

Birdwatching Centre

Lagoon I

Browns Island

South Arm III

Hambleton

Lax Hill

South Arm I

Gorse Close

South Arm II

Gibbet Gorse

NO ACCESS

Interpretative Centre

Lyndon Reserve

Edith Weston & A1

Manton &A6003 A47

250 yards

NO ACCESS Beyond This Point

Lyndon

ATTENBOROUGH GRAVEL PITS

NOTTINGHAMSHIRE WILDLIFE TRUST

Nearest town: Nottingham
OS Map 129 SK 513342

360 acres (146 ha) of flooded gravel pits recolonised over 50 years by marginal and wetland vegetation. It is an SSSI. There is a birdwatching hide and a nature trail. The reserve is owned by Butterley Aggregates and is jointly managed with the Trust.

Location and access: The reserve is at Beeston, at the southern edge of Nottingham, and the main car park (SK 516340) is signposted via Barton Lane, off the A6005 Nottingham to Long Eaton road.

Please keep to the footpaths. A key to the bird hide may be purchased (contact the wardens on site or the Trust office).

The gravel pits were worked between 1929 and 1967, and the process of recolonisation since these years has created a wide range of aquatic and waterside habitats. The water-linked insect life is interesting - damselflies and dragonflies include the four-spotted chaser and the magnificent southern and migrant hawkers. The great diving beetle is a fierce predator, attacking even small fish. There are also zebra and swan mussels here.

The reserve is best known for its birds, however. It is an important site for winter wildfowl and often holds a high

WILDLIFE FEATURES
%% **Dragonflies** 🐦 **Winter wildfowl**

proportion of Nottinghamshire's shoveler and diving ducks, with larger numbers of mallard and teal, and occasionally wigeon too. But what is exciting is that scarcer wildfowl such as sawbills and sea ducks are regularly seen; and cormorant frequently. The delta area attracts small numbers of a wide range of migrating waders (the bird hide is opposite the delta).

In summer, great crested grebe, little ringed plover and common tern nest, as well as quite a number of reed and sedge warblers, and you may also be able to hear the extraordinary call, a machine-like whirring, of the rarer grasshopper warbler from the bushes. It's a bird that rarely reveals itself.

Map

Legend:
- MARSH
- BOUNDARY
- WOODLAND
- POND
- PATH
- RAILWAY
- SCRUB
- HIDE

Labels: Beeston Pond, Meadow Lane, Delta Sanctuary, Long Lane, Works, Attenborough Lane, Attenborough Village, Station, Works Pond, A6055, Main Pond, River Trent, Church, Barton Lane, Church Pond, Tween Pond, Clifton Pond, 500 yards, N, P

173

BUNNY OLD WOOD

NOTTINGHAMSHIRE WILDLIFE TRUST

Nearest town: Nottingham
OS Map 129 SK 579283

38.5 acres (15.6 ha) of what was a very old coppiced wych elm wood, though it suffered greviously in the outbreaks of Dutch elm disease in the 70s onwards. The elms are suckering, but the aim is to restore the wood with other tree species as necessary.

Location and access: The wood is due south of Nottingham, about 4 miles (6.5 km) south of the A52 loop, south of Bunny on the A60 running towards Loughborough (just past the works and a farm on the right). The wood is to the left (east) of the road. There is limited parking on the road verge.

Alternatively, the reserve may be reached by footpath from the Silver Seal mine entrance (SK 584293) off Wysall Lane to the north of the reserve.

Visitors should keep to the rides and dogs should be kept under control.

This wood is an old one - confirmed by documents and indicators such as the fact that it edges a parish boundary and that there is plenty of dog's mercury and bluebell on the clayey soil that they find hard to colonise. It lies on a steep north-facing slope, and as well as the decimated wych elm coppice, there is ash coppice with oak and field maple as tall standard trees. Look also for wild cherry and

WILDLIFE FEATURES
✿ **Woodland flowers**
✗ **Woodland birds**

crab apple along the southern boundary, and wood anemone, yellow archangel and sanicle among the wild flowers.

About 30 species of birds have been seen here, including great and lesser spotted woodpeckers, and summer visitors include spotted flycatcher, blackcap and tree pipit. The hawfinch has also been seen - heavy headed with its formidable beak which helps it crack even cherry stones.

The butterflies to be seen include the white letter hairstreak which has a preference for wych elm as host plant for its eggs.

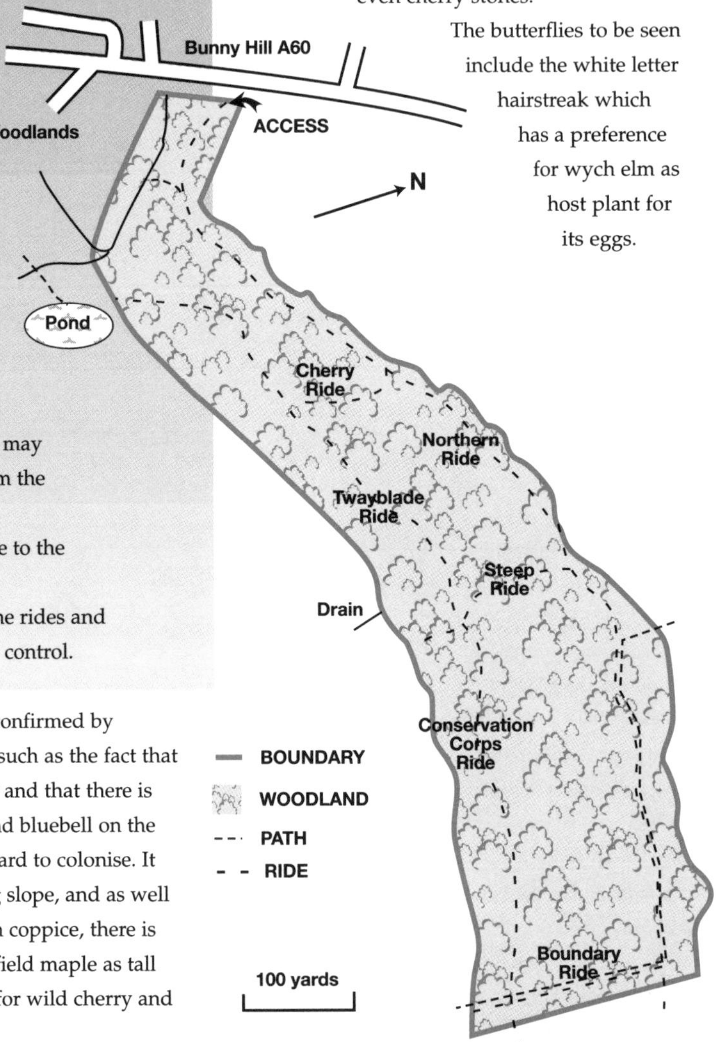

Map labels: Bunny Hill A60 · Woodlands · ACCESS · N · Pond · Cherry Ride · Northern Ride · Twayblade Ride · Steep Ride · Drain · Conservation Corps Ride · Boundary Ride

— BOUNDARY
WOODLAND
- - - PATH
- - RIDE

100 yards

DUKE'S WOOD

NOTTINGHAMSHIRE WILDLIFE TRUST

Nearest town: Newark
OS Map 120 SK 677603

20 acres (8 ha) of mixed deciduous woodland and an industrial archaeology site (the UK's first onshore oilfield), part of a larger SSSI, the remainder of which is private. There is a nature trail and information centre for guided parties.

Location and access: The wood is about 2 miles (3 km) south of Eakring which itself is (as the crow flies) about 9 miles north-westwards of Newark. From the A617 Newark-Mansfield road, about 8 miles from Newark, just past Kirklington, take the side road north towards Eakring. You pass Whip Ridding Farm on the right, then a stretch of woodland on the right. Shortly after this is White Stub Lane on the right, which leads to the reserve entrance. There is some car parking here, but if full please return to park on the main road, and not in the lane. Please keep to the marked trails and paths and keep dogs on leads.

This is a marvellous example of cooperation between industry and the Wildlife Trust. It combines an area of ancient and secondary woodland with what was the site of the UK's first onshore oilfield. Some of the 'nodding donkey' pumps have been restored and can be seen on the trail.

The wood, on a ridge of high ground, is dominated by oak, ash, hazel and birch. The shrub layer also contains guelder rose (flowering white with shiny red poisonous berries), dogwood (flowering white, black berries) and wild privet (white blossom, shiny black berries) - these all like a rather limy soil.

WILDLIFE FEATURES
- Woodland birds
- Woodland flowers

There are usually a good many spring and early summer flowers - bluebell, primrose, wood anemone, yellow archangel among them - and quite a range of butterflies.

And among the songbirds you may hear the nightingale: it has nested in the area for some years but this is the northern edge of its range, so that it cannot be guaranteed.

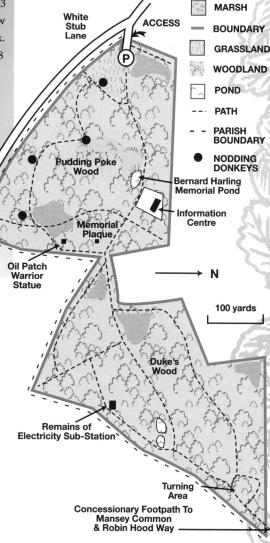

White Stub Lane

ACCESS

P

To Nut Wood

Pudding Poke Wood

Bernard Harling Memorial Pond

Information Centre

Memorial Plaque

Oil Patch Warrior Statue

N

100 yards

Duke's Wood

Remains of Electricity Sub-Station

Turning Area

Concessionary Footpath To Mansey Common & Robin Hood Way

MARSH
BOUNDARY
GRASSLAND
WOODLAND
POND
PATH
PARISH BOUNDARY
NODDING DONKEYS

TRESWELL WOOD

NOTTINGHAMSHIRE WILDLIFE TRUST

Nearest town: Retford
OS Map 120 SK 762798

118 acres (48 ha) of woodland, one of the best examples of a mixed ash, oak and maple wood to be found in Nottinghamshire, and an SSSI. It has ponds of interest. There is a nature trail.

Location and access: The wood is south of the (northerly) minor road between the villages of Grove and Treswell, about 3 miles east of Retford. Leave Retford for North Leverton, turn right (south) towards Grove and then left (east) towards Treswell on Wood Lane. The main entrance gate and car park are about half way along the wood, just before a farm on the left.

Sporting rights are held by the previous owners who shoot occasionally in winter, normally on weekdays.

Treswell Wood was mentioned in the Domesday Book and has probably covered much the same area ever since. It was worked of course, in the coppice-with-standards tradition, until this century when there have also been major fellings, leaving few tall oaks. The use of heavy machinery instead of horses has also damaged the drainage, leading to water-logging at certain times.

So, the intention is to restore the oak-ash woodland, coppicing some areas while letting others develop without intervention.

WILDLIFE FEATURES
❀ **Woodland flowers**
✕ **Woodland birds**

Plants and shrubs to look for include species usually found only in old woodland; they include wild service tree (to the right of trail marker post 8, for example) - and by post 9 are some wych elm which have survived Dutch elm disease. Among the plants of old woodland are dog's mercury, herb Paris with its quartet of leaves (sometimes difficult to pick out among the former) and early purple orchid. And there are yellow flag and marsh marigold by the new ponds - both are handsome flowers.

The birdlife is superb, with woodcock, the two spotted woodpeckers and a host of other species, (a great grey shrike was ringed here in 1974 and a red-breasted flycatcher in 1993).

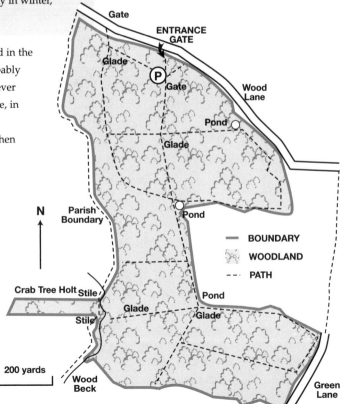

176

Northern England

With its vast areas of open countryside, from the peaks of the Lake District to the wild Northumberland coast, there are many spectacular places to see wildlife in northern England. And even in some of the most heavily industrialised places, havens for wildlife still survive, such as around the Tees estuary, where a colony of seals lives at the river mouth. Further up the valley in Upper Teesdale is the spectacular High Force waterfall, the highest in England. The Durham Wildlife Trust's Bowlees visitor centre nearby explains the surrounding landscape, famous for arctic-alpine plants and invertebrates. Much of Cumbria and Yorkshire are protected as National Parks, but beyond those boundaries, Wildlife Trusts are caring for some vital habitats. At South Walney at the tip of Walney Island on Cumbria's coast, are huge breeding colonies of lesser black-backed and herring gulls, while on the Yorkshire coast, Spurn is a narrow sand and shingle spit stretching for 3.5 miles into the Humber estuary, and one of Europe's finest places for seeing migrant birds.

This region includes four reserves on the Isle of Man in the middle of the Irish sea, which has a considerable diversity of unspoilt habitat.

NORTHERN ENGLAND

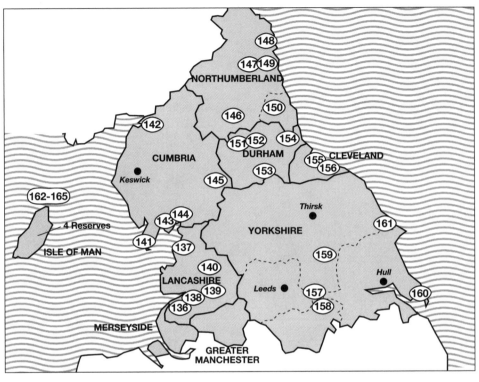

MERE SANDS WOOD

LANCASHIRE WILDLIFE TRUST

Nearest towns: Ormskirk/Southport
OS Map 108 SD 447157

104 acres (42 ha) of deciduous (with some
conifer) woodland enclosing lakes created by
sand extraction. It is an SSSI. There are a visitor
centre, seven bird-watching hides (two with
wheelchair access), nature trails, wheelchair
access paths and a site warden.

Location and access: Rufford is about 4.5 miles
north of Ormskirk and the reserve is 0.5 mile
west of Rufford, south of the B5246, the
Southport road. A donation is requested for
parking.

Geologically this is a text-book reserve with
layers of sand and peat charting changes to the
local coastline since the last Ice Age. It is an SSSI
for this reason. It has been dug for sand in
some areas, but from an early stage, extraction
was planned to leave a site suitably landscaped
for development as a nature reserve, with belts

WILDLIFE FEATURES
 Wildfowl and waders
 Red squirrel

of woodland left undisturbed and shallow-
edged lakes and marsh and dry heath created.

The mature woodland is mainly birch with
some oak, but there is also a Scots pine
plantation which is where the red squirrels are
seen. There was a problem with rampaging
rhododendron, planted last century, but much
has been removed to allow native flowers to
grow. Other flowers such as common spotted,
early and southern marsh orchid, bee orchid,
marsh helleborine, yellow bartsia and golden
dock, are seen in areas refilled after sand
digging.

The lakes have reedbeds in places and it is
the water birds which are the main wildlife
interest. Wintering wildfowl include teal,
gadwall, goldeneye, pochard, wigeon and
shoveler, while nesting birds include grebes,
tufted duck, mallard, gadwall, shelduck and
ruddy duck. The little ringed plover is one of
the waders. There are also many woodland
birds, including woodcock.

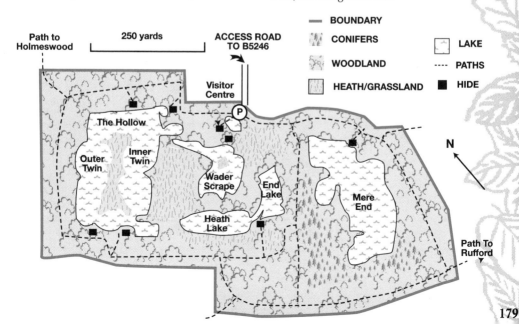

WARTON CRAG

LANCASHIRE WILDLIFE TRUST

Nearest town: Carnforth
OS Map 97 SD 493728

85 acres (35 ha) of the summit and wooded eastern slopes of a limestone hill, with a Local Nature Reserve and RSPB land alongside. Most of the area is an SSSI.

Location and access: The hill is about 1 mile north of Carnforth. From Carnforth take the unclassified road for Warton (alternatively go north up the A6 and then turn off left for Warton). In the village there is parking in a disused quarry about 100 yards along Crag Road from its junction with Main Street at the Black Bull inn near the church. Follow the concessionary path onto the Crag, heading north to Potts Wood through the LNR. (There is also a second car park 600 yards further along Crag Road.)

Warton Crag is a heady jumble of habitats – bare limestone, sparse grassland dotted with flowers, scrub, grown-up coppice and woodland – fascinating for anyone interested in

WILDLIFE FEATURES
✿ Woodland flowers and butterflies
🐿 Red squirrel

wild flowers. Even on almost bare rock, yellow rockrose and purple mats of thyme are a fine sight in summer. Low they may be, but they can have roots a yard deep into cracks in the rock, remaining green while grasses around wither from drought. April and May are spectacular for the woodlands, the ground carpeted with a mosaic of wood anemone, bluebell, primrose, early purple orchid and others. Strickland Wood is good for ferns.

The scrub has spindle, dogwood and wild privet amongst others shrubs (easier to identify by their autumn berries maybe).

The area is also notable for its butterflies - fritillaries, northern brown argus, dingy skipper and green hairstreak among them. There are many warblers in early summer - there are also woodpeckers - and in winter fieldfare, redwing and occasionally waxwing.

The red squirrels are a southern outpost of the Lake District tribe. There are some greys, but they are probably based outside the reserve.

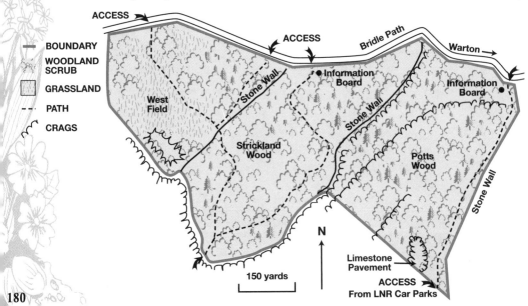

BOUNDARY
WOODLAND SCRUB
GRASSLAND
PATH
CRAGS

ACCESS
ACCESS
Bridle Path
Warton →
Information Board
Information Board
West Field
Stone Wall
Strickland Wood
Stone Wall
Potts Wood
Stone Wall
N
Limestone Pavement
150 yards
ACCESS
From LNR Car Parks

CUERDEN VALLEY PARK

LANCASHIRE WILDLIFE TRUST

Nearest towns: Leyland/Bamber Bridge
OS Map 102 SD 565238

650 acres (240 ha) along the valley of the River Lostock, with woods, grasslands, ponds and river, managed by the Wildlife Trust on behalf of The Cuerden Valley Park Trust. There is a ranger service and guided walks and conservation activities are organised.

Location and access: Cuerden Valley Park is south of Preston reached via the A6 and with (as the map shows) easy access from Junctions 28 and 29 on the M6 and from Junctions 8 and 9 on the M61. There are access routes for the disabled. An electric scooter is available for the less able.

The park stretches along the valley of the River Lostock as it meanders from Whittle-le-Woods

WILDLIFE FEATURES
Wildfowl and other birdlife
Woodland flowers

to Bamber Bridge. About half the land is let for farming, mainly grazing. Apart from the river there is an artificial lake stocked for fishing and several ponds. Great crested grebe, heron, mallard and moorhen are among the birds nesting here and coot and kingfisher are frequently seen. (And the dipper can sometimes be seen along the river.)

There is a variety of small broadleaved and mixed woodlands which have been extended by mainly broadleaved planting. Most woods have carpets of bluebell in the spring, together with wood sorrel and other woodland plants. The meadows are good for butterflies. A range of birds is commonly seen, including sparrow-hawk, great spotted woodpecker, nuthatch, treecreeper, long-tailed tit and goldcrest.

Further variety is provided by the willow-alder plantings by the river and the grassland areas - apart from the picnic areas, grass is cut as a hay crop to encourage wild flowers and butterflies.

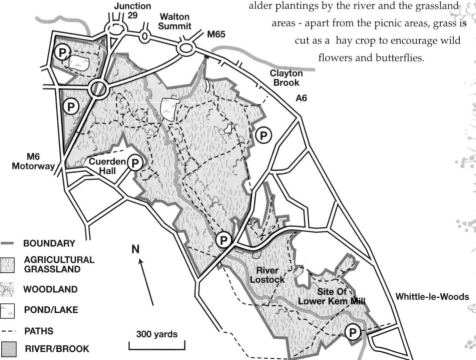

BOUNDARY

AGRICULTURAL GRASSLAND

WOODLAND

POND/LAKE

PATHS

RIVER/BROOK

N

300 yards

Junction 29
Walton Summit
M65
Clayton Brook
A6
M6 Motorway
Cuerden Hall
River Lostock
Site Of Lower Kem Mill
Whittle-le-Woods

FOXHILL BANK

LANCASHIRE WILDLIFE TRUST

Nearest town: Oswaldtwistle
OS Map 103 SD 740278

A 19 acre (8 ha) valley reserve, an urban site with a variety of habitats.

Location and access: The reserve is close to the centre of Oswaldtwistle, 0.5 mile south-west of the railway station in the valley of Tinker Brook. From the main road (Union Road) turn down Mill Hill opposite the war memorial. There is parking for three cars at a time. The main access is here. There is wheelchair access. Please keep dogs on a lead.

Hidden away in a shallow valley, this reserve has historic ties with local industry. The two lodges (pools) were constructed as reservoirs for a fabric dye and print factory. Having fallen into disuse, major work was needed to convert the concrete-sided tanks into something more welcoming to wildlife. Plants have now colonised, creating a mosaic of open water, reedbeds with reedmace ('bulrush') and rushes. This, together with the undisturbed scrub, offers secluded nest sites for coot, moorhen, tufted duck, little grebe, mallard and many warblers.

WILDLIFE FEATURES
Woodland birds

The banks of the brook are another habitat, with mosses and ferns. In fact the real delight of this reserve is the mixture of habitats in such a small area. Together with the wetland there is a small wood of sycamore and ash between the brook and Foxhill Bank Lodge.

The birdlife reflects this diversity - birds respond to the structure of a site. So there's the chance of seeing great spotted woodpecker, siskin, reed bunting, blackcap and maybe heron in winter.

ACCESS

ACCESS

ACCESS

ACCESS

Playing Fields

Foxhill Bank Lodge

Weir Stream Section

N

ACCESS

Tinker Brook

Heart Lodge

ACCESS

ACCESS

Oswaldtwistle Union Road

SCRUB

SCRUB & WETLAND HABITATS

BOUNDARY

WOODLAND

OPEN WATER

PATH

100 yards

CROSS HILL QUARRY

LANCASHIRE WILDLIFE TRUST

Nearest town: Clitheroe
OS Map 103 SD 745434

17 acres (7 ha) of abandoned limestone quarry with some older woodland. It is a Local Nature Reserve.

Location and access: The quarry is just north of Clitheroe along the Ribble Way, and is continuous with Brungerley Park. Approach from Waddington Road (through Brungerley Park) or from West Bradford Road (opposite Castle Cement works). There is parking at the east end of Pimlico Road. Climbing is forbidden without written permission from the Wildlife Trust.

Note: another reserve, Salthill Quarry, can also be visited nearby, a mile north-east of the town at OS 758426.

Cross Hill was abandoned as a working quarry in the early 1900s, since when it has become an exceptional wildlife refuge. Once abandoned, the thin soils became colonised by a natural succession evolving from flower-rich grassland to scrub to woodland.

The main quarry has a fine display of wild flowers in June - the mounds of spoil are lime-rich and fairy flax and lady's bedstraw can be seen alongside wild thyme and marjoram. At the eastern end of the reserve, however, further quarrying was infilled during the 1970s and the heavy clay used as capping underpins a damp grassland.

WILDLIFE FEATURES
✘ **Birdlife**
✿ **Limestone flowers**

The scrub casts dense shade, with ivy covering the ditches and mounds. However bluebell, wood anemone, wood sanicle and woodruff can be seen in the more open, undisturbed western woods towards Brungerley Park; this area was never quarried.

The flower-rich grasslands of the main quarry attract a number of butterflies - the common blue, orange tip and meadow brown are often seen. As for the birds, summer warblers sing here and grey wagtail and sand martin are seen from April onwards. Heron fish the river and the kingfisher is seen throughout the year.

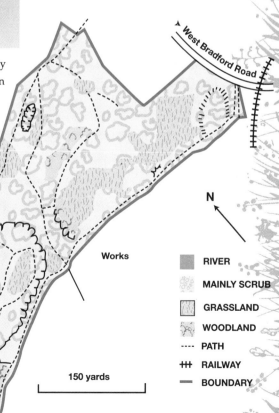

Ribble Way

River Ribble

West Bradford Road

Works

N

150 yards

RIVER
MAINLY SCRUB
GRASSLAND
WOODLAND
---- PATH
╫ RAILWAY
— BOUNDARY

183

SOUTH WALNEY

CUMBRIA WILDLIFE TRUST

Nearest town: Barrow in Furness

OS Map 96 SD 215620

A coastal reserve of sand dunes, mudflats, saltmarsh and freshwater marsh totalling 325 acres (130 ha). There are waymarked trails and six bird-watching hides, one with wheelchair access. There is also a summer sales kiosk; toilets (suitable for the disabled) are near the car park.

Location and access: The reserve is at the southern tip of Walney Island, 6 miles (10 km) south of Barrow. Follow the A590 to Barrow and cross Jubilee Bridge onto Walney Island. Turn left immediately and follow Ocean Road for 0.75 mile. Turn left onto Carr Lane and follow the road for 4 miles, passing Biggar village. An unmetalled road beginning near the entrance to South End caravan site leads to the reserve car park after one mile.

The reserve is open 1000-1700 (1600 winter) all days except Mondays (bank holidays excepted). Dogs are only allowed between September and March, and must be kept on a lead.

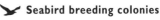

WILDLIFE FEATURES

Seabird breeding colonies

Sand dunes, mudflats, saltmarsh, freshwater marsh and brackish pools - this reserve has them all. The waymarked trails offer a passport to them, and they each have their own distinct character. The blue trail for example passes the oyster farm to fresh and salt pools which attract many waders and duck, including red-breasted merganser and goldeneye; and great black-backed gulls nest on the encircling shingle ridges. The green trail, on the other hand, leads through the dunes to a hide overlooking Morecambe Bay. Four species of tern may be seen, while grey seals are regular visitors offshore and occasionally haul out.

This reserve is also noted for its massive populations of breeding lesser black-backed and herring gulls (maybe 30,000 pairs in all) as well as a large colony of eider duck - their most southerly breeding location in Britain.

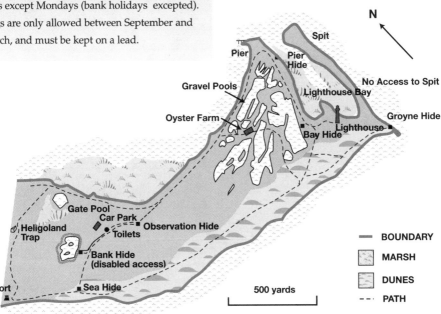

DRUMBURGH NATIONAL NATURE RESERVE

CUMBRIA WILDLIFE TRUST

Nearest town: Carlisle
OS Map 85 NY 256590

A peatbog of about 220 acres (90 ha) together with areas of heath.
It is a National Nature Reserve.

Location and access: The reserve is immediately south of the village of Drumburgh, a village about 8 miles (13 km) north-west of Carlisle reached via the B5307. Leave the village on the narrow road next to the post office. After about 200 yards, the road becomes a track. Cars may be parked on the verges here. The main part of the reserve is 0.75 mile further on, but if you do continue along the track by car please make sure that you do not obstruct access when you park - the track is in frequent use. Dogs must be controlled on the reserve.

WILDLIFE FEATURES
❋ **Peatbog, now rare**

This site is one of the best and least damaged bogs in England. Bogs create themselves only very slowly and they remain a fragile habitat. Together with the sphagnum moss (in fact there are 13 different species of sphagnum moss to be found here, each adapted to its own 'micro-habitat') grows the small sundew, which boosts its mineral intake by absorbing tiny insects trapped on its sticky hairs. However, in drier areas, heathers grow, and sometimes tussocks of purple moor grass.

There is a surprising variety of animal life to be seen in what are on the face of it poor conditions. Dragonflies are fairly common, and emperor and drinker moths and large heath butterflies are typical of these surroundings. Adders and lizards might be seen. Waders such as curlew and redshank nest here, while sparrowhawk and short-eared owl may be seen hunting.

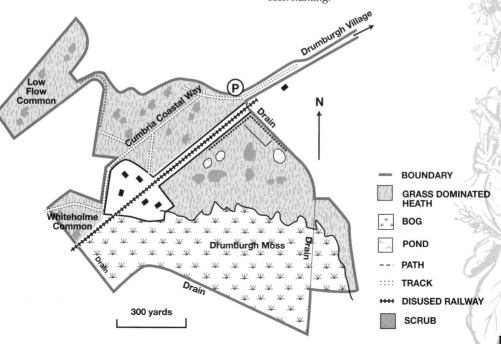

BOUNDARY
GRASS DOMINATED HEATH
BOG
POND
PATH
TRACK
DISUSED RAILWAY
SCRUB

300 yards

185

BROWN ROBIN

CUMBRIA WILDLIFE TRUST

Nearest town: Grange over Sands
OS Map 97 SD 415790

67 acres (26 ha) of old woodlands and pasture.
There is a waymarked trail.

Location and access: The reserve lies on the edge
of Grange. From the A590 there is access via the
B5271 and the B5277. There is a small lay-by for
parking on the B5271 and steps up to the reserve.
Alternatively there is pedestrian access from the
south past Blawith Farm, as the map shows.
Dogs must be kept on leads at all times.

Parts of this woodland are ancient and these
areas are probably marked by the yew and ash
trees which naturally adopt limy soil (the rock
here is limestone). Spindle also grows here
(with pink berries in autumn), and look for the
unusual spurge laurel, a waist-high shrub with
glossy rhododendron-like leaves gathered at the
tips of the shoots. It has green flowers in
spring. There are good spreads of bluebell
together with wood anemone, primrose and
wild garlic.

Some of the pasture is also colourful with
flowers - have a look especially at Merlewood
Bank. Here the underlying limestone and thin
soil deter rampant grasses, and flowers such as
white pignut (a fine member of the cow parsley
clan) and yellow rockrose can flourish. The
rabbits also help low plants by keeping the
grass short. The Top Fields are rather similar
except that they have a thicker soil (left by
glaciers) which allows oxeye daisy, knapweed
and other flowers to thrive here. Park Fields,
however, have been artificially fertilised (the
nettles are one sign of this), and as a result there
aren't so many different flowers.

WILDLIFE FEATURES
✿ **Wild flowers**

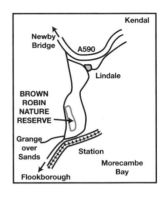

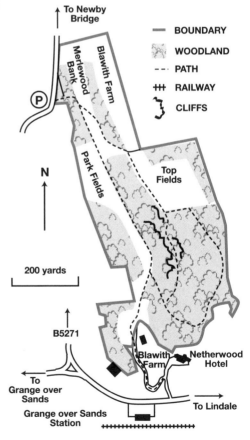

LATTERBARROW

CUMBRIA WILDLIFE TRUST

Nearest town: Kendal
OS Map 97 SD 440828

10 acres (4 ha) of limestone grassland, woodland and scrub.

Location and access: Latterbarrow lies just off the A590 between Grange over Sands and Kendal. Take the turning signposted Witherslack and Halecat (about 8 miles south of Kendal). Pass the Derby Arms and turn left immediately onto the old A590 (marked as a dead-end). The reserve entrance lies about 300 yards along the old road where a bridleway is signposted to the right. Dogs should be on leads when ponies or other livestock are grazing.

Two hundred species of wild flowers and ferns have been recorded here, an impressive total for such a small site. The rock is limestone and the soil is mostly very thin; there are even small areas of exposed limestone 'pavement' to be seen. This thin limy soil has a very characteristic plant tally. In spring early purple orchid and cowslip cover the central open area while violets thrive in the light shade of the woodland edge. In high summer rockrose, salad burnet and kidney vetch cluster around the rocky outcrops. It's interesting that wild thyme grows here, as it prefers slightly acid soils but you'll see that it grows on the tops of the old anthills, where the soil is dry and slightly acid! And there is more flower interest besides.

The reserve is also noted for its butterflies, from the yellow brimstone in spring (buckthorn is the host plant

WILDLIFE FEATURES
❀ **Limestone flowers and butterflies**

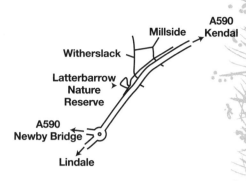

on which it lays its eggs and this grows on Latterbarrow) to two species of fritillary - the high brown and the pearl-bordered - which are attracted to lay their eggs on the violets. They are seen flying between May and July. The grayling is another inhabitant, often seen resting on the ground, angling its wings to the sun to control its body temperature.

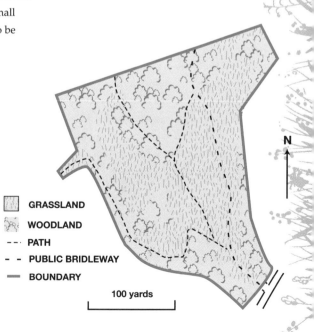

▨	GRASSLAND
▨	WOODLAND
---	PATH
- -	PUBLIC BRIDLEWAY
▬	BOUNDARY

100 yards

SMARDALE GILL

CUMBRIA WILDLIFE TRUST

Nearest town: Kirkby Stephen
OS Map 91 NY 738083

The reserve is about 100 acres (40 ha) in size, a 3.3 mile (5 km) length of disused railway line, with, at the northern end, the steep wooded slopes of the gill. The gill is an SSSI and NNR.

Location and access: Smardale is signposted off the A685 about 1 mile south of Kirkby Stephen and immediately before the junction with the A683 to Sedbergh. Continue following the signs to Smardale. Cross the railway, then the disused railway, and turn left towards the line again. There is a large car park here.

For access from the south, park at Newbiggin and cross the A685 where a small lane turns off towards Friars Bottom Farm; take the left hand fork and follow the footpath to the line.

The railway line is open, but a permit is needed for other areas. Dogs should be kept on short leads.

When the railway was in use, its banks would have been kept clear, but since it closed down in the 1960s birch, willow and hazel have invaded, quite thickly in places. The Wildlife Trust has started coppicing here, to create a mosaic of wooded and open grassy banks. But the woodland seen beyond this on either side is old coppice judging by the multi-stemmed trees, with bluebell, primrose and wild garlic in spring, and a good many ferns. Look out for red squirrels in these woods and redstart and pied flycatcher among the summer birds. Buzzard and

WILDLIFE FEATURES
❀ Wild flowers and butterflies

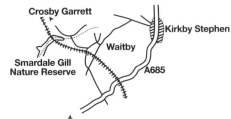

sparrowhawk may be seen all year round.

It's interesting that most of the grassland is dominated by blue moor grass, found only on limestone. This underlying rock flavour is also reflected in the rockrose, the purple-crimson bloody cranesbill and other flowers.

There are butterflies too - look for the Scotch argus, now rare in England, a brown butterfly (on the wing in August) with a slow fluttering flight. It has quite strong wing 'eyespots'. Its host plant is the moor grass.

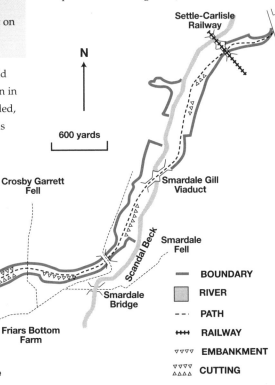

▬	**BOUNDARY**
▨	**RIVER**
- - -	**PATH**
╋╋╋	**RAILWAY**
▽▽▽▽	**EMBANKMENT**
△△△△	**CUTTING**

BRIARWOOD BANKS

NORTHUMBERLAND WILDLIFE TRUST

Nearest town: Hexham
OS Maps 86/87 NY 791620

47 acres (19 ha) of ancient woodland, an SSSI.
There is an interpretation board.

Location and access: The reserve is 3 miles
(5 km) south-west of Haydon Bridge (which is
6 miles west of Hexham on the A69). It is at the
meeting of the Kingswood Burn with the River
Allen, near Plankey Mill. There is parking at
Plankey Mill, where the farmer may make a
charge, and access on foot is across a narrow
suspension bridge. Alternatively there is a
National Trust car park at Allenbanks a mile
downstream. The nearest picnic site and toilets
are at this NT car park.

Please keep to the paths to protect the flowers.

This is one of the best areas of ancient
woodland in the county, a marvellous wood to
explore, with rock outcrops and tumbling
streams - note that the paths are steep and fairly
strenuous and the route may be impassable at
the Kingswood Burn waterfall after heavy rain.

There is a variety of trees, with ash
dominating some of the ground while oak and
birch are common where the soil is more acid.
Alder fringes the stream and grows in the
wetter areas. The many dead trees (which
attract the great spotted woodpecker and other
hole nesting birds) are wych elms, killed by the
last outbreak of Dutch elm disease. There is also
yew, holly and beech and old hazel coppice. All
this means a good birdlife - including the wood
warbler and pied flycatcher - the result of the
varied structure of the woodland rather than
the actual species of trees.

The woodland floor has many typical flowers;

WILDLIFE FEATURES
✿ Woodland flowers
🐿 Red squirrel   ✕ Woodland birds

look out for the reddish flowers of wood
cranesbill and, in shaded areas, the
honey-coloured bird's nest orchid - it has no
green leaves, but gains nourishment solely from
decaying mould.

And look out for red squirrels, especially in
autumn, when the bright chestnut coat of
summer is becoming chocolate brown, with the
back perhaps greyish in colour. Soon after
dawn is a good time of day to spot them!

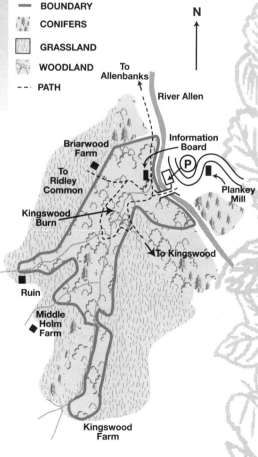

500 yards

HARBOTTLE CRAGS

NORTHUMBERLAND WILDLIFE TRUST

Nearest town: Alnwick
OS Map 80 NT 922040

366 acres (148 ha) of open moorland, part of a lough (lake) and some bog land. Part of the Harbottle Moors SSSI, managed in partnership with the Forestry Commission.

Location and access: Harbottle village is about (20 miles) 32 km south-west of Alnwick via the B6341. Travel west through the village and on for a while to park in the Forestry Enterprise car park on the left of the road. There is a picnic area here. A footpath from the north-eastern corner leads uphill and onto the reserve through a wicket gate. The army's red flag normally flying here does not apply to the reserve, but do not cross the western boundary fence onto the range. You should also remain in the Drake Stone area if grouse shooting is in progress; the shooting season is August 12th - December 12th, but not Sundays.

Here you have great sweeps of heather and mossy bog broken by riven sandstone outcrops which were, in the Drake Stone area, scratched and polished by the glaciers of the last Ice Age. When that came to an end, these hills became wooded with oak and birch but firing and grazing destroyed the tree cover and in time heather moor took its place. However, the cliff gullies still shelter one or two plants from that earlier time. Look for chickweed wintergreen for example, a charmer with a white starlike flower held above a whorl of leaves (it flowers June-July).

The moorland has the usual heathers, bilberry and other familiars, the bog areas can be a vivid green and are usually flagged by cotton grass. Here, in close up, sundews, sprawling cranberry

WILDLIFE FEATURES
🐾 Crags and outcrops and glorious sweeps of moorland

and orchids grow. Beware the trembling bog at the eastern end of the lough - it is a 'schwingmoor' developed over a deep pool, but in any event bogland should not be walked on, it is a very fragile habitat.

Apart from the grouse and other moorland birds, look out for the fast flying emperor moth, its 6 cm span wings carry handsome eyespots; it is related to the silk moth.

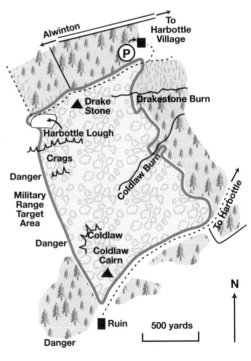

ARNOLD MEMORIAL RESERVE

NORTHUMBERLAND WILDLIFE TRUST

Nearest town: Alnwick
OS Map 81 NU 255197

A 3 acre (1.2 ha) reserve with woodland and scrub and with quarry faces and quarry spoil. There are interpretation boards and an information centre at the entrance, open in summer.

Location and access: The reserve is south-west of Craster village. There is a car park in the disused quarry besides the reserve with picnic area and toilets (including disabled). Entry is from the car park access road, from beside the interpretation board.

The reserve is within an outcrop of the Whin Sill, a hard lava rock which has been quarried for whinstone. Since quarrying ended, the rock faces and spoil heaps have been colonised by woodland and scrub of sycamore, ash, elm, Scots pine together with bramble, honeysuckle and gorse. There are also willows fringing the stream.

Below the rock crags grow bluebell, primrose, foxglove and wood sage and many other wild flowers.

This is one of the few areas of 'wild' semi-natural woodland and scrub to be found along this stretch of coast. It is a pit stop for migrating birds - an open invitation to rest and feed. Among the rarities that have been seen here have been wryneck,

WILDLIFE FEATURES
❀ **Woodland flowers**
✖ **Resident and migrant birds**

icterine and barred warblers, red-breasted flycatcher and bluethroat. The last is a charming relative of the wheatear, complete with bold eye stripe and (obviously) with a blue throat. The reserve is also a moulting refuge for the lesser redpoll.

And of course it offers nesting sites - sedge and willow warblers, chiffchaff and blackcap nest here. The reserve can be alive with birdsong.

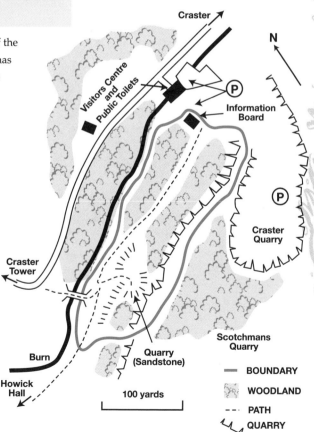

HAUXLEY

NORTHUMBERLAND WILDLIFE TRUST

Nearest town: Alnwick
OS Map 81 NU 285023

A 79 acre (32 ha) reserve with a freshwater lake with islands and some surrounding land, a former open-cast coal mine. There is a visitor's centre with toilets (suitable for the disabled) and 5 bird-watching hides, one suitable for wheelchairs. Wardens are on site at most times.

Location and access: The reserve is at Hauxley, about 8 miles (13 km) south-east of Alnwick on the A1068. The map gives details of location. Enter by the track which leaves the minor road between Low and High Hauxley, sharing access with the caravan site.

This is a superb example of forward-planned conservation. The site was an open-cast coal mine, which was landscaped to the Trust's specifications by the National Coal Board, to create a lake with islands.

Trees have been planted around the boundary and near the hides. There are five of these in all, but please note that there is no access between Hide No 5 and Ponteland Hide.

There are reedbeds in some areas, their birdlife adding further to the already impressive lists of waders, seabirds and wildfowl to be seen here.

WILDLIFE FEATURES
- **Wildfowl, waders and terns**
- **Summer flowers**

The roseate tern is just one example - the most graceful of the tern tribe, with long tail streamers which single it out (the rosy breast is only seen briefly during breeding). It is one of Britain's rarest nesting seabirds, a scarce visitor.

There is also wild flower interest - look for kidney vetch with rather silky stems and leaves and the blue-flowered viper's bugloss. The bloody cranesbill also grows here, one of our most handsome wild flowers, a bushy plant with purple-crimson flowers in July and August.

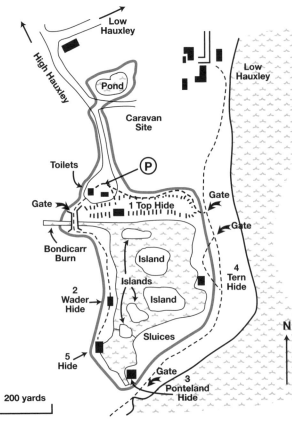

BOUNDARY

WATER

PATH

200 yards

WALLSEND SWALLOW POND

NORTHUMBERLAND WILDLIFE TRUST

Nearest town: Newcastle
OS Map 88 NZ 301693

A 35 acre (14 ha) reserve with a shallow pool formed by flooded mining subsidence and woodland. A Local Nature Reserve, it is part of the Rising Sun Country Park. There is one birdwatching hide, adapted for wheelchair use. There are also pond dipping platforms.

Location and access: The reserve is about half way between Gosforth and Whitley Bay, in the Rising Sun Country Park south of the A191. There is parking at the Rising Sun Centre, and the picnic area and toilets are at the centre.

The reserve contains a shallow lowland pool, formed as a result of mining subsidence from the Rising Sun colliery. The pool is of fairly recent origin, but it does now have stands of

WILDLIFE FEATURES
🐦 Wintering and migrating wildfowl and waders

yellow flag iris, branched bur-reed (a rather handsome tall erect plant) and greater reedmace around the water margin. This last is usually called the bulrush - wrongly, as the bulrush is a separate species. However, the Victorian artist Alma-Tadema showed the reedmace in his famous painting 'Moses in the Bulrushes' - and the name has stuck!

There are also areas of carr (wet marginal woodland) together with grassland and plantation woodland. The plantation was part of the reclamation scheme and contains a mixture of Corsican pine, ash, alder, Swedish whitebeam and sycamore. There are plans to plant in more native species, and to create clearings to encourage ground-level variety.

Wintering and migrating birds are the main interest of the reserve - passage waders include redshank and greenshank and among the winter wildfowl are teal and whooper swan (with a really loud trumpeting call - hence its name). Little grebe, mute swan, coot and mallard all nest here.

Both hides give excellent views. And also keep an eye out for brown hare - they are frequently seen.

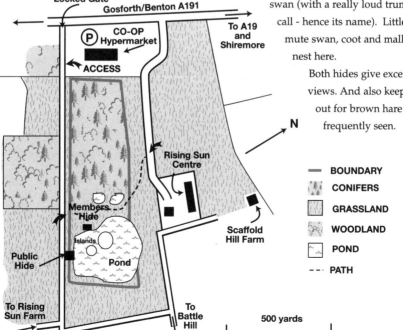

BOUNDARY

CONIFERS

GRASSLAND

WOODLAND

POND

PATH

500 yards

BOWLEES VISITOR CENTRE

DURHAM WILDLIFE TRUST

Nearest town: Middleton in Teesdale
OS Map 93 NY 907282

A visitor centre open 1 April - 31 October
1030 - 1700 all week 1 November - 31 March
1100 - 1600 Sat & Sun, with local walks.

Location and access: The centre is about 12 miles as the crow flies, north-west of Barnard Castle. It is reached by the B6277 from Barnard Castle to Alston. The centre is well signposted 0.75 mile west of the village of Newbiggin. There is a free Durham CC car park.

The centre demonstrates the natural history of Teesdale with superb two- and three-dimensional displays on the geology, wild flowers, birds, trees and the wildlife of the River Tees.

FEATURES
Moorland and waterfall walks

Having visited the centre, take the opportunity to see the area for yourself. There are interesting walks from the centre. Gibson's Cave is just a third of a mile away and many streamside birds, including the dipper and wagtail, can be seen along the nature trail. Low Force waterfall, also known as Salmon Leap, is close by. Middleton is an easy 4 mile walk downstream and High Force is 2 miles upstream from Low Force. Alternatively, you can drive on to park near High Force. There is a small entry fee to the waterfall which has been charged since 1897!

High Force is by far the most dramatic waterfall in Britain with peat-stained water tossed with white foam tumbling in a wooded gorge like a natural theatre. One of the rock layers exposed here is the Whin Sill, a columnar volcanic intrusion.

From here, the Pennine Way leads to open moorland and Cow Green. This was flooded in the early 1970s, drowning a unique collection of arctic-alpine flowers which had bloomed here since the last Ice Age. However, mountain pansy, spring gentian and saxifrages still survive in the Upper Teesdale National Nature Reserve.

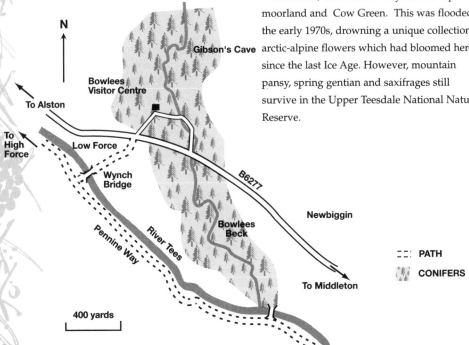

194

LOW BARNS

DURHAM WILDLIFE TRUST

Nearest town: Bishop Auckland
OS Map 93 NZ 160315

123 acres (50 ha) of wetland together with mixed woodland and grassland. It is an SSSI. There are bird hides, a nature trail and a visitor centre (1000-1600) and the Wildlife Trust's HQ is also here.

Location and access: The reserve is west of Bishop Auckland, close to the A68. From the A68 you want the side road to the east of Witton-le-Wear; follow the brown signposts (Low Barns Nature Reserve) through Witton-le-Wear, turning right at the Victoria pub. Once over the level crossing, the reserve and visitor centre is 0.5 mile along the road, again signposted in brown.

From the A689, it is 0.75 mile west of High Grange.

There is car parking around the centre together with a small picnic area.

Low Barns Reserve developed following gravel extraction on the farmland edging the River

WILDLIFE FEATURE
✕ Birdlife

Wear. This ended in 1964, and the former owners allowed the Wildlife Trust to take over the now water-filled pools. Both naturally and by design, it has become a very diverse wildlife area, including some mature alder woodland.

The wetland features include three lakes, inter-connecting streams and a number of ponds which are, from a wildlife point of view, mature with balanced and regular wildlife. The small ponds especially are good for damselflies and dragonflies, including the impressive southern hawker dragonfly. Butterflies include brimstone, ringlet, holly blue - this last a woodland butterfly unlike the other blues, the host plants on which the eggs are laid being holly and ivy.

There is a rich and abundant birdlife, including the kingfisher. In summer the reserve is alive with birdsong, residents being joined by many summer migrants - redstart, pied flycatcher and several warblers. In winter, large numbers of wildfowl can be seen and the grey heron is present throughout the year.

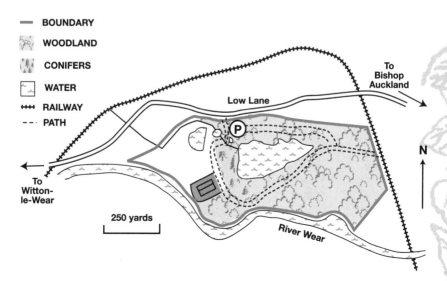

BOUNDARY
WOODLAND
CONIFERS
WATER
RAILWAY
PATH

To Bishop Auckland

Low Lane

To Witton-le-Wear

N

250 yards

River Wear

HANNAH'S MEADOW

DURHAM WILDLIFE TRUST

Nearest town: Barnard Castle
OS Map 93 NY 933186

Old unimproved meadowland, an SSSI. An old barn in the north-west corner of the top meadow has been converted into an unmanned visitor centre.

Location and access: The reserve is about a 10 mile drive from Barnard Castle. Take the B6277 Alston road via Lartington and Cotherstone to Romaldkirk, and then turn left (west) to follow the Balderhead road via Hunderthwaite and Hury. The reserve is adjacent to the road, a quarter of a mile east of the Balderhead reservoir car park. Please keep to the footpath as the reserve is in active farming use and very fragile. Please keep dogs on a lead and avoid trampling the hay crop.

WILDLIFE FEATURES
✿ Meadow flowers

Until they were acquired by the Wildlife Trust in 1988, Hannah Hauxwell farmed these fields using only traditional methods. There was no ploughing and re-seeding and no use of artificial fertilisers - hence the wealth of wild flowers and the SSSI status.

The meadows are still grown, cut and grazed in the traditional way. Sheep lamb in April and May. The fields are closed during June/July to let the hay mature. Once cut, the grass is allowed to grow again and cattle graze in September and October. Sheep are brought back in November before the winter rest period and the cycle begins again in the spring.

Flowers include wood cranesbill, ragged-robin and globeflower, a member of the buttercup family flowering March-May. Look also for two small ferns: adder's-tongue, with its tongue-like leaf enfolding its upright spore stem, and moonwort with golden brown 'flowers' in August which are in fact spore fronds. The pasture is more acid and has fewer flowers.

Lapwing, redshank, skylark and meadow pipit all nest here.

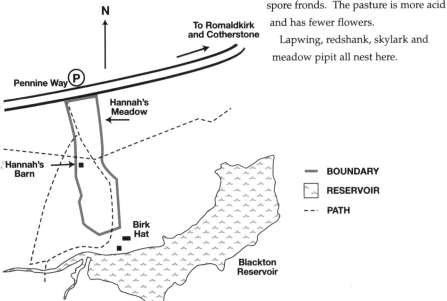

N

To Romaldkirk and Cotherstone

Pennine Way Ⓟ

Hannah's Meadow

Hannah's Barn

Birk Hat

Blackton Reservoir

━━ BOUNDARY

▨ RESERVOIR

--- PATH

JOE'S POND

DURHAM WILDLIFE TRUST

Nearest town: Houghton-le-Spring
OS Map 88 NZ 329488

A 10 acre (4 ha) reserve with a deep freshwater pool surrounded by dense hawthorn scrub and with an area of damp meadow at the southern end. It is an SSSI.

Location and access: The reserve is 1.25 mile (2 km) south-west of Houghton-le-Spring, near the A690. From the B1284 between Chilton Moor and Great Lumley, a minor road gives access to a rough track leading to Joe's Pond. There is room to park one or two cars at the north end of the reserve. There is also a footpath from East Rainton on the A690.

WILDLIFE FEATURES
❀ **Meadow flowers** ✕ **Birdlife**

pondweeds, reedmace ('bulrush'), watermint and water buttercup and other flowers in the marshy edge. There are six species of dragonfly to be seen.

Joe Wilson also built bird-nesting islands: these and the mature appearance of the reserve as a whole attract many nesting and wintering waterfowl including great crested grebe and ruddy duck in summer and teal, pochard and tufted duck in winter. The scrub also attracts birds including flocks of thrushes in winter. All five owls are regularly seen.

There is a population of water vole, now somewhat endangered in many areas of Britain.

Joe's Pond is a deep freshwater site surrounded by dense hawthorn scrub and willow. To the southern end there are damp meadows marked out by hemlock and great willowherb and a dry meadow filled with cowslips in spring

The pond was an old clay pit, once used as a reservoir, subsequently developed and managed by Joe Wilson for 25 years. He stocked it with aquatic plants including

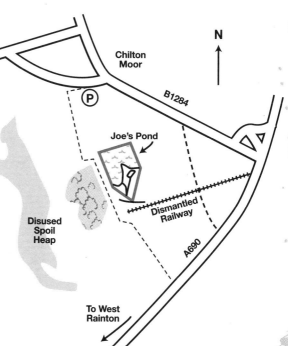

- — **BOUNDARY**
- 🟦 **WOODLAND**
- ☐ **POND**
- --- **PATH**

197

COATHAM MARSH

TEES VALLEY WILDLIFE TRUST

Nearest town:: Redcar
OS Map 93 NZ 586247

134 acres (54 ha) in all, with 50 acres of ancient marsh bounded by grazed meadows and man-made lakes, together with 80 acres of lime-rich grassland. There are bird-watching hides (one with disabled access) and viewing platforms; there is a warden.

Location and access: The reserve is about 2 miles (3 km) west of Redcar, best reached via the A1085 Redcar-Middlesbrough trunk road, turning up Kirkleatham Lane as the map explains. The car park is reached from Tod Point Road.
   To prevent disturbance, some areas are out-of-bounds.

This reserve may have steel works to one side, a trunk road to another and be cut by a railway line, but its wetland features attract a large and diverse bird population.
   In the 16th century, the marshes were used as

WILDLIFE FEATURES
- Waders and wildfowl
- Lime-rich grassland

saltings, and 50 acres remain, chiefly in the centre of the reserve. A freshwater fleet (a run of water) crosses nearby, broadening into a sedge-fringed pool. There are also two man-made freshwater lakes, formed in the 1970s from what was a refuse tip.

   The reserve also includes 80 acres of dry grassland growing on dumped furnace slag, and the lime in the waste encourages a fascinating summer library of yellow-wort, stonecrop and other lime-loving flowers.

   In spring, the skylark, meadow pipit, wheatear and whinchat are commonly seen, and bluethroat and black redstart can be seen occasionally. Summer sees the reed bunting and sedge warbler in the tall vegetation to the north. But winter is the most spectacular when flocks of 1,000 lapwing, 500 teal and wigeon and shoveler can fill the sky. Many of these are attracted to the scrape on West Marsh (a hide nearby).

   More than 200 species have been recorded here, with little egret and black-winged stilt two of the real rarities.

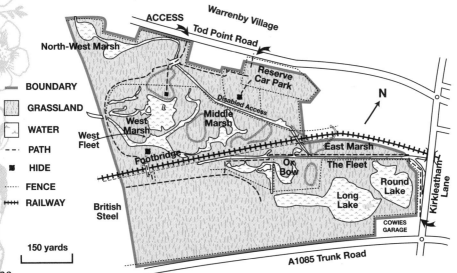

198

SALTBURN GILL

TEES VALLEY WILDLIFE TRUST

Nearest town: Redcar
OS Map 94 NZ 674205

52 acres (21 ha) of mixed SSSI woodland in a steep-sided coastal dene together with some open ground. There are toilets at the boating lake car park.

Location and access: The reserve extends south-east from Saltburn. Access with convenient parking is near Mill Farm, from the boating lake where the Gill flows into the sea. Otherwise it can be reached via the playing fields on the north-west edge of Brotton, using their car park. Walk westwards across the playing fields and drop down into The Griff. Dogs must be kept under control.

WILDLIFE FEATURES
❋ **Flowers of ancient woodland**
✕ **Birdlife**

Two side valleys (Darn Bottle and The Griff) run into steep-sided Saltburn Gill, with the higher ground between them open. In the main, however, this is an undisturbed mixed woodland with oak and ash the main trees, and wych elm and sycamore. But the invasive and aggressive sycamore must be felled. It is not a British native, by the way, but a mountain tree from southern Europe.

From spring on, the woodland floor can be a blaze of colour with glossy yellow lesser celandine leading the way and violets and wild garlic scenting the air and sheets of bluebell later. This woodland is sheltered in winter and humid in summer - hence the plentiful ferns!

The birdlife is rich, with chiffchaff usually the first of the summer migrants to arrive, followed by blackcap and spotted flycatcher, with even kingfisher being seen. There are moorhen, mallard and grey wagtail along the streams.

The open areas of the upper slopes (which until the 1960s were pig fields) are clothed with bracken or gorse and scattered with young trees. It's worth going to Bennison Banks to find yellow tormentil and cow-wheat with yellow rather snapdragon-like flowers which indicate a patch of acidy soil.

BOUNDARY
GORSE & BRACKEN
WOODLAND

300 yards

199

BROCKADALE

YORKSHIRE WILDLIFE TRUST

Nearest town: Doncaster

OS Map 111 SE 499176/508168 (access points)

A 91 acre (37 ha) valley gorge reserve

Location and access: Take the Kirk Smeaton road running east of the A1 just south of the Wentbridge viaduct. At the village of Kirk Smeaton take the road to Little Smeaton. In the village take the road to Stapleton and Durrington. After leaving Little Smeaton a track (Leys Lane) is on the right after some 400 yards. A car park is provided on the left hand side.

Because of vandalism, the reserve signs are not conspicuous.

The River Went has cut itself a deep gorge in the limestone; the rock itself outcrops on the valley sides beneath the trees and there is also evidence of old quarries. The valley bottom is flat, however, with silt brought by the river (it still sometimes floods).

WILDLIFE FEATURES
A picturesque site ❀ Woodland and grassland wild flowers

The trees are a mixture, with poplar by the river and areas of larch, but much of the cover is ash-sycamore woodland.

The limy soil encourages a good number of wild flowers: rockrose and the prickly carline thistle with straw yellow flowers for example, are typical of limy grasslands. There are cowslip and orchids such as early purple orchid in spring and twayblade later. Have a look for the delightful quaking grass, dancing in the breeze, while on the grassland by the river hemlock, hound's-tongue, yellow flag and several of the geranium clan are found.

Plants apart, there are a good many warblers nesting each year, with occasional visits from nightingale and even kingfisher. Slow worm, common lizard and grass snake can also be found in this interesting reserve.

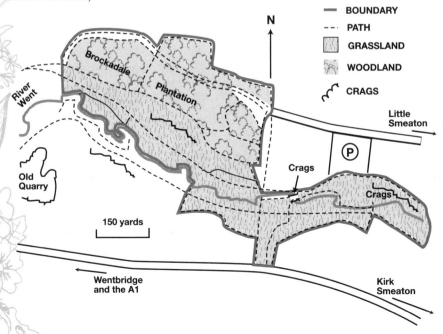

POTTERIC CARR

YORKSHIRE WILDLIFE TRUST

Nearest town: Doncaster
OS Map 111 TA 598010

A 350 acre (140 ha) wetland reserve with drainage dykes and subsidence pools and with some grassland and woodland. There is a field centre and viewing hides and some 6 miles of footpaths.

Location and access: The reserve is about 2 miles south-east of Doncaster town centre. The main entrance to the reserve is at the western edge along the A6182. Arriving via the A6182 either from Doncaster or the M18, take the turnoff at the roundabout shown on the map, signposted 'No Through Road'. After 50 yards turn right onto the reserve car park. Alternatively travel out of Doncaster on the A630, turn left (first traffic lights) onto Carr Hill to reach the same roundabout after about1 mile.

WILDLIFE FEATURES

- ➤ Wildfowl
- ❀ Wild flowers
- ✺ Dragonflies

The reserve is at the lowest point of a shallow basin with mainly peat deposits on top of clay and gravel scrapings left by glaciers at the end of the last Ice Age. Poor drainage and mining subsidence since 1959 have created pools - the largest being the 10 acre pool at Low Ellers - attractively wild most of them, fringed with reeds and sausage-headed 'bulrush' (correctly this is greater reedmace). The pools and marshy areas are often bright with flowers, with shiny yellow marsh marigold in spring and later yellow iris, yellow water lily and others.

But the reserve is best known for its nesting wildfowl - hence the hides. Shoveler, tufted duck, pochard and water rail are among the number, with colonies of reed and sedge warblers.

The visiting birds can be equally interesting, though what you see is more a matter of luck of course: great crested grebe, bittern, marsh harrier, wryneck are among those that have been seen here. The name wryneck comes from the bird's unusual habit of twisting its neck when startled.

There are also many dragonflies.

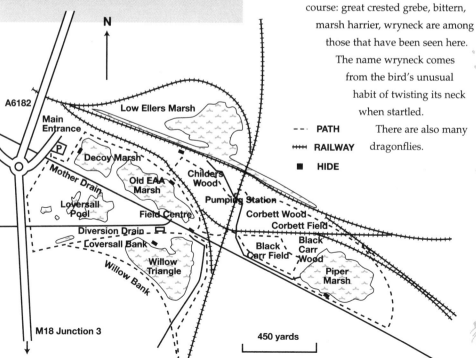

- - - **PATH**
╫╫╫ **RAILWAY**
▪ **HIDE**

N

A6182
Main Entrance
P
Decoy Marsh
Low Ellers Marsh
Mother Drain
Old EAA Marsh
Childers Wood
Loversall Pool
Field Centre
Pumping Station
Corbett Wood
Corbett Field
Diversion Drain
Loversall Bank
Black Carr Field
Black Carr Wood
Willow Triangle
Willow Bank
Piper Marsh

M18 Junction 3

450 yards

WHELDRAKE INGS

YORKSHIRE WILDLIFE TRUST

Nearest town: York
OS Map 105 SE 694444

A 395 acre (160 ha) flood meadow reserve, it is part of an SSSI and National Nature Reserve. There are two birdwatching hides, one placed for winter viewing, the other for summer.

Location and access: The reserve is about 8 miles south-east of York. It can be reached either from Wheldrake or Thorganby villages, which are about 3 or 4 miles (6 km) east of the A19. Leaving Wheldrake for Thorganby, the road takes a sharp turn to the right. Half a mile further on, a narrow road forks to the left and leads down to the Wheldrake bridge. There is (limited) parking here. Please keep to the riverside path which leads to the two hides - the rest of the reserve is a refuge area.

Dogs are not allowed.

This old meadow flood plain reserve extends across one of the wider parts of the lower Derwent Valley SSSI. It is crossed by drainage channels and there is a pool.

For centuries this land has been managed traditionally, being cropped for hay and grazed afterwards. It has never been artificially fertilised (the soil is enriched with the silt brought by the winter floods). All a recipe for a rich flower tally. One flower typical of places such as this is the tall (it can grow up to waist height)

WILDLIFE FEATURES
🐦 Winter wildfowl and waders
🌼 Plant communities of ancient grassland

great burnet with an unmistakable crimson 'sausage' flower head. For the specialist the narrow-leaved water dropwort (one of the cow parsley tribe) grows by the river.

The winter flooding of the reserve attracts Bewick's swan, geese and other wildfowl, often in large numbers, while the breeding birds in summer include snipe, curlew, redshank and lapwing, with mallard, coot and moorhen often busy on the pond. At dusk you might also see a barn owl (and a short-eared owl in daylight).

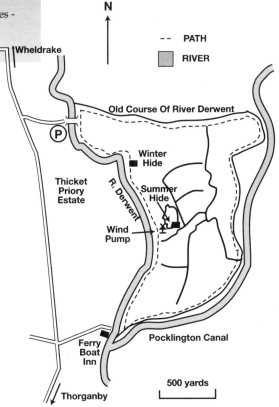

N

- - - PATH

▨ RIVER

Wheldrake

P

Old Course Of River Derwent

Winter Hide

Thicket Priory Estate

R. Derwent

Summer Hide

Wind Pump

Ferry Boat Inn

Pocklington Canal

Thorganby

500 yards

SPURN

YORKSHIRE WILDLIFE TRUST

Nearest town: Kingston upon Hull

OS Map 113 TA 417151 (access)

A 3.5 mile (5.5 km) sand and shingle spit, with 280 acres (113 ha) above and 477 acres (193 ha) below high-water mark, the area of mudflat and saltmarsh beyond the ridge. There is an information centre and there are wardens.

Location and access: The reserve is about 20 miles (32 km) south-eastwards from Hull. From Hull take the A1033 to Patrington and then the B1445 to Easington, and then on to Kilnsea and Spurn. The Trust owns the road to the car park near the lighthouse - cars may be charged a fee (except Fridays).

Certain areas may be closed to the public for obvious reasons.

The dunes carry plants which can cope with loose sand: marram grass, sea bindweed and sea-buckthorn (which has to be controlled) for example. Look also for sea-holly, one of the most handsome shore plants (and unmistakable - it lives up to its name).

It's a breezy, invigorating place, with the chance of spotting seals. But what brings many visitors is the fact that this is one of the finest sites in Europe for seeing migrant birds. Wildfowl such as mallard and shelduck might shelter here in winter, but at passage times curlew, dunlin, knot, oystercatcher, redshank and turnstone arrive. Terns also pass through - and you may see them being harried by arctic skua (efforts are being made to encourage the little tern to breed here). Other arrivals can include pied and spotted flycatchers, redstart, whinchat and fieldfare and redwing - these last feed on the berries on the sea buckthorn bushes.

WILDLIFE FEATURES

🦅 Migrating birds in amazing numbers and occasional seals

The number of these birds using Spurn as a staging post can be amazing - an estimated 6,000 blackbirds once arrived on a single day.

The Spurn Bird Observatory, maintained by the Yorkshire Naturalists' Union, keeps the records.

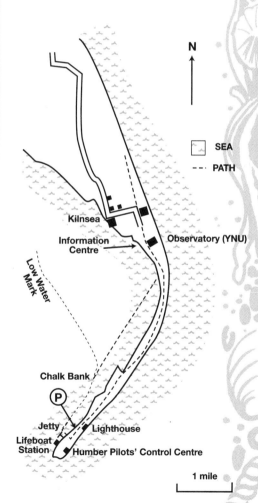

BURTON RIGGS

Nearest town: Scarborough
OS Map 101 032832

About 37 acres (15 ha) of old gravel pits with two big freshwater lakes with islands and a variety of surrounding habitats. There is a waymarked trail.

Location and access: The reserve is at the east end of the Vale of Pickering, close to the village of Seamer on the outskirts of Scarborough. Scarborough's new industrial estate runs along its east side while the A64 (Seamer by-pass) and the Scarborough-Filey railway line lie immediately to the west. There is parking off the roundabout on the A64, opposite Morrisons supermarket and the industrial estate.

WILDLIFE FEATURES
✖ **Birdlife**
✾ **Orchids and other wild flowers**

Sand and gravel were extracted here until 1974, when the land was left to itself and it now has a very varied wildlife. Two big freshwater lakes occupy the deepest parts of the pits and shallows have been created to attract waders. Around the lakes is a bumpy terrain with various soils. Trees have been planted but there are now some fairly well established areas with bee, pyramidal and common spotted orchids to be seen on the steep banks to the north of the larger lake.

A total of 168 birds have been listed, of which 32 have nested - one being the little grebe in most recent years and the little ringed plover. Others in the 'Top Ten' list of breeding birds are great crested grebe, sand martin, yellow wagtail, sedge warbler, whitethroat and lesser whitethroat, reed bunting and the kingfisher - this is a new arrival.

The lakes have pike and other coarse fish, while the pools have both common and great-crested newts (the last is now quite rare).

N
↑

Ⓟ

SAND MARTIN CLIFFS

LIGHT INDUSTRY

FOSSIL BAY

BALANCING POOL

ANGLING LAKE

FOSSIL BAY

APPLEBY ISLAND

DAVES HILL

MAGIC POOL

— BOUNDARY
WOODLAND
SCRUB
SHINGLE
LAKE/POOL
--- PATH
+++ RAILWAY

150 Yards

THE AYRES VISITOR CENTRE

THE MANX NATURE CONSERVATION TRUST

OS Map NX 4350038

The Ayres is a stretch of coast reached via a mile of side road from the A10. It has shingle, dunes and heath and is home to some of the island's rarest plants. There is a nature trail leading to the beach through the dunes and across a 'lichen heath'.

There are plenty of wild flowers to be seen - wild orchids in the spring and burnet rose and bird's-foot-trefoil among the others to be seen later.

There is also a good bird life - you should see gannet, shag and cormorant diving for fish, while oystercatcher, curlew and other waders feed on the shore. Some of these also nest on the upper shore dunes and heath, together with the little tern.

CLOSE SARTFIELD

THE MANX NATURE CONSERVATION TRUST

OS Map SC 358956

About 1.5 miles (2.5 km) north-west of Ballaugh, this wetland reserve of 31 acres (12.5 ha) is part of the Ballaugh Curragh wetland and one of the larger Manx reserves. It has areas of fen, wet hay meadow, marshy grassland and some birch woodland.

This variety attracts a number of birds and the area has one of the largest winter roosts of hen harrier in western Europe.

The birds can be viewed from a hide (with wheelchair access).

There is also a host of interesting plants to be seen, including stands of the luxuriant royal fern in the wetter areas, six species of orchid and yellow rattle, cuckoo flower and other grassland flowers.

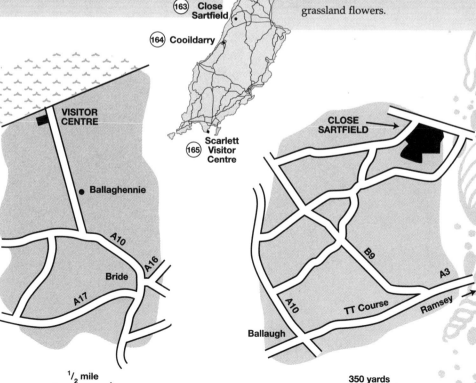

(162) Ayres Visitor Centre

(163) Close Sartfield

(164) Cooildarry

(165) Scarlett Visitor Centre

VISITOR CENTRE

Ballaghennie

A10

A16

Bride

A17

¹/₂ mile

CLOSE SARTFIELD

B9

A3

A10

TT Course

Ramsey

Ballaugh

350 yards

COOILDARRY

THE MANX NATURE CONSERVATION TRUST

OS *Map* SC 314901

This deep wooded valley is just to the south-west of Kirk Michael, reached by the A4 or A3 roads. The woodland is varied with elm, ash, alder, beech, lime, chestnut and the Mediterranean holm oak (the valley held a Victorian pleasure garden). There are also some large Corsican pines on the drier rim of the valley. In spring the woodland floor is carpeted with bluebell, primrose, wood anemone and wild garlic.

Among the 35 birds known to have nested here are raven and sparrowhawk. The reserve is one of the few places where the wood warbler has been recorded.

SCARLETT VISITOR CENTRE

THE MANX NATURE CONSERVATION TRUST

OS *Map* SC 258664

Scarlett, which is some 2 miles (3 km) south-west of Castletown has some spectacular geology, with an old limestone quarry near the visitor centre and rugged volcanic columnar basalt protruding as the "Stack".

The nature trail starts by the quarry. Most of the vegetation of Scarlett is maritime heath, with a range of plants that includes bulbous buttercup, stonecrop and, in the spring, sheets of the beautiful blue spring squill.

Shag, cormorant, gulls and auks are often seen perched on the "Stack".

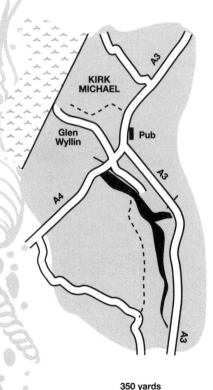

KIRK MICHAEL

Glen Wyllin

■ Pub

A3

A4

A3

A3

350 yards

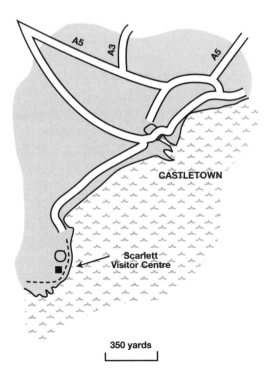

A5

A3

A5

CASTLETOWN

○ ■ → Scarlett Visitor Centre

350 yards

Wales

This section covers a vast range of habitats from shingle and lagoon on the north coast of Anglesey, to the magnificent cliffs of the Gower Peninsula on the south coast of Glamorgan. Powys is a county of rounded hills in the heart of Wales, taking in Radnorshire, Montgomeryshire and Brecknock, where sheep greatly outnumber people. Glaslyn in Montgomeryshire has some of the finest heather moorland in Wales and supports birds of prey such as peregrine and red kite, and a breeding population of red grouse. In the centre of Powys, near Rhayader is the unspoilt Gilfach Farm, with the River Marteg tumbling through its grounds, as well as oak woodland, meadows and moorland. Off the west coast of Wales are some spectacular islands such as Skomer, internationally important for seabirds such as kittiwake, guillemot, razorbill and puffin. Fenland was once extensive on the Gwent levels close to the Severn estuary, but it has mostly been lost through drainage and development. The last remaining fragment can be seen at Magor Marsh with its pattern of drainage ditches, wet rush pasture and reedbeds. Two hay meadows support attractive wild flowers such as yellow rattle and ragged-robin and a whole host of birds can be seen including kingfisher, heron, reed, sedge and grasshopper warblers, and sparrowhawk and buzzard.

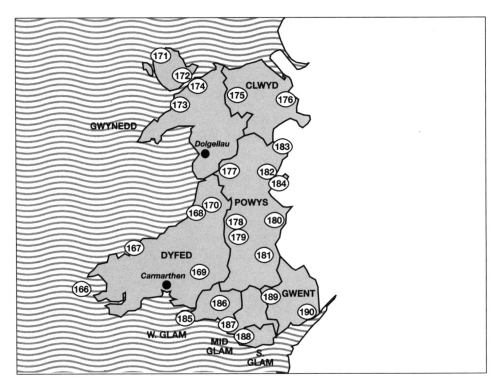

SKOMER

THE WILDLIFE TRUST, WEST WALES

Nearest town: Haverfordwest
OS Map 157 SM 730090

A spectacularly eroded island, which together with the neighbouring Skokholm and Midland Island is of international importance for large numbers of breeding birds. It is a National Nature Reserve (NNR).

Location and access: Boats cross from Martinshaven, beyond Marloes via the B4327 south-west from Haverfordwest. Cars can be left in the National Trust car park. There are boats at 1000, 1100 and 1200 every day except Mondays (Bank Holidays excepted) for daily visits from April to October. There is also limited chalet accommodation for overnight stays.

(Skokholm may also be visited on Mondays only, from early June to late August. Full board accommodation is also available. Details from the Wildlife Trust.)

Dogs are not allowed on the islands.

WILDLIFE FEATURES
Seabirds and migrants
Breathtaking island scenery

Whatever the time of year, Skomer provides much pleasure. The early spring arrival of the puffin and other seabirds to their colonies. The riot of flowers in May and June, when the bluebell reigns, followed by red campion and foxglove while sea campion and thrift carpet the cliff tops. The heather of late summer, the nightly departure of young Manx shearwaters, and then the autumn seal pups.

The Skokholm-Skomer islands are the largest seabird colonies in southern Britain with fulmar, kittiwake, guillemot and razorbill on the cliffs, puffin on the cliff slopes and large gulls on flatter ground. At night they are alive with immense numbers of Manx shearwater and smaller numbers of storm petrel. Add to this nesting birds like buzzard, peregrine, short-eared owl, chough and raven and rare visitors which have included Cory's shearwater, frigate bird, black kite, Caspian tern, hoopoe and black-headed bunting.

Skomer is also one of the largest archaeological sites in Britain with the remains of an Iron Age community, as well as much evidence of farming in its Victorian hey-day.

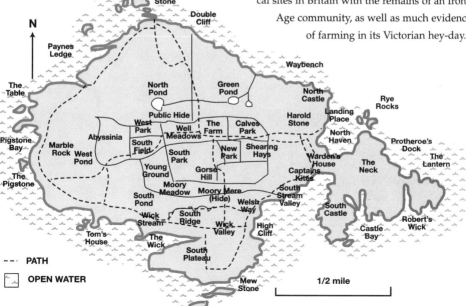

PATH - - -

OPEN WATER

1/2 mile

209

THE WELSH WILDLIFE CENTRE

THE WILDLIFE TRUST, WEST WALES

Nearest town: Cardigan
OS Map 145 184455

Location and access: The Centre is less than a mile from Cardigan. Take the A487 Fishguard road south from the town and then the A478 Tenby road for nearly 2 miles and turn left (east) towards Cilgerran. The entrance on the north side of this road is signposted.

A 250 acre (105 ha) reserve incorporating an NNR, SSSI land and a very popular, and prizewinning, visitor centre. The habitats include reedbed, wild flower meadow, ancient woodland, lagoons, and the gorge of the River Teifi. There are various nature trails; there are 5 miles of paths in all, and most of them are wide enough for wheelchair use. Many different workshops and wildlife events are held. There are seven hides in all, including a treetop hide, for observing heron, wildfowl and waders, but also one for otter watching.

Cottage accommodation is available for weekend and for week-long stays. Dogs must be kept on leads.

WILDLIFE FEATURES

🦆 **Wildflowl and waders**   🦦 **Otter**
🌼 **Woodland and meadow flowers**

To help costs towards maintaining the site, an entrance charge is made.

There is a wide range of habitat types at this all-season reserve, and the rich variety of wildlife includes grey heron and Cetti's warbler, birds of prey and wintering wildfowl and waders. Sightings in 1997 included red kite, marsh harrier and common crossbill. There are woodland and meadow flowers, and badger, fox, deer and bats are present. The reserve is also one of the best sites in Wales for the otter - the artificial holt is in use.

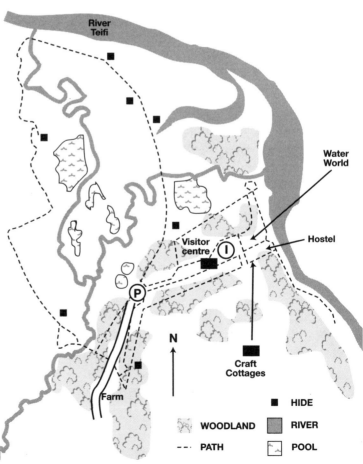

LLYN EIDDWEN

THE WILDLIFE TRUST, WEST WALES

Nearest town: Aberystwyth
OS Map 135 SN 607674

A natural and unpolluted lake, 26 acres (10.5 ha) in extent together with grassland and a small bog. The reserve forms the major part of an SSSI, while the lake itself is a National Nature Reserve.

Location and access: From Aberystwyth take the A487 and then the A485 south (towards Lampeter), turning right onto the B4576 at Abermad. Follow this road to the village of Llangwyryfon then turn left and head south on a very narrow unclassified road to Trefenter. Continue through Trefenter and over the Hafod Ithel from where you obtain a fine view of the lake.

Parking is possible at several places along the road. Access to the lake is possible only along the western shore and those wishing to reach the extreme southern end of the reserve should use the path which passes above Glan-llyn .

Care should be taken not to damage the boggy flushes to the north of the lake - these are a fragile habitat.

The lake, never more than 4 yards deep, is remarkable for its plants. Here grow stands of the attractive water lobelia, with carpets of shoreweed and quillwort and others visible in the clear unpolluted water. Another plant to spot is the floating water plantain with (often) floating stems and leaves.

WILDLIFE FEATURES

Wintering wildfowl ✽ **Lake plants**
Dragonflies & damselflies

There are beds of sedge and water horsetail, grading at the southern end of the lake into a bogland with a good cover of bog mosses and with cotton grass, sundew and the very handsome yellow-flowered bog asphodel. The surroundings are largely typical upland grassland, but there is some heather too.

The lake attracts wintering wildfowl, mainly coot, pochard, mallard, wigeon and teal together with part of a flock of 20-30 whooper swan which winter in central Ceredigion.

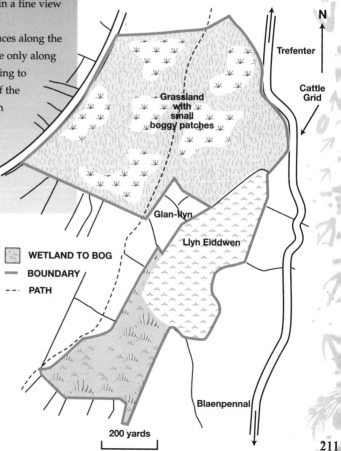

Grassland with small boggy patches

Glan-llyn

Llyn Eiddwen

Trefenter

Cattle Grid

Blaenpennal

N

WETLAND TO BOG
BOUNDARY
PATH

200 yards

CASTLE WOODS

THE WILDLIFE TRUST, WEST WALES

Nearest town: Llandeilo
OS Map 159 SN 610225

About 60 acres (24 ha) of fine mixed woodland on steep limestone slopes overlooking the River Tywi and its floodplain.

Location and access: The woods extend about a mile west of Llandeilo town centre. There is a public car park next to the fire station (on the A40) from where visitors can walk through Penlan Park to the north-west of the town centre to the entrance to the reserve. From here, the footpaths are indicated by the Badger Footprint signs.

The main native trees here are common oak and wych elm (but the latter is mainly dead from Dutch elm disease) together with ash, hazel and (flagging the limestone rock) spindle. But conifers have been planted in places, along with some beech. In spring, the ground is carpeted with wood anemone, bluebell and primrose.

WILDLIFE FEATURES
 ✾ **Woodland flowers**   ✗ **Birdlife**

You can sometimes find the parasitic toothwort (lacking green, with a whitish flower head) on the roots of holly. Another plant to look out for is the lungwort, a large lichen loosely attached to the tree bark, green and leathery when wet. Indeed, the woods are noted for their impressive range of lichens.

The woodland attracts all three woodpeckers and nuthatch and treecreeper, and summer visitors include warblers, redstart and both pied and spotted flycatchers (after a flycatching sortie, the former rarely returns to the same perch - unlike the latter!). And the water meadows which border the reserve below the woods are one of the most important areas in inland Dyfed for mallard, teal, wigeon, goosander, shoveler, tufted duck and pochard.

The woodland clearings are good for butterflies, while several species of bat occur.

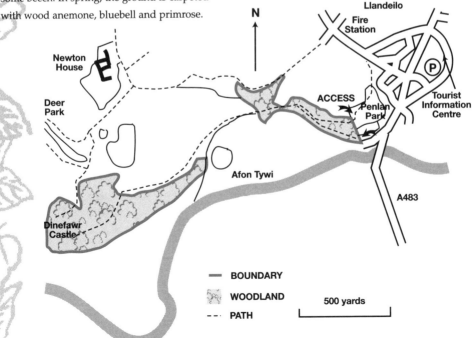

N

Llandeilo
Fire Station

Newton House

Deer Park

ACCESS
Penlan Park

Tourist Information Centre

P

Afon Tywi

A483

Dinefawr Castle

— BOUNDARY
 WOODLAND
--- PATH

500 yards

COED SIMDDE LWYD

THE WILDLIFE TRUST, WEST WALES

Nearest town: Aberystwyth

OS Map 135 SN 713787 (main entrance)

89 acres (36 ha) of oakwood, mainly on a steep south-facing slope and with a waterfall at the western end where the Nant Bwadrain cascades into the valley. It is a National Nature Reserve (NNR).

Location and access: The reserve is situated on the north bank of the Rheidol Valley above the minor road to Cwm Rheidol, 10 miles (16 km) east of Aberystwyth.

A small car parking space is provided off the road beside the Nant Bwadrain. Cars can also be left at the disused mine heaps a little further east, from where a footpath enters the reserve.

The reserve is part of the largest remaining intact area of valleyside sessile oakwood in this

WILDLIFE FEATURES
✿ Sessile oak woodland

part of mid Wales. The trees are almost wholly sessile oak, with leaves which merge smoothly with a longish leaf stalk (without the lobes of the common or pedunculate oak) and with acorns with a short or no stalk. But there are also birches dominant in some areas - both the silver birch and the downy birch, the latter with downy twigs and often brownish bark. In the enclave of the stream you can also find alder, ash, wych elm and small-leaved lime.

Flowers include bilberry, heather and cow-wheat, typical of acid soil. You may also see yellow pimpernel and sheep's-bit. And for the specialist there are numerous mosses and some interesting leafy liverworts.

Birds which might be seen include buzzard, red kite, jackdaw, jay, raven, long-tailed tit, pied flycatcher, redstart and wood warbler.

And of great interest are the large and active wood ant nests at the lower eastern end of the reserve. These insects can be dominant within their territories, foraging up to the highest twigs. The trackways of the different colonies do not cross, but dovetail like a Chinese puzzle.

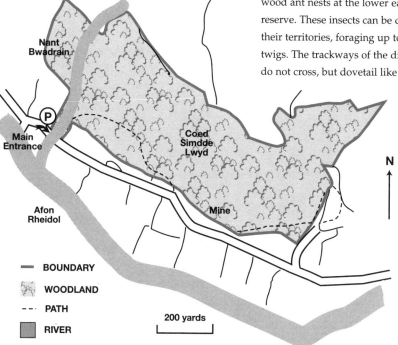

Nant
Bwadrain

P

Main
Entrance

Coed
Simdde
Lwyd

Afon
Rheidol

Mine

N

— **BOUNDARY**

WOODLAND

--- **PATH**

RIVER

200 yards

213

CEMLYN NATURE RESERVE

NORTH WALES WILDLIFE TRUST

Nearest town: Holyhead (Bangor)
OS Map 114 SH 331932

62 acres (25 ha) of brackish lagoon and associated shingle ridges, a mecca for birds at all times of year.

Location and access: The reserve is on the north coast of Anglesey, 2 miles west of the Wylfa nuclear power station. From Bangor, follow the signs for Menai Bridge and then take the A5025 to Amlwch and Tregele. At Tregele, turn right to follow the signposts to the reserve.

From Holyhead, take the A5 and then turn left onto the A5025, to Tregele. Park in one of two car parks close to the reserve.

There is a reserve warden on site between May and August. Visitors are asked not to walk on the crest or lagoon side of the ridge from May to mid-August.

WILDLIFE FEATURES
✖ Birdlife ✤ Maritime plants

As soon as shingle and sand are thrown out of reach of the tides, specialised maritime plants can colonise. A striking feature of the shingle ridge here is the fine stand of sea-kale, but sea campion, thrift and yellow horned-poppy can also be seen. There are clumps of sea beet along the drift line and saltmarsh specialists fringe the lagoon.

But the main interest must be the birdlife. The lagoon has been managed as a wildfowl refuge for more than half a century and this has included installing a weir to manage water levels and increasing the area of nesting islands. Summer breeding birds include several hundred pairs of terns (roseate regularly being one of the species; and the only substantial colony of sandwich tern in Wales) and ringed plover and oystercatcher for the waders - but also grasshopper and sedge warblers and reed bunting.

Rarities have also been seen here: bridled tern, squacco heron and black-headed bunting among others.

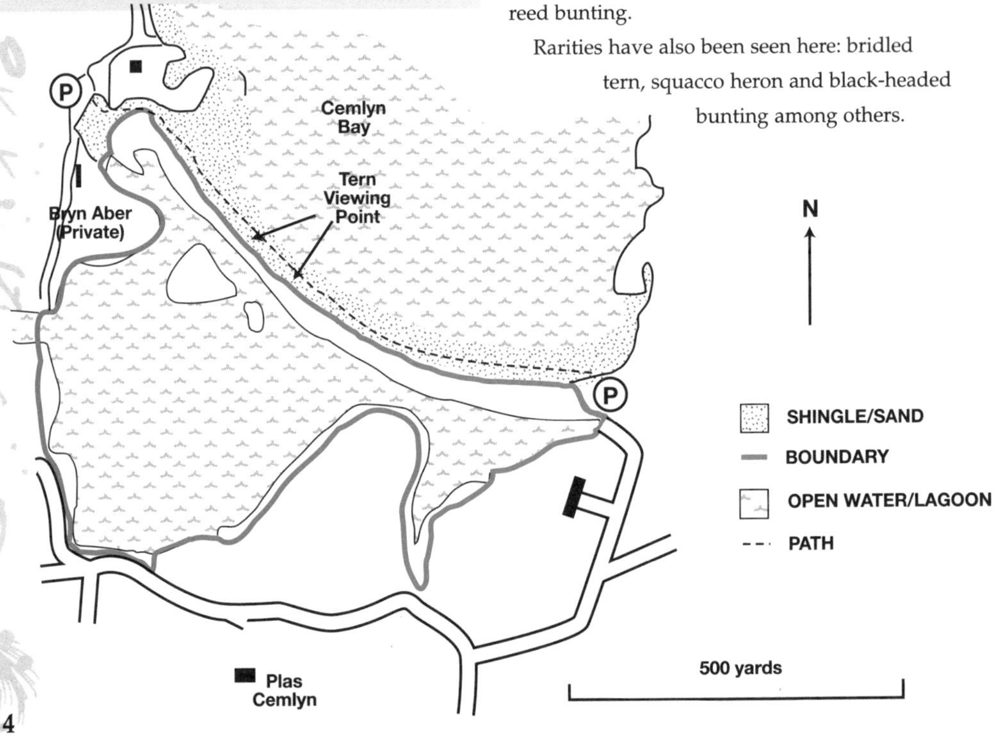

Map legend:
- SHINGLE/SAND
- BOUNDARY
- OPEN WATER/LAGOON
- PATH

Map labels: Cemlyn Bay, Tern Viewing Point, Bryn Aber (Private), Plas Cemlyn, N, 500 yards

CORS GOCH

NORTH WALES WILDLIFE TRUST

Nearest town: Bangor
OS Map 114 SH 503817

A valley reserve of 167 acres (68 ha) with one of the finest fen communities in Britain and also some acidic heathland and limestone grassland.

Location and access: From Bangor follow signs for Menai Bridge and then take the A5025 north. 1.5 miles past Pentraeth turn left onto the road signed for Llanbedrgoch. About 1 mile past Llanbedrgoch, cars can be parked in the lay-by on the left, just north of the track which leads to the reserve.

A reserve of splendid variety with both limestone and sandstone outcrops. The fen is rich because drainage from limestone high ground creates a calcareous (limy) peat - great stands of reeds grow, scented with myrtle and mint. Saw sedge is another species, and here you can find royal fern. In the marshy areas where there is

WILDLIFE FEATURES

❀ **Marsh orchids and other fen plants**
✖ **Birdlife**

mineral soil, marsh helleborine and other orchids can be seen.

There are orchids too on the limestone grassland - the often diminutive green-winged orchid and the fragrant orchid, with the lesser butterfly orchid in the damp areas between the grassland and the fen.

Where the sandstone rock outcrops, or is near the surface, the soil is acid and here there is a heath community with, in the south of the reserve, the now rare brilliant blue marsh gentian the highlight.

More than 20 butterfly species, including small pearl-bordered fritillary, have been seen, and 12 species of dragonfly.

The variety has evolved over centuries of traditional management - and the Trust continues this with grazing, reed cutting and haymaking.

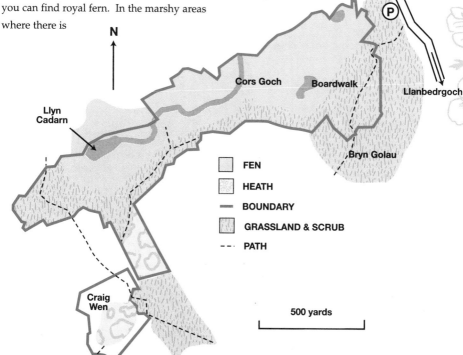

N

Llyn Cadarn

Cors Goch

Boardwalk

Llanbedrgoch

P

Bryn Golau

☐ FEN
▨ HEATH
— BOUNDARY
▨ GRASSLAND & SCRUB
--- PATH

Craig Wen

500 yards

CAEAU TAN Y BWLCH

NORTH WALES WILDLIFE TRUST

Nearest town: Caernarfon
OS Map 115 SH 431488

A reserve of traditional fields, with meadow, scrub and wetland.

Location and access: From Caernarfon, take the A499 (towards Pwllheli). At Clynnog-fawr (about 10 miles - 16 km - from Caernarfon) take the sharp left turning just before the church; signposted for Llanllyfni, and then immediately turn right onto a narrow road. Continue uphill for about three quarters of a mile then take an unexpected right hand turn. Continue on this winding lane for about 1 mile. After a right-angled turn to the left, continue for about 150 yards to the gateway to Caeau Tan y Bwlch on the left. Park in the small parking area.

Caeau Tan y Bwlch means 'the fields below the mountain pass' and the reserve lies on the northern slopes of Bwlch Mawr with views across Caernarfon Bay and Anglesey and beyond. They have earth and stone walls.

WILDLIFE FEATURES
❀ Meadow flowers

They are a reminder of the colourful meadows which could be found everywhere in the past.

In the upper fields grow black knapweed, bird's-foot-trefoil, lady's-mantle, heath and common spotted orchids and the adder's-tongue fern (a good indicator of old meadowland). Greater butterfly orchid flowers in July, filling the air with its sweet scent. On the lower, wetter slopes a variety of ferns and sedges and other wetland plants thrive - wood horsetail, marsh violet, bogbean (which many consider our most handsome wild flower) and lady's smock.

From the scattered willow scrub you'll hear the whitethroat's song and the unusual chirring of the grasshopper warbler.

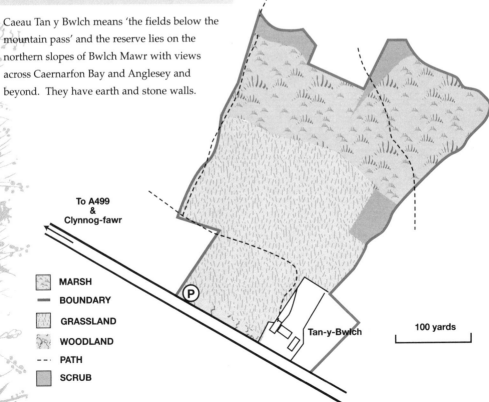

To A499
&
Clynnog-fawr

Tan-y-Bwlch

100 yards

- ▦ MARSH
- ▬ BOUNDARY
- ▥ GRASSLAND
- ▨ WOODLAND
- --- PATH
- ▓ SCRUB

216

SPINNIES, ABER OGWEN

NORTH WALES WILDLIFE TRUST

Nearest town: Bangor
OS Map 115 SH 613721

A 9 acre (3.5 ha) reserve with a brackish coastal lagoon and other open water, grassland, scrub and woodland. There is a large bird hide overlooking both the lagoons and the estuary.

Location and access: The Spinnies reserve is slightly less than 2 miles (3 km) east of Bangor, near the estuary of Afon Ogwen at the eastern end of the Menai Straits. From Bangor, take the A5122 and at Penrhyn Castle turn left onto the road for Tal-y-bont. After passing over the river, take the road on the left (the only road on this side). Follow this for about half a mile to the entrance to the reserve. Do not park here, but in the car park, 300 yards further along the road.

WILDLIFE FEATURES
Estuary and woodland birds

The reserve is one of the North Wales Wildlife Trust's most popular reserves because of the birdlife it attracts. More than 85 species have been seen either on or around the reserve, including rarities such as pied-billed grebe, surf scoter, spoonbill, bittern, marsh harrier and yellow-browed warbler.

Regular winter visitors include greenshank, water rail, teal, kingfisher and occasionally firecrest, while the estuary alongside attracts several thousand oystercatcher and curlew, several hundred redshank, dunlin, shelduck and wigeon and smaller numbers of other waders and wildfowl. Several hundred red-breasted merganser and great crested grebe congregate to moult in late summer, while the list of birds breeding on the reserve is impressive.

The name Spinnies is derived from the small wooded areas which surround the central lagoon. And this lagoon was originally a meander of the Afon Ogwen, before it was canalised as part of the drainage of the original saltmarshes of the area. Today this lagoon is brackish, influenced by the tides.

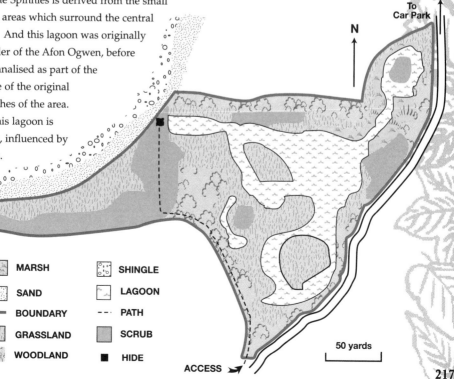

N

To Car Park

MARSH	SHINGLE
SAND	LAGOON
BOUNDARY	PATH
GRASSLAND	SCRUB
WOODLAND	HIDE

ACCESS

50 yards

GORS MAEN LLWYD

NORTH WALES WILDLIFE TRUST

Nearest town: Denbigh
OS Map 116 SH 970580

A reserve at the northern end of the lake Llyn Brenig. There is a bird hide.

Location and access: Gors Maen Llwyd is 7 miles (11 km) south-west of Denbigh on the B4501. From Denbigh take the A543 Pentrefoelas road and after 7 miles turn left on the road signposted to Llyn Brenig. After 1 mile turn left again; the road runs across the reserve. Park at the top car park or near the bird hide
   Heathland is very vulnerable to damage by erosion and nesting birds can easily be disturbed, so please keep to the footpaths and keep dogs on a lead.

This varied reserve is particularly attractive in August when the heather is in flower. Heather and bell heather signal the drier areas, and the paler rose-pink flowers of cross-leaved heath the wetter.

WILDLIFE FEATURES
❀ Heathland ✕ Birdlife

   The lake attracts many birds. Goosander, great crested grebe, cormorant and heron fish it; common sandpiper and mallard nest near it. Raptors and the raven are seen here all year, but birdwise, the reserve really comes into its own in spring and autumn when migrant waders descend on it.

   There is a strong insect tally, including the emperor moth, a relative of the silk moth with noticeable eye spots, seen flying fast in early summer. Dragonflies haunt the boggy areas.

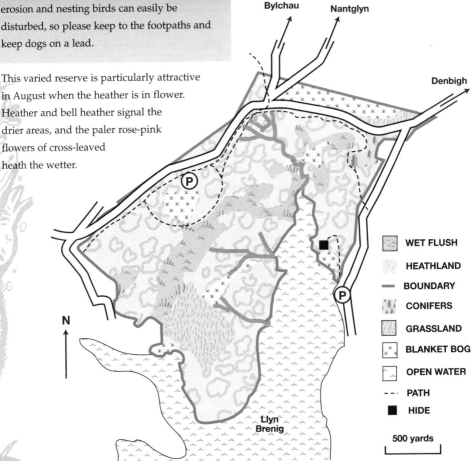

Bylchau
Nantglyn
Denbigh

N

WET FLUSH
HEATHLAND
BOUNDARY
CONIFERS
GRASSLAND
BLANKET BOG
OPEN WATER
PATH
HIDE

Llyn Brenig

500 yards

MARFORD

NORTH WALES WILDLIFE TRUST

Nearest town: Wrexham
OS Map 117 SJ 357560

A disused sand and gravel quarry of 38 acres (15.3 ha), which since 1971 has been allowed to regenerate naturally. The variety of habitats includes cliff faces, grassland, scrub, some areas of woodland (some ancient) and a pool. It is designated as an SSSI.

Location and access: The reserve is 2.5 miles (4 km) north-north-east of Wrexham near the village of Marford. From Wrexham follow signs for the A483 (to Chester) and just past a roundabout turn right onto the B5445, for Gresford and Marford. At Marford, turn left into Springfield Lane, 50 yards past the Trevor Arms Hotel. The entrance to the reserve is a further 400 yards, on the left just before the railway bridge. Cars can be parked either side of the bridge.

The limy grassland and the barer areas of the reserve have a splendid plant list, including restharrow and kidney vetch which are normally found on coastal sand dunes. Bird's-foot-trefoil, yellow-wort, white mullein and other early colonisers are seen on the barer soil, while areas which are now being grassed over sport a colourful summer display of vetches, campions, bellflowers and others.

The reserve as a whole is a super place for butterflies. They total more than 30 species including grayling (which does favour

WILDLIFE FEATURES
🦅 **Birdlife**
🦋 **Butterflies** 🌿 **Wild flowers**

the bare ground over the grassland), purple and white-letter hairstreaks and dingy skipper.

As for the birds, the three woodpeckers are attracted to the woodland together with nuthatch and treecreeper, spotted flycatcher, wood warbler and greenfinch, while the scrub and rough grassland are notable for long-tailed tit and bullfinch. Linnet, yellowhammer and whitethroat nest in the gorse.

Springfield Lane
entrance

P

BOUNDARY
GORSE SCRUB
WOODLAND
BARE GROUND
PATH

100 yards

GLASLYN

MONTGOMERYSHIRE WILDLIFE TRUST

Nearest town: Machynlleth
OS Map 136 SN 828942

535 acres (216 ha) of some of the finest heather moorland in Wales, together with a lake, a blanket bog, a deep ravine and extensive scree slopes and crags. There is an information panel.

Location and access: From Machynlleth take the A489 eastwards as far as Penegoes and then turn off right (south-east) onto the minor road that runs steeply over the hills to the B4518 Llanbrynmair to Lanidloes road. About 1 mile before you reach Dylife (about 2 miles from the B4518) a track leaves to the south. Go down the track for about 1 mile and park at the reserve entrance. Take care in poor weather, and you should keep out of the ravine.

This reserve is truly out in the wilds and, by nature reserve standards, it is a really extensive tract of countryside. It embraces many different habitats and is large enough to have a significant impact on local wildlife, providing a worthwhile territory for birds of prey such as the peregrine.

It supports a breeding population of red grouse, which depend on the variety and health of

WILDLIFE FEATURES
✕ Birdlife including peregrine

the heather moorland, seeking cover from the older tussocks while feeding particularly on the young heather shoots. Heather moorland is a threatened habitat, and (as you will see on some of the land outside the reserve) much has been replaced with conifer plantation or by ploughing and reseeding. Sometimes you will see the 'natural' heather remaining only on the tracksides outside the fields.

Apart from the three members of the heather family, typical plants to look for are bilberry with edible black berries, cowberry with edible red berries (both have rather oval leaves) and crowberry with heather-like leaves and black berries, edible but flavourless.

The bog areas and the natural lake are other highlights of this marvellous reserve.

Ravine

Heather

Regenerating
Heather

Heather &
Rough Grass

P

☀ **VIEWPOINT**

HEATHER MOORLAND

— **BOUNDARY**

--- **PATH**

LAKE

500 yards

GILFACH FARM

RADNORSHIRE WILDLIFE TRUST

Nearest town: Rhayader
OS Map 147 SN 965717

A 418 acre (169 ha) farm (with a lovingly restored medieval Welsh longhouse) which has escaped many of the changes in farming in the last 20 years. The reserve includes a tumbling river, oak woodland, meadows and moorland. It has SSSI status. There is a waymarked trail with interpretation boards. There is a fee for entry to the longhouse and visitor centre.

Location and access: From Rhayader take the A470/A44 north towards Aberystwyth and Llangurig. About 2 miles north of Rhayader, where the road bends sharply back on itself, take the right hand turning (at the apex of the bend, just over the River Marteg) towards St Harmon. The cattle-grid marks the beginning of the reserve, and a second grid after about 0.75 mile marks its other boundary. Cars can be parked at the Marteg Bridge car park. There are livestock, so dogs must be kept on a lead and gates closed after use.

This unimproved farm contains a rich variety of habitats and many increasingly uncommon species of plants and animals. Even the tunnel of the now disused railway is a favourite bat roost and hibernation site - with five species, including Daubenton's bat (notable for fishing the surface of rivers and ponds). Along the river, the golden-ringed dragonfly is one of the species seen.

Dipper, grey wagtail and common sandpiper are river

WILDLIFE FEATURES
- **Birdlife including red kite**
- **Dragonflies**

birds here, with pied flycatcher, redstart and wood warbler among those of the sessile oak woodland above the house. Wheatear, whinchat and stonechat nest on the hill and buzzard and kestrel, and even red kite and raven may be seen up here, typical upland species.

There are many mosses in the river gorge, and lichens too - and also sun-loving lichens on the rock outcrops of the hill. Wild flowers include the handsome globe flower and mountain pansy.

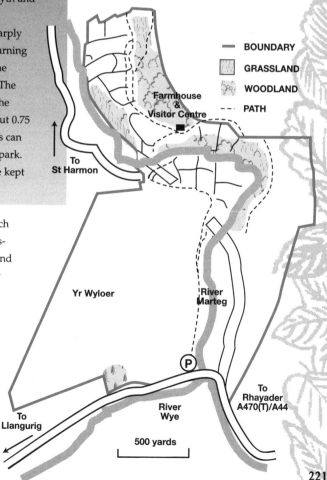

BOUNDARY
GRASSLAND
WOODLAND
PATH

Farmhouse & Visitor Centre

To St Harmon

Yr Wyloer

River Marteg

To Llangurig

River Wye

To Rhayader A470(T)/A44

500 yards

221

BAILEY EINON

RADNORSHIRE WILDLIFE TRUST

Nearest town: Llandrindod Wells
OS Map 147 SO 083613

A woodland reserve, 11 acres (4.5 ha) in area, on the bank of the River Ithon, a good example of the original rich lowland valley woods of the area. There is a waymarked trail.

Location and access: The reserve is about 2 miles east of Llandrindod Wells. From the town centre take Craig Road leading to Cefnllys Lane. After a short while you come to Shaky Bridge with a car park and picnic site. A kissing-gate just downstream from the picnic site marks the entrance to the reserve. Please do not park in front of the kissing-gate.

The wood has many characteristics of the 'wildwood' that covered much of Wales thousands of years ago. It is a varied woodland. Around the trail the tall canopy

WILDLIFE FEATURES
❀ Spring flowers ✕ Woodland birds

trees are mainly ash, with hazel as the lower shrub layer. Wetter areas have alder while the dry rocky part beyond the end of the trail has oak with field maple. The flowers also vary - bluebell, dog's mercury and early purple orchid and orpine in places, with wetter areas flagged by kingcup. Coppicing encouraged these in the past, by regularly opening the woodland floor to sunlight and the Wildlife Trust continues coppicing today. The open glades also attract butterflies.

Tits are a common sight, acrobatically searching for caterpillars and aphids on the shrubs, but you'll have a good chance of seeing pied flycatcher (these birds make regular use of the nesting boxes), redstart, willow and wood warbler as well as the great spotted woodpecker. Pairs of buzzard sometimes nest in the treetops, while the otter can sometimes be seen along the river here.

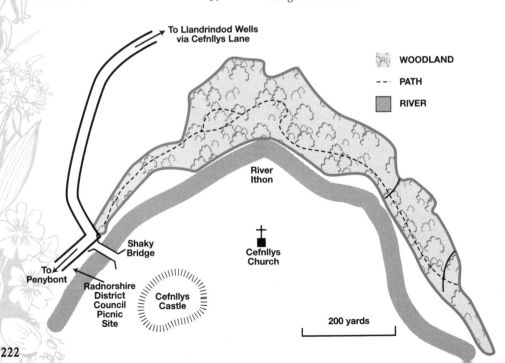

To Llandrindod Wells
via Cefnllys Lane

WOODLAND
- - - PATH
RIVER

River
Ithon

Shaky
Bridge

Cefnllys
Church

To
Penybont

Radnorshire
District
Council
Picnic
Site

Cefnllys
Castle

200 yards

222

BURFABOG

RADNORSHIRE WILDLIFE TRUST

Nearest town: Presteigne
OS Map 148 SO 275613

24 acres (9.5 ha) of grassland, within which two alder-lined streams bisect, leading to Knobbley Brook which forms the southern boundary of the reserve. There is a motte-and-bailey castle within the reserve, of unknown history and date. The reserve has SSSI status.

Location and access: From Presteigne take the B4362 south-west to Knill and Ditchyeld Bridge. At Ditchyeld Bridge turn right (west) onto an unclassified road leading to Evenjobb. The reserve is located on this road, about 100 yards before a turning for Burfa and Barland on the left hand side; the entrance is marked by a gate and a sign. Livestock graze to maintain the great variety of plants, so dogs must be on leads. Footbridges and duckboards are installed to secure the visitors' route around the reserve.

WILDLIFE FEATURES
✿ **Wetland and meadow flowers**
✕ **Birdlife**

Despite its name, this is a mosaic of grasslands, but of considerable interest - more than 140 species of plants have been listed. In the wetter acid areas, heath spotted orchid grows in large numbers, along with purple moor-grass and devil's-bit scabious. In the less acid areas golden saxifrage abounds, along with kingcup, meadowsweet and ragged-robin.

On the drier ground you find pignut and harebell, with bluebell, dog's mercury and red campion in the hedgerows. Although basically a woodland flower, the bluebell flourishes in hedgerows in wetter western regions of the country, in the west and south-west.

Along the streamsides you can find raspberry, guelder-rose and yellow flag iris.

The birds are interesting: snipe, heron, lapwing and mallard visit the reserve along with nesting whitethroat and garden warbler.

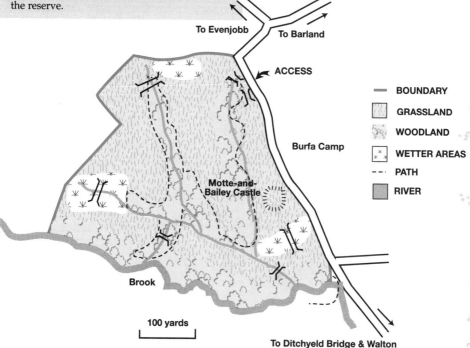

To Evenjobb

To Barland

◄ ACCESS

Burfa Camp

Motte-and-Bailey Castle

Brook

100 yards

To Ditchyeld Bridge & Walton

— BOUNDARY
GRASSLAND
WOODLAND
WETTER AREAS
--- PATH
RIVER

PWLL-Y-WRACH

BRECKNOCK WILDLIFE TRUST

Nearest town: Talgarth (Hay on Wye)
OS Map 161 SO 165326

21 acres (8.5 ha) of broadleaved woodland of considerable botanical interest, set in a narrow steep-sided valley. The reserve also holds a fine sculpted waterfall, some quarry faces and an old tramway.

There is also a geology trail and leaflet to the geological features.

Location and access: Talgarth is located between Hay on Wye and Brecon, at the foot of the Black Mountains, within the Brecon Beacons National Park. The wood is about half a mile south-east of Talgarth, on the north bank of the River Enig. To get to the parking (six cars maximum) take the A479 south from the square in Talgarth (first left over the bridge) and fork left almost immediately into Pendent Road. Continue over the river and up the hill past the hospital and follow the narrow lane for a further 250 yards to a reserve entrance on the right; there is another entrance and parking area a little further on. About 650 yards of the path to the waterfall are suitable for wheelchairs.

Variations in soil chemistry and drainage make this a varied

WILDLIFE FEATURES
❀ **Woodland flowers**
🐾 **Dipper and other stream wildlife**
〰 **Geological features**

woodland. Sessile oak grows on the upper, rain-leached valley sides with heather and hard fern pointing to an acid soil. Lower down, however, where nutrients drain down from richer rock bands in the sandstone, there are ash trees and lime-loving shrubs such as spindle and dogwood and plants such as herb Paris, and bluebell carpets the ground in springtime.

As for butterflies, they are often attracted to the sunny glades. The speckled wood, with brown and cream spotted wings, is one example - the males are strongly territorial and may be seen fighting in aerial combat.

The wood warbler and pied flycatcher are among the woodland birds here, with dipper and grey wagtail by the stream. There are often woodpeckers. The wood is home to the most important colony of dormouse in the region - coppicing encourages the soft fruits and hazelnuts they need. The otter is occasionally present.

Rock exposures at the waterfalls and the quarry reveal interesting geological features. An interpretation panel explains the rocks revealed at the main waterfall. A leaflet guiding walkers around the geology trail provides a fuller explanation.

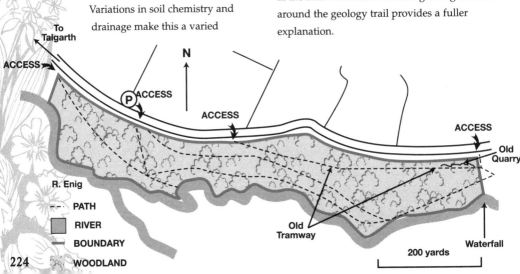

224

PATH
RIVER
BOUNDARY
WOODLAND

R. Enig

To Talgarth
ACCESS
P ACCESS
ACCESS
ACCESS
Old Quarry
Old Tramway
Waterfall
200 yards
N

DOLYDD HAFREN

MONTGOMERYSHIRE WILDLIFE TRUST

Nearest town: Montgomery
OS Map 126/137 SJ 208005

The River Severn (Afon Hafren) when looping across a relatively flat valley has formed oxbow lakes, an excellent wetland habitat for waterfowl. There are two observation hides.

Location and access: From Montgomery take the B4388 (towards Welshpool). Nearly 3 miles (5 km) north of Montgomery, turn left onto an unclassified road for Forden village and drive through the village and on for about 1.5 miles to the Gaer Farm, sited at a sharp left hand bend. Turn right at the bend down a track and park in the car park. Keep to the footpath which leads to the observation hides.

The reserve is open from August to March, but closed April to July to avoid disturbing nesting birds.

As a river like the Severn works its way down through the gravels of the valley, it winds in great loops, eroding material from the outside of the bends and depositing it on the inside. From time to time a loop breaks across at the neck, and the loop remains as a cut-off oxbow. Old oxbows account for the pattern of wet hollows cut into the riverside meadows here. The Wildlife Trust has dredged some of these deeper to give more standing water.

WILDLIFE FEATURES
Wildfowl and waders

Like many wetland sites, winter is the best time for a visit, when waders and wildfowl are clustered along the water's edge or in the shallows. On the stubble of the nearby fields, large flocks of skylark and yellowhammer may be feeding. In spring, the sand martin, common sandpiper and little ringed plover return from foreign parts. And the occasional peregrine may sweep across in the hope of making a meal.

The site is proving attractive to the otter; the best chance to see them is from the hide furthest from the car park. Hare are seen on the fields throughout the year.

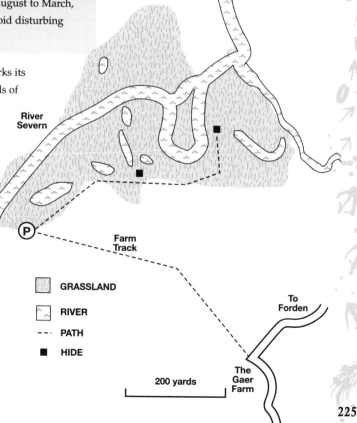

River
Severn

Farm
Track

To
Forden

GRASSLAND

RIVER

- - - PATH

■ HIDE

200 yards

The
Gaer
Farm

225

LLANYMYNECH ROCKS

**MONTGOMERYSHIRE WILDLIFE TRUST
& SHROPSHIRE WILDLIFE TRUST**

Nearest town: Oswestry
OS Map 126 SJ 265220

An old limestone quarry, a reserve of 6 acres (2.4 ha) straddling the border between England and Wales. Quarrying stopped in the 1920s and the site has reverted to nature, with bare rock faces and scree, grassland, scrub and woodland.

Location and access: From Oswestry take the A483 south (towards Welshpool). About 200 yards south of the Cross Guns pub (the village of Pant), take Underhill Lane on the right. Follow this lane round two bends and up to the end of the rough track, where cars can be parked.

There is also parking in the village of Llanymynech, about 1 mile south of Pant.

This reserve is a fascinating example of the healing power of nature. The limestone grassland and the woodland which are now main features have developed since quarrying stopped in the 1920s. But the sheer, towering quarry faces are themselves an important aspect, providing nest sites for the jackdaw and the decidedly

WILDLIFE FEATURES
🦋 **Wild flowers** 🦋 **Butterflies**

rare peregrine.

The old spoil heaps are colonised by grasses and scrub, with dogwood and hawthorn and ash among the species, and this has become more or less woodland in places. But the highlight of the reserve is where the thinly turfed quarry floor is scattered with flowers marking the seasons. You see cowslip and early purple orchid in spring, an early summer flowering of spotted, pyramidal and bee orchids together with tiny blue milkwort, fairy flax and other limestone flowers, while late summer flowers include marjoram, star-like yellow-wort and carline thistle, followed by the small purple-pink trumpets of autumn gentian.

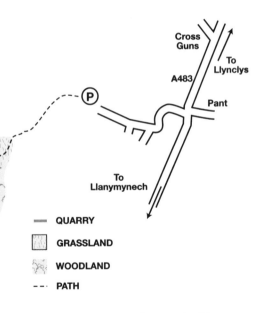

— QUARRY

▨ GRASSLAND

▨ WOODLAND

--- PATH

Butterflies are attracted to this riot of wild flowers; particularly noticeable, although small, is the common blue.

And the sheer rock face echoes with the sound of birdsong.

300 yards

ROUNDTON

MONTGOMERYSHIRE WILDLIFE TRUST

Nearest town: Bishop's Castle
OS Map 137 SO 293947

A prominent craggy hill rising from woodland (some marred by Dutch elm disease), with grassland and exposed rock faces. There are waymarked trails, the longer one very steep and rough.

Location and access: From Bishop's Castle follow the signs for the A488 north towards Shrewsbury. After about a mile it crosses the A489 running west to Churchstoke and then Newtown. Before Churchstoke turn right onto either of two unclassified lanes, clearly signposted for the reserve with brown and white signs. There is a car park inside the reserve entrance, but please remember to shut the gate.

WILDLIFE FEATURES
❀ Grassland flowers

The best way to take in all features of interest here is to keep to the waymarked path. This starts with a small pond, an additional habitat added by the Wildlife Trust. It has a good display of monkeyflower (*Mimulus*), an escape from cultivation which has naturalised well in recent years.

Over the stile, the path goes through a woodland with ash, oak, rowan and some invasive sycamore, occupying the lower slopes. Look out for the green woodpecker here, which may be digging at one of the anthills. If you don't want the steep climb of the whole walk, turn back when the path crosses the stream.

To complete the circuit, however, walk out onto the lane and back into the reserve about 400 yards further up. There is a steep climb to the summit, crowned with a hill-fort, and the crags here reveal the volcanic nature of the rock.

The soil is usually very thin here and dries quickly in summer: the hill is well known for its spring ephemerals, a group of short-lived plants which grow and flower early, at the beginning of the season. They include shepherd's cress, vernal whitlow grass (not a grass but a plant with a stem of small white flowers rising from a rosette of leaves) and upright chickweed.

The adits (tunnels) of the old mines are a feature of the reserve and, together with the hollow trees, provide bat roosts.

Hill-fort

ACCESS

P

UPLAND PLANTS

WOODLAND

PATH

RIVER

200 yards

SOUTH GOWER CLIFFS

GLAMORGAN WILDLIFE TRUST

Nearest town: Swansea
OS Map 159 SS 470844

Six nature reserves on the Gower Peninsula covering 238 acres (96 ha) of SSSI, including cliff and shore, limestone grassland and heath.

Location and access. From Swansea, take the A4118 west to the village of Port Eynon, a drive of about 16 miles (10 km). Follow the road through the village, to the car park by the beach. Take the footpath on the west side of the beach to the reserves. Five of them form a chain here, the sixth (Deborah's Hole) being about 1.25 miles further west along the coast. The OS Map reference is for the first (eastern) reserve, Sedger's Bank, near the car park

These reserves have some of the most magnificent sea cliffs in the whole of Wales, limestone riven and torn by the seas and the

WILDLIFE FEATURES
↟ Wildfowl   ✽ Lime-rich grassland

wind into bays and coves, pinnacles and caves. The cliffs are also extraordinarily rich botanically, with more than 200 species of plants, some real rarities, backed up by the interest of the shore flowers. These coastal flowers are glorious in summer. In winter, the main interest lies with the sea birds.

Sedger's Bank is a good place for sub-littoral animals and plants exposed by the low tides, summer shore-nesting birds and grey seals in winter. The next reserve, Port Eynon Point, is an important sea watching site - late July and early August see largescale seabird movements of large numbers of Manx shearwater and gannet and others (and it's best to be on site at daybreak). Deborah's Hole has spring coastal flowers and summer coastal breeding birds as its speciality - well worth the extra walk.

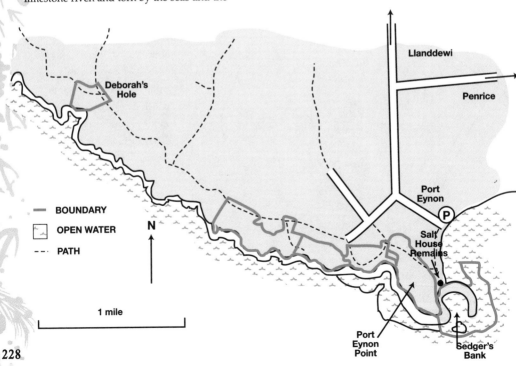

BOUNDARY

OPEN WATER

PATH

N

1 mile

Deborah's Hole

Llanddewi

Penrice

Port Eynon

Salt House Remains

Port Eynon Point

Sedger's Bank

MELINCWRT WATERFALLS RESERVE

GLAMORGAN WILDLIFE TRUST

Nearest town: Neath
OS Map 160 SN 825017

A narrow gorge with oak woodland up its steep sides and a spectacular 80 foot high (24 metre) waterfall.

Location and access: The reserve is signposted from the A465(T) road, 5 miles (8 km) north-east of Neath. The car park is on the west side of the B4434 (south of Resolven), the entrance to the reserve being on the opposite side of the road via a public footpath.

A tributary of the Neath river has created this gorge with the spectacular waterfall which was painted by Turner in 1794.

The remains of a seventeenth century blast furnace and iron works can be found on the reserve's northern boundary. Today, however, it is a magnificent wildlife haven.

The woodland is mature sessile oak interspersed with gnarled silver birch, wild cherry, rowan and crab-apple. In early summer the woodland floor carries a carpet of bluebell, with enchanter's-nightshade taking over later in the year (a somewhat modest plant with small white flowers for such a lovely name!).

WILDLIFE FEATURES
❀ **Woodland flowers, woodland ferns**
✗ **Birdlife**

In the wet flushes you can find golden saxifrage and tutsan, more handsome plants by far, with yellow flowers.

There are plenty of ferns in these damp and somewhat sheltered conditions. Twenty species have been recorded, including green spleenwort, brittle bladder fern, hay scented buckler fern and Wilson's filmy fern (which does live up to its name).

Birdlife includes redstart and pied flycatcher, with dipper and grey wagtail being regularly seen along the stream at all times of the year.

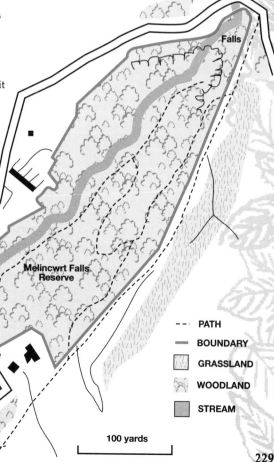

Falls

Melincwrt Falls Reserve

Resolven B4434

- - - **PATH**
— **BOUNDARY**
GRASSLAND
WOODLAND
STREAM

100 yards

229

PARC SLIP NATURE PARK

GLAMORGAN WILDLIFE TRUST

Nearest town: Bridgend

OS Map 170 SS 880840

250 acres (101 ha) of restored land with recreated semi-natural habitats such as grassland, marsh and wader scrape together with young woodlands. There are three bird hides and a nature trail and visitor centre.

Location and Access: From Bridgend take the A4063 north. Just past the M4, turn left at the roundabout onto the B4281 (to Aberkenfig). The reserve is signposted off this road. Park in the car park. There is disabled access to the park, reserve and bird hides.

This is a many-and-varied reserve, rather wonderfully created from dereliction. In addition to the habitats listed above, there are four flower-rich fields which are being managed as pasture and as hay meadows and (although not a feature for visitors because of the danger of disturbance) an artificial sett has been constructed away from the footpaths to help the local badger population move into the park to live, rather than just use it for feeding.

Mining ended in the 1980s, yet already the bird tally includes nesting lapwing and skylark with, in winter, snipe and migrant waders such as little

WILDLIFE FEATURES
Wild flowers   Birdlife

ringed plover, green sandpiper and little gull. Heron haunt the northern wetlands, while from the bird hides here, moorhen can be watched nesting and the kingfisher dashes past between its favourite streams.

In winter large flocks of mallard and teal roost overnight. The green woodpecker is already seen around the new broadleaved woodland - one large area and several shelter belts have been planted up.

And the flowers include marsh, common spotted and bee orchids.

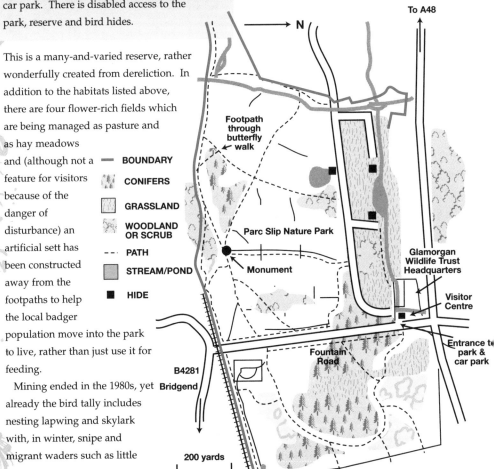

BOUNDARY

CONIFERS

GRASSLAND

WOODLAND OR SCRUB

PATH

STREAM/POND

HIDE

CWM COLHUW

GLAMORGAN WILDLIFE TRUST

Nearest town: Llantwit Major
OS Map 170 SS 960674

A coastal reserve holding the remains of a 2700 year old Iron Age hill fort, edged by cliffs and commanding panoramic views of the Bristol Channel. The reserve has open grassland fringed with woodland or scrub. There are information boards.

Location and access: The reserve is near Llantwit Major, about halfway between Bridgend and Rhoose. From Bridgend take the B4265 south until the turning on the right, signposted for Llantwit Major. In the village follow the road signposted for the beach. Park in the seafront car park and climb up the steps past the information boards to gain access to the reserve. There are all-year toilet and café facilities at the car park.

The reserve is set on Jurassic Blue Lias, a fossil-rich rock, part of the only area in Wales with this geology. The open grassland is notable for limestone flowers in the summer months May-August. Another of the reserve's special features is the maritime field, with a diverse plant list which includes the scarce wild cabbage. This robust herb with lemon yellow flowers and thick, greyish fleshy leaves (which distinguish it from the mustards) is the ancestor of today's cabbages and kales - the stout stem bears scars reminiscent of brussels sprout plants.

WILDLIFE FEATURES
* Limestone flowers
* Autumn migrant birds

The sheltered open limestone grassland glades of the reserve provide habitats for butterflies such as meadow brown, small heath and common blue. Birds such as bullfinch, goldfinch, yellowhammer and whitethroat nest in the scrub.

It is also a notable site for sightings of migrant birds.

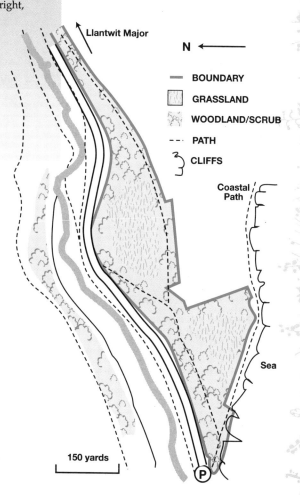

Llantwit Major

N ←

— BOUNDARY
GRASSLAND
WOODLAND/SCRUB
--- PATH
CLIFFS

Coastal Path

Sea

150 yards

P

SILENT VALLEY

GWENT WILDLIFE TRUST

WILDLIFE FEATURES
🟤 Beech woodland 🦅 Woodland birds

Nearest town: Ebbw Vale
OS Map 171 SO 187062

This reserve, a Local Nature Reserve managed jointly with Blaenau Gwent County Borough Council, contains interesting beech and alder carr woodland and areas that were once meadows (there was once a farm here). There is an old coal pit, now being reclaimed by nature. Some of the reserve has SSSI status.

Location and access: From Ebbw Vale take the A4046 south. After about 2.5 miles (4 km) you reach the village of Cwm. Go through the village one-way system and exit on the northern side. Take the second turning on the right (by a corner shop). About a third of a mile further on there is a car park on the right (the cemetery is just ahead, on the left). Walk northwards across the flat grass playing area to get to the reserve entrance.

The beech woodland up the steep climb is the highest and most westerly natural beechwood in Britain.   The production of mast (beech nuts) is sometimes so great that huge flocks of chaffinch and brambling come to feed in the winter months.

The mounds of greater tussock sedge and the alder carr mark out wet ground, and there are usually plenty of ferns to be seen. The coal tip is also prominent, now being colonised by a green patchwork of mosses, lichens, heather and grasses.

In the south of the reserve, once open pasture contains anthills in the open spaces. The green woodpecker feeds here - more commonly heard with its laughing yaffle call than seen. Pied flycatcher and redstart are among the birds that also nest on the reserve.

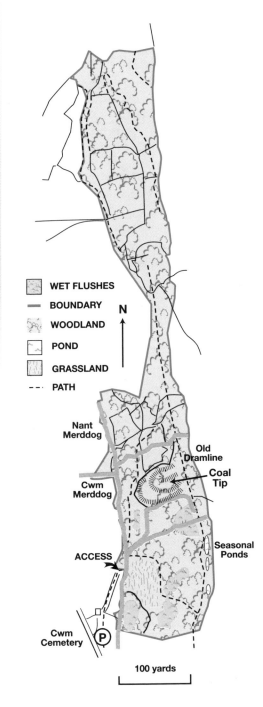

WET FLUSHES
BOUNDARY
WOODLAND
POND
GRASSLAND
PATH

N

Nant Merddog
Cwm Merddog
Old Dramline
Coal Tip
Seasonal Ponds
ACCESS
Cwm Cemetery

100 yards

MAGOR MARSH

GWENT WILDLIFE TRUST

Nearest town: Newport
OS Map 171 ST 427867

A 64 acre (26 ha) reserve, the last remnant of fenland on the Gwent levels, a prime example of the succession of plant communities from open water to marsh and scrub woodland. It is an SSSI. There is a bird hide.

Location and access: From Newport take the A48 east (towards Chepstow) and turn right onto the B4245 for the village of Magor. Turn off the road into the village and follow the signs for Redwick, passing the priory ruins on the left. Immediately after the railway bridge turn left and follow the road for about half a mile. The reserve entrance is on the right; park in the car park.

Magor can also be reached from junctions 23 and 23A of the M4 motorway.

WILDLIFE FEATURES
❀ **Wetland flowers**   ✕ **Birdlife**

A long history lies behind this reserve: it is the last remnant of traditionally managed fenland to be found on the Gwent levels, with a pattern of drainage ditches and other features which have remained unchanged for centuries.

There is wet rush pasture in the south-east and two notable hay meadows in the south-west corner. These last are maintained traditionally and only grazed after the hay cut, with the result that in late spring they are a mass of flowers and you will see yellow flag, yellow rattle and ragged-robin among them. Marsh marigold is common over the whole reserve in spring.

The reedbeds provide nest sites for sedge, reed and grasshopper warblers. The rare marsh warbler might also be seen, along with mallard, moorhen, heron, kingfisher and water rail. Snipe and reed bunting nest in the rough pasture while garganey, green sandpiper and night heron pass through on their way to winter feeding grounds. Overwintering birds include numerous teal. Sparrowhawk, buzzard and even peregrine may be seen at any time of year.

BOUNDARY
GRASSLAND
WOODLAND
POND
PATH
HIDE

233

Scotland & Ulster

Scotland offers a profusion of unspoilt wild places for people to visit and just a few Scottish Wildlife Trust reserves are featured in this section. A spectacular place to visit is the Isle of Eigg, now managed by a community trust including the Scottish Wildlife Trust. Dominating the island is the volcanic ridge of the Sgurr. Crofted fields and sand dunes are rich in wild flowers, and 68 bird species nest on Eigg, including the magnificent golden eagle. Even more remote is Handa island, off the north-western tip of Scotland, home to incredible numbers of nesting seabirds. More accessible are the Falls of Clyde, close to New Lanark village in Strathclyde. Ancient woodlands cover this dramatic gorge on the River Clyde where visitors can watch badgers emerge from their setts and peregrine falcons nesting on eyries.

On the east coast, is Montrose Basin, with a visitor centre overlooking the changing life of the River South Esk tidal basin. Many birds are attracted by its mudflats, saltmarsh and reedbeds, including curlew, oystercatcher, dunlin, and in winter, internationally important populations of pink-footed geese.

This section also includes reserves managed by the Ulster Wildlife Trust in Northern Ireland. Much of the countryside appears quite undeveloped, with many small fields and hedgerows still remaining. It has some beautiful scenery including the Giant's Causeway on the north coast of Antrim. This is the end of a basalt plateau, the eastern edge of which is intersected by the Glens of Antrim. One of these, Glenarm is a reserve which has been undisturbed for many years. The woodland and river are rich in birdlife including buzzard, woodcock and dipper.

SCOTLAND & ULSTER

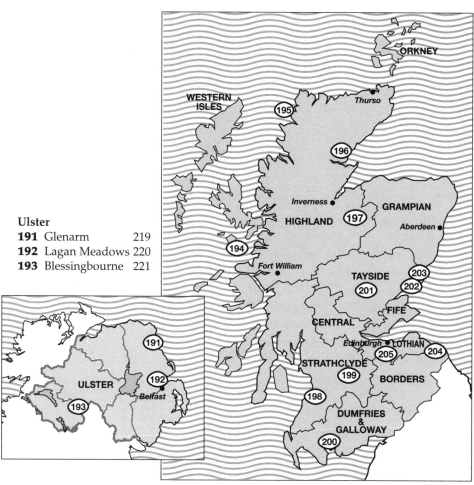

ISLE OF EIGG

**ISLE OF EIGG TRUST
SCOTTISH WILDLIFE TRUST**

Nearest town: Mallaig
OS Map 39 NM 474875

The island of Eigg offers 7400 acres (2995 ha) of fine rough uplands with alpine plants, hazelwood on steep coastal cliffs, lochans and bogs. About half the island has SSSI status. Interpretation boards and exhibits are being developed and a ranger leads guided walks in summer. The Isle of Eigg Trust includes the Scottish Wildlife Trust working in partnership with the island community and Highland Council.

Location and access: The nearest mainland town is Mallaig, some 16 miles (26 km) from Eigg by the Caledonian MacBrayne ferry. Access is for foot passengers only; cars cannot be taken.

To reach Mallaig, take the A82 north from Fort William and about 1.25 miles from the town turn west (left) onto the A830. During the summer months a private ferry runs each day except Thursday from Arisaig, about 9 miles south of Mallaig.

The most striking feature on the island is the narrow volcanic ridge of the Sgurr and the heather moorland lying between it and the north-west coast. The Atlantic gales prune the vegetation here. Less common plants able to tolerate the wet and windy conditions include least willow and Wilson's filmy fern. A lime-rich mineral dyke is signposted by pink moss campion, white mountain avens and the woolly yellow heads of kidney vetch.

The slopes below the craggy cliffs which edge the Beinne Bhuidhe plateau are largely covered with hazel scrub,

WILDLIFE FEATURES
* ❋ **Wild flowers**
* ✖ **Birdlife including golden eagle**

with ferns among the boulders and also wood anemone, great patches of bluebell and other woodland flowers. There is a colony of Manx shearwater on the steep grassed slopes, while you might see buzzard and raven riding the air currents overhead.

The crofted fields at Cleadale are rich in wild flowers as are the dunes behind the large sandy beach at Laig.

Sixty-eight bird species nest on Eigg, including snipe in the marshes, the red-throated diver and the golden eagle. It is hoped that the corncrake can be encouraged to return. Otters are frequently seen and the ferry is an excellent vantage point for spotting cetaceans.

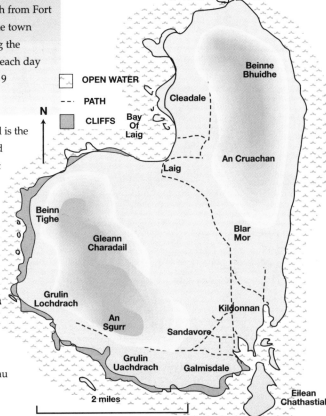

OPEN WATER

PATH

CLIFFS

N

Eilean Thuilm

Beinne Bhuidhe

Cleadale

Bay Of Laig

Laig

An Cruachan

Beinn Tighe

Gleann Charadail

Blar Mor

Grulin Lochdrach

An Sgurr

Kildonnan

Sandavore

Grulin Uachdrach

Galmisdale

Eilean Chathastial

2 miles

HANDA ISLAND

SCOTTISH WILDLIFE TRUST

Nearest towns: Scourie, Tarbet
OS Map 9 NC 138480

Handa is a 896 acre (363 ha) island with sea cliffs which are one of the largest seabird nesting sites in north-west Europe. The island has SSSI status. A small visitor centre is open during the summer and there is a ranger.

Location and access: The island is reached for day visits by boat from the village of Tarbet, Sundays excepted and weather permitting. To reach Tarbet take the A894 north from Unapool and continue on this road past Scourie. About 3 miles north of Scourie turn left onto an unclassified road, signposted for Tarbet, a further 3 miles.

Visitors must keep to a waymarked circular path around the island.

16,000 razorbill and 8,000 kittiwake. In addition there are around 3,500 pairs of fulmar and a few hundred pairs of puffin and shag.

The tops of the cliff carry some interesting plant communities, including a fine thrift and sea plantain 'meadow' and maritime heaths, both rich and poor in species. In less-exposed areas away from the sea there is some grassland with Yorkshire fog and heathland with ling or crowberry, and with bog asphodel flagging the damper areas. Lochans enliven the moorland interior, a number supporting red-throated divers.

This moorland has been colonised by both great and arctic skuas; numbers breeding seem to be increasing and have reached national significance in recent years. Other nesting birds here include shelduck, ringed plover, wheatear, skylark and meadow pipit.

The cliffs, reaching 460 ft (140 metres) high on the west of the island, decreasing to the south-east (where there are sandy bays), have weathered into ledges which attract up to 114,000 guillemot,

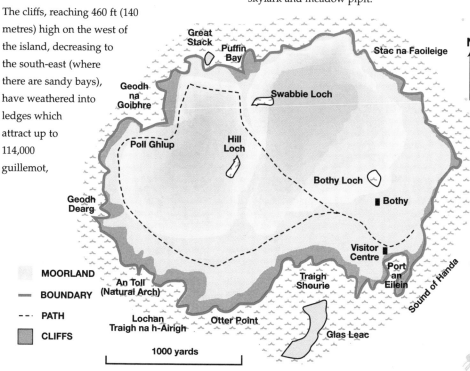

MOORLAND

BOUNDARY

PATH

CLIFFS

1000 yards

LOCH FLEET

Nearest towns: Golspie, Dornoch

OS Map 21 NH 794965

2,833 acres (1,147 ha) of tidal basin and sand dunes, coastal heath and some planted pine woodland. It is an SSSI.

In the summer, the ranger leads guided walks around the reserve. A cottage next to the reserve is being developed as an educational and interpretative centre.

Location and access: Loch Fleet lies 2 miles (3 km) south of Golspie on the A9, and about 5 miles north of Dornoch. Cars can be parked at Little Ferry or in lay-bys around the basin.

The reserve contains a number of different habitats lying within and around the basin of Loch Fleet, the most northerly inlet of water on the east coast. To the north and south the basin is bordered by sand dune and shingle ridge systems.

WILDLIFE FEATURES

 Wading birds and wildfowl

 Seals

As for the woodland, much of the blown sand to the north is planted with conifers and natural seeding of Scots pine is occurring. However, there may have been woodland here for centuries, because you can find flowers such as twinflower and twayblade which are typical of old pinewoods.

Both Ferry Wood and Balblair Wood contain numerous woodland birds, including the Scottish crossbill, capercaillie and siskin.

The dune systems also contain diverse plant communities, including marram grass on the newer dunes and birch and juniper scrub on the older, more stable ones.

The dunes, beaches and saltmarshes fringing the estuary also support many breeding birds, including the little tern. Thousands of waders and wildfowl throng the basin during the winter months. Mallard, teal and wigeon keep to the basin while goldeneye, common scoter, eider and long-tailed duck venture out onto the open sea in calmer weather.

The common seal can often be seen hauled out on the sandbanks.

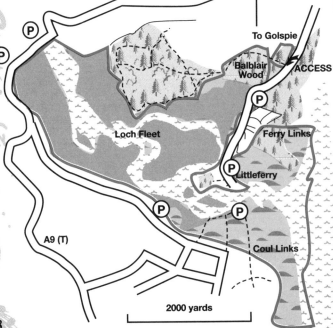

DUNES

TIDAL MUDFLATS

BOUNDARY

CONIFERS

WOODLAND

OPEN WATER

PATH

PASS OF RYVOAN

SCOTTISH WILDLIFE TRUST

Nearest town: Aviemore
OS Map 36 NJ 998104

300 acres (122 ha) of native pinewood and scree slopes lying in spectacular scenery within the Glenmore Forest Park. The reserve is managed jointly with Forestry Enterprise who provide a ranger service based in the Glenmore Visitor Centre.

Location and access: The reserve is 7 miles (11 km) east of Aviemore. From Aviemore take the B9152 south and turn left onto a side road for Coylumbridge. From here, take the unclassified road east to Glenmore Lodge, passing Loch Morlich on the right. Cars can be left in the car park opposite the campsite in Glenmore. Walk up the road past Glenmore Lodge to reach the Pass of Ryvoan.

This is an important corridor between the Abernethy and Glenmore forests, a steep sided pass - extending from 1150 to 2050 ft (350 to 622 metres) with a loch which a trick of the light makes a strange olive green colour. It is anyway a colourful place, with slopes of bilberry and birch, and some bright bogland in the valley, while the mineral-rich northern slope carries a host of plants. Primrose, violet, moschatel and

WILDLIFE FEATURES
✿ Native pinewood flowers
✕ Birdlife

wintergreen are amongst the attractive flowers to be seen. There is plenty of heather, and juniper, both upright and sprawling, spreads through the open pinewood.

This woodland is naturally regenerated native Caledonian pine forest. Timber has been felled, and the area has also been used as a hunting ground as well as rough grazing, but it has survived here as woodland since first colonised at the end of the last Ice Age.

Crossbill, goldcrest and crested tit are among the resident birds, while summer visitors number tree pipit, redstart and grey wagtail.

Red deer and red squirrel are also regularly seen here.

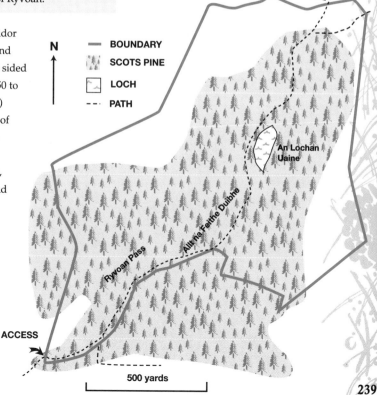

	BOUNDARY
	SCOTS PINE
	LOCH
	PATH

ACCESS

An Lochan Uaine

Allt na Feithe Duibhe

Ryvoan Pass

ACCESS

N

500 yards

AYR GORGE WOODLANDS

SCOTTISH WILDLIFE TRUST

Nearest town: Ayr
OS Map 70 NS 457249

A 99 acre (40.2 ha) reserve of oak and birch woodland in a ravine in the valley of the River Ayr. Nearly half the reserve has SSSI status. There are interpretation boards at the reserve and a leaflet is available.

Location and access: The reserve is near Failford village, on the B743. From Ayr take the A719 north-east for about 3 miles to the junction with the A77. Continue straight over the roundabout onto the B743 and continue until Failford. Cars can be parked in the lay-by in the village.

There is a well-maintained network of footpaths on the west side of the river.

WILDLIFE FEATURES

🐦 **Spectacular scenery** ✾ **Rare cow-wheat among the typical woodland plants**

are partly semi-natural - dominated by sessile oak and some birch - and partly conifer plantation, the majority of which has recently been felled. A sparse shrub layer of holly, hazel and rowan can be found in the deciduous woodland, and the locally rare cow-wheat grows on the more acidic soil. There are also several uncommon invertebrates.

Sessile oak is typical of valley woods in the uplands of the west and north of Britain. This oak differs from its cousin the common (or pedunculate) oak by having leaves which smoothly join the stalk (the common oak has lobes here) and acorns with no or only a short stalk.

Ayr Gorge is an impressive steep ravine in the river valley. The woodlands

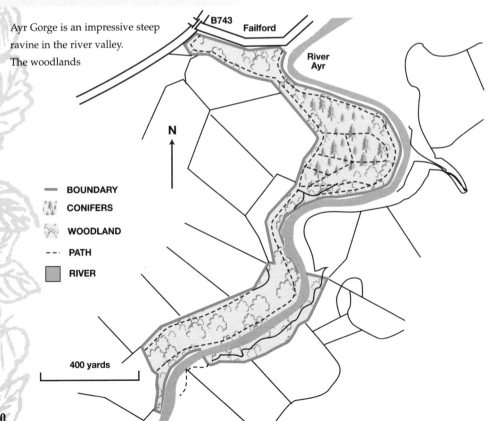

BOUNDARY
CONIFERS
WOODLAND
PATH
RIVER

400 yards

FALLS OF CLYDE

SCOTTISH WILDLIFE TRUST

Nearest town: Lanark
OS Map 71/72 NS 882425

145 acres (58.6 ha) of ancient gorge woodland stretching alongside the River Clyde, with its spectacular and famous falls. 46 acres are of SSSI status. There is a Visitor Centre in Lanark and interpretation boards on the reserve.

Location and access: The reserve is one mile south of Lanark on an unclassified road; from the centre of Lanark follow signs for New Lanark. There is parking available in New Lanark village. The Visitor Centre is open every day April-October and at weekends the rest of the year. There is a good network of footpaths, some with wheelchair access.

From the historic village of New Lanark the reserve stretches south along the River Clyde. The famous falls at Corra Linn have been an attraction for at least two centuries - Coleridge and Wordsworth visited and many artists have propped their easels here.

On both sides of the river stand a mixture of natural and plantation woodland, with established oak, ash, birch, beech and Douglas fir. Much of the reserve on the east side is conifer plantation, but flowers such as dog's mercury and bluebell recall that this was originally oakwood. The west side has introduced species such as rhododendron and sequoia, along with oak, alder and yew.

WILDLIFE FEATURES
🦅 **Birdlife**
🦇 **Natterer's bat** 🐿 **Red squirrel**

The conifers are gradually being replaced with native broadleaves.

The kestrel nests on inaccessible ledges in the gorge; dipper and grey wagtail can be seen, and the waters are well stocked with fish - minnow, trout, grayling and pike. Other nesting birds include both green and great spotted woodpeckers, spotted flycatcher and five species of tit, including the long-tailed tit and the very local willow tit.

During the summer, Natterer's bat roosts in the reserve. Badgers are regular breeders and a badger-viewing platform has recently been built above the sett. Contact the ranger service for viewing arrangements.

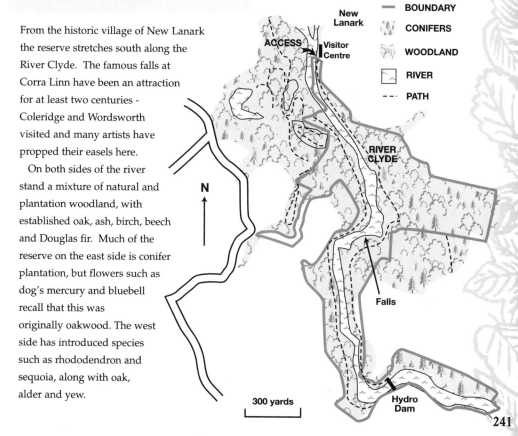

	BOUNDARY
	CONIFERS
	WOODLAND
	RIVER
	PATH

New Lanark

ACCESS

Visitor Centre

RIVER CLYDE

N

Falls

300 yards

Hydro Dam

241

CARSTRAMON WOOD

SCOTTISH WILDLIFE TRUST

Nearest town: Kirkcudbright

OS Map 83 NX 592605

198 acres (80.3 ha) of ancient oak woodland, a remnant of the once extensive Galloway woodlands. The reserve is an SSSI. There are interpretation boards.

Location and access: The reserve is 2 miles (3 km) north of Gatehouse of Fleet. From Kirkcudbright take the A755/B796 north-west to Gatehouse. From the village take the unclassified road north for Barlay and Carstramon. Cars may be parked in lay-bys on this road. A number of good footpaths provide a circular route.

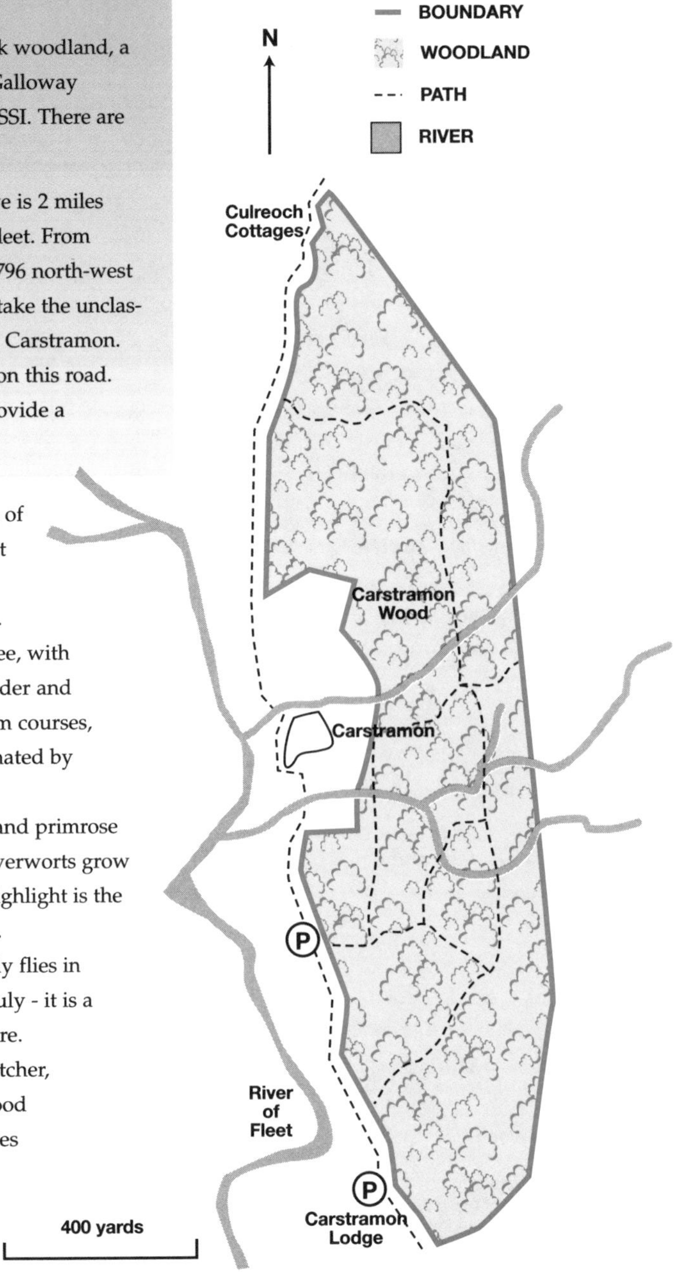

Carstramon Wood is the largest of four relic oak woods in the Fleet Valley, all remnants of the once extensive Galloway woodlands.

Sessile oak is the dominant tree, with hazel in the shrub layer. Ash, alder and wych elm grow along the stream courses, and the wettest areas are dominated by ash and alder.

Dog's mercury, wood violet and primrose and a number of mosses and liverworts grow beneath the tree canopy. One highlight is the sheet of bluebells in late spring.

The purple hairstreak butterfly flies in the canopy of the oak trees in July - it is a local and declining butterfly here.

As for the birdlife, pied flycatcher, redstart, green woodpecker, wood warbler and tree pipit are species to look out for.

WILDLIFE FEATURES

❀ **Bluebell**　　✕ **Woodland birds**

N

— **BOUNDARY**

WOODLAND

--- **PATH**

RIVER

Culreoch Cottages

Carstramon Wood

Carstramon

P

River of Fleet

P

Carstramon Lodge

400 yards

LOCH OF THE LOWES

SCOTTISH WILDLIFE TRUST

Nearest town: Blairgowrie
OS Map 52/53 NO 050440

A freshwater loch with fringing marsh and woodland, totalling some 235 acres (95 ha), with SSSI status. There is a bird-watching hide and visitor centre. A ranger service operates throughout the year.

Location and access: The reserve is 2 miles (3 km) north east of the village of Dunkeld, from which it is signposted. There is a car park as indicated on the map.

The hide (with wheelchair access) is open all year, the centre April-September.

WILDLIFE FEATURES

✖ **Birdlife including osprey**
✿ **Wetland plants**

The reed- and tree-fringed loch is picturesque, and a main interest here is the diversity of habitats to be found. Here at the edge of the Scottish Highlands, plants and animals typical of both lowland and upland Scotland can be discovered.

A good example of semi-natural, mixed deciduous woodland fringes the lochs. The water is unpolluted and, for example, quillwort, shoreweed, water lobelia and bogbean usually seen in bare, rocky Highland lochs grow near yellow water-lily and other plants typical of a silty lowland lake.

The birdlife is splendid, especially in mid-summer when you can expect a bustle of birds - mallard, water rail and great crested grebe among the number. Teal and tufted duck also breed here and goldeneye, goosander, red-breasted merganser, wigeon and pochard are regularly seen, with maybe a thousand greylag geese roosting here in late autumn. However, the main feature for many years has been a pair of breeding ospreys, and the reserve provides one of the best sites in Scotland for viewing them.

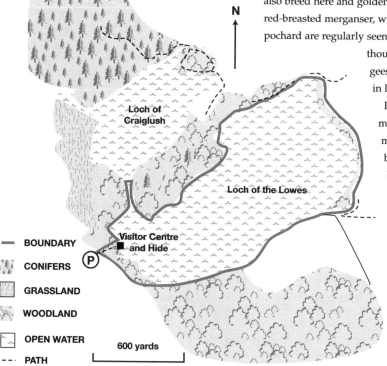

N

Loch of Craiglush

Loch of the Lowes

Visitor Centre and Hide

P

— **BOUNDARY**

CONIFERS

GRASSLAND

WOODLAND

OPEN WATER

--- **PATH**

600 yards

SEATON CLIFFS

SCOTTISH WILDLIFE TRUST

Nearest town: Arbroath
OS Map 54 NO 667416

A 30 acre (12 ha) SSSI stretching north along the coast from Arbroath. The red sandstone cliffs display interesting rock formations with a range of plants and wildlife. There is a nature trail with interpretation boards.

Location and access: The reserve begins three quarters of a mile (about 1 km) from the centre of Arbroath. Cars may be parked on the town promenade.

The reserve is colourful with flowers at many times of year: in early summer sweet-smelling white scurvy grass cascades down the slopes and clumps of thrift and bird's-foot-trefoil splash pink and yellow. Primrose and violet can be found in nooky corners, with meadowsweet and cranesbill where springs create marshy ground.

This flowery abundance attracts many butterflies - the green-veined white is maybe the earliest to be seen, with common blue and meadow brown abundant in summer. The vivid day-flying six-spot burnet moth is also common.

The reserve isn't so good for nesting birds, however - the sloping geology of the sandstone and pebbly conglomerate

WILDLIFE FEATURES
🦋 **Butterflies** ❁ **Maritime plants**
🦅 **Birdlife**

doesn't provide suitable nest sites. But arches and caves have been weathered and some house martins nest in these. Fulmar, kittiwake and guillemot can be seen offshore in summer and eider duck, and there are migrant birds to be seen in autumn and winter. The area is nationally important for wintering purple sandpiper.

Seals are regular visitors to the bays.

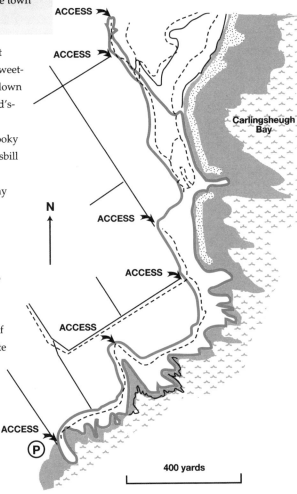

CLIFFS
BOUNDARY
OPEN WATER
PATH
SAND

Carlingsheugh Bay

N

ACCESS
ACCESS
ACCESS
ACCESS
ACCESS
ACCESS

400 yards

MONTROSE BASIN

SCOTTISH WILDLIFE TRUST

Nearest town: Montrose.
OS Map 54 NO 694576

2,550 acres (1,030.3 ha), encompassing tidal mudflats, with zones of saltmarsh, reedbed and unimproved grassland, together with some arable land. Most of the reserve is an LNR and SSSI.

There is a visitor centre from where the reserve can be viewed. There are also birdwatching hides and a ranger service operates throughout the year.

Location and access: The reserve is immediately west of Montrose. The best starting point is the visitor centre (open all year) where there is ample car parking. You can obtain directions to other hides and keys from staff at the centre. The car parks at Old Montrose and Taycock also provide easy access to the basin.

The basin of the River South Esk forms a tidal area of about 1,800 acres (750 ha), more or less rectangular in shape. The river itself winds close to the southern shore of the basin. Most of the reserve is beneath the high water mark of ordinary spring tides, but slightly more elevated areas, particularly at the western

WILDLIFE FEATURES
- Wildfowl and waders
- Occasional seals

end, provide saltmarsh and reedbeds (brackish and fresh water), and unimproved grassland.

The basin carries large populations of curlew (peak numbers in August and March), oystercatcher (October-November), knot (January) and dunlin (February), usually feeding near the river channel and roosting in the north-west corner or on the fields behind the sea bank at high tides. The oystercatcher prefers the shingle bank to the south-east. There are also many other waders seen on migration.

Duck are also attracted - wigeon in thousands and mallard, teal and pintail. Shelduck and eider are seen all year. Mute swan is most numerous in July when moulting. Really special are the numbers of overwintering pink-footed and greylag geese, the former of international importance.

Other birds include cormorant and terns while the sedge warbler nests in the reedbeds.

Seals occasionally follow the salmon into the estuary.

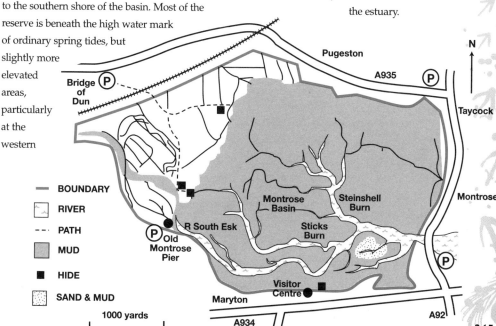

245

RED MOSS OF BALERNO

SCOTTISH WILDLIFE TRUST

Nearest town: Edinburgh
OS Map 65/66 NT 164636

A raised bog with heather, bog plants and a small birch wood, 57 acres (23 ha) in area. It is an SSSI. There are several interpretation panels on the reserve.

Location and access: The reserve lies 9 miles (14 km) south-west of Edinburgh, 1.5 miles south of the village of Balerno. From Edinburgh take the A70 south-west to the village and through to the Pentland Hills Regional car park, by Little Redford Wood.

An aqueduct and raised broadwalk runs around the reserve, and visitors must keep to these for a bog (despite its 'dirty and smelly' image) is a fragile - and colourful habitat.

Formerly a peat 'common' cut for fuel, the reserve is the largest remaining raised bog and the finest peatland left in the Edinburgh area. The peat reaches a depth of about 6 yards, rising with a noticeable dome at the centre. Mainly birch woodland (with some willow and rowan) fringes the moss, which carries heather and is dotted with birch and Scots pine.

It is the wet boggy areas which carry the most variety of plant life - including six different bog mosses (Sphagnum) which can vary in colour, and the handsome yellow-flowered bog asphodel, with scatters of cotton grass. Also on the bog are scatters of the

WILDLIFE FEATURES
❀ Bog plants

sundew, with sticky hairs to trap small insects to supplement its nutrient uptake. In summer the marshy margins of the reserve are colourful with ragged-robin, marsh ragwort, cuckoo flower and heath spotted orchid.

There are abundant insects. Swarms of small moths flit over the heather, while dragonflies haunt the pools. The common lizard can be seen, sunning itself on the drier hummocks.

There is also a good birdlife; the most notable being redpoll and tree pipit.

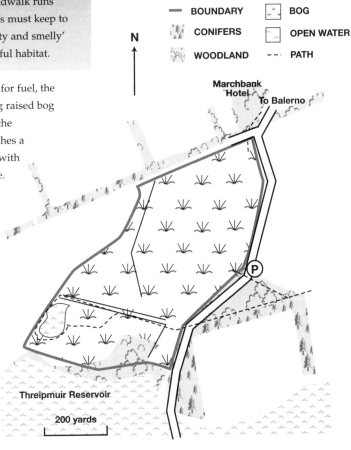

	BOUNDARY		BOG
	CONIFERS		OPEN WATER
	WOODLAND		PATH

N

Marchbank Hotel
To Balerno

P

Threipmuir Reservoir

200 yards

ST ABB'S HEAD

SCOTTISH WILDLIFE TRUST

Nearest town: Eyemouth
OS Map 67 NT 914688

A 311 acre (126 ha) reserve of magnificent sea cliffs, a freshwater loch and coastal grasslands. There is a visitor centre here, open April-October; and a ranger service operates throughout the year. The reserve is managed jointly with the National Trust for Scotland.

Location and access: The reserve is best approached from the visitor centre, where there is parking. Take the minor road between Coldingham and St Abb's and look out for the reserve sign.

A reasonable footpath runs through the reserve.

The reserve stretches north from St Abb's to St Abb's Head, a complex coastline with cliffs which can rise to 300 ft (90 metres), with many offshore stacks and rocks, all providing nesting sites for large numbers of seabirds including up to 10,000 guillemot, and also razorbill, kittiwake and a small number of puffin. Deep gaps or inlets give good viewing of these.

Many migrant birds can also be seen from the headland vantage points. In summer gannet pass to Bass Rock, their breeding ground, but in autumn you should be able to see offshore both sooty and Manx shearwaters, and arctic and great skuas.

Behind the cliffs, humps and hollows of turf run down to the ribbon of Mire Loch.

Sometimes on the reserve you will see the unexpected rarity blown off course - the red-breasted flycatcher and greenish warbler have been recorded, for example.

WILDLIFE FEATURES
 Nesting seabirds 🌿 Wild flowers

The wild flowers are a feature - the rock is acid in parts, here you find tormentil and the acid-liking heath milkwort, and it is mineral-rich in others, with natural gardens of yellow rockrose and bird's-foot-trefoil and purple mats of thyme and pink cushions of thrift.

There is a good butterfly count, with common blue and grayling and others, but migrants such as the Camberwell beauty are also sometimes seen. Day-flying moths (burnet, silver Y) can be numerous.

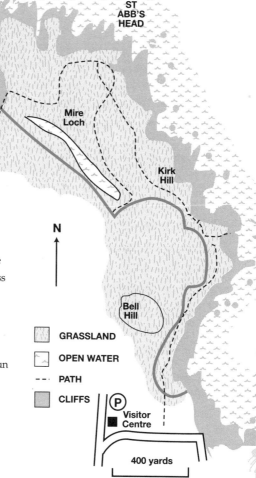

ST ABB'S HEAD

Mire Loch

Kirk Hill

N

Bell Hill

GRASSLAND

OPEN WATER

PATH

CLIFFS

Ⓟ Visitor Centre

400 yards

GLENARM

ULSTER WILDLIFE TRUST

Nearest village: Glenarm
OS map ref: 9 D305135

445 acres (180 ha) of semi-natural oak
woodland, hazel coppice and scrub, alder/birch
woodland, unimproved grassland and a
wide river.

Location and access: Glenarm village is on the
A2 between Larne and Carnlough. Access is
from the B97 leaving Glenarm by the cemetery
for Ballymena. The track from the B97 crosses a
bridge over to the other (east) bank of the
Glenarm river and there is car parking about a
mile further on. Check with the Trust to confirm
the gates will be open.

The reserve occupies the floor of Glenarm Glen,
one of the famous Glens of Antrim. As it is
within a private estate, it has rested undisturbed
for a long time, with only light grazing in the
woodland.

There is a rich birdlife (and many nest boxes
have been put up to encourage others),
including buzzard and woodcock and dipper
along the river. Mammals are usually retiring,
but the red squirrel should be seen.

WILDLIFE FEATURES
❀ **Wild flowers** 🐿 **Red squirrel**
✖ **Birdlife**

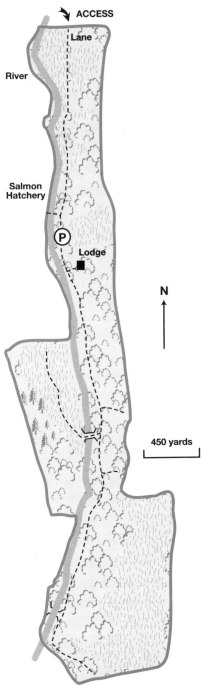

N

450 yards

— **BOUNDARY**
CONIFERS
GRASSLAND
WOODLAND
‑‑‑ **PATH**
RIVER

248

LAGAN MEADOWS

ULSTER WILDLIFE TRUST

Nearest town: Belfast

OS map ref: 15 J335703

57 acres (23 ha) of meadow, scrub, marsh, quaking mire and woodland.

WILDLIFE FEATURES
Wildlife in an urban setting

Location and access: This reserve lies within the Lagan Valley Regional Park on the outskirts of Belfast.

This reserve is heavily used by the public for a variety of outdoor pursuits, and the way that nature conservation is integrated on this site should be a model for future urban nature reserves.

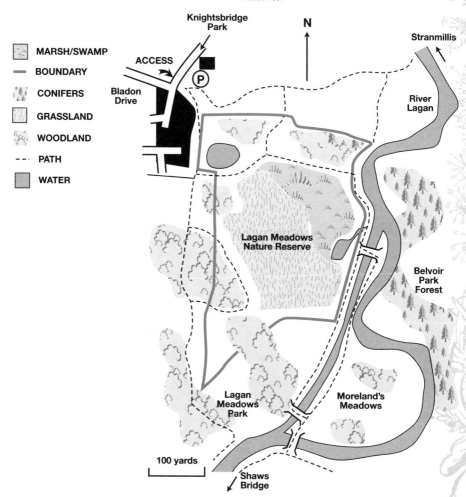

MARSH/SWAMP
BOUNDARY
CONIFERS
GRASSLAND
WOODLAND
PATH
WATER

Knightsbridge Park

ACCESS

Bladon Drive

N

Stranmillis

River Lagan

Lagan Meadows Nature Reserve

Belvoir Park Forest

Lagan Meadows Park

Moreland's Meadows

100 yards

Shaws Bridge

BLESSINGBOURNE

ULSTER WILDLIFE TRUST

Nearest village: Fivemiletown
OS map ref: 18 H449484

35 acres (14 ha) of private estate parkland (the manor is occupied) including a 6 acre (2.5 ha) lake. The habitats include swamp, open water, estate woodland and pasture.

Location and access: Blessingbourne is on the outskirts of Fivemiletown village, where there are car parking and toilet facilities.

WILDLIFE FEATURES
Birdlife including kingfisher
Dragonflies

The lake is particularly clean and species-rich with a well-developed fen margin (which has to be prevented from encroaching further into the open water). Brown trout and crayfish are among the aquatic species here, with kingfisher and water rail among the birdlife.

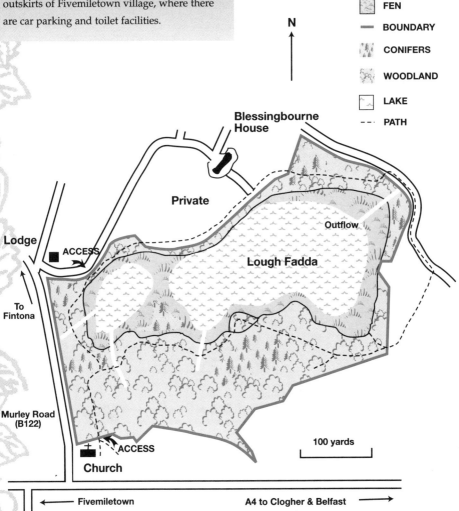

FEN
BOUNDARY
CONIFERS
WOODLAND
LAKE
PATH

N

Blessingbourne House

Private

Lodge
ACCESS

To Fintona

Outflow

Lough Fadda

Murley Road (B122)

ACCESS

Church

100 yards

Fivemiletown ← | → A4 to Clogher & Belfast

250

INDEX BY SPECIES

INDEX BY NAME